The Creative Enterprise

The Creative Enterprise
Managing Innovative
Organizations and People

EXECUTION

VOLUME 3

Edited by
Tony Davila
Marc J. Epstein
and
Robert Shelton

Praeger Perspectives

Westport, Connecticut
London

Library of Congress Cataloging-in-Publication Data

The creative enterprise : managing innovative organizations and people / edited by
Tony Davila, Marc J. Epstein, and Robert Shelton.
    p. cm.
    Includes bibliographical references and index.
    ISBN 0-275-98685-3 (set : alk. paper) — ISBN 0-275-98686-1 (vol. 1 : alk. paper) —
ISBN 0-275-98687-X (vol. 2 : alk. paper) — ISBN 0-275-98688-8 (vol. 3 : alk. paper)
    1. Organizational change—Management. 2. Technological innovations—Management.
3. Creative ability in business—Management. 4. Industrial management. I. Davila, Tony.
II. Epstein, Marc J. III. Shelton, Robert D.
HD58.8.C727   2007
658.4'063—dc22   2006030628

British Library Cataloguing in Publication Data is available.

Library of Congress Catalog Card Number: 2006030628
ISBN: 0-275-98685-3 (set)
        0-275-98686-1 (vol. 1)
        0-275-98687-X (vol. 2)
        0-275-98688-8 (vol. 3)

First published in 2007

Praeger Publishers, 88 Post Road West, Westport, CT 06881
An imprint of Greenwood Publishing Group, Inc.
www.praeger.com

Printed in the United States of America

∞

The paper used in this book complies with the
Permanent Paper Standard issued by the National
Information Standards Organization (Z39.48-1984).

10 9 8 7 6 5 4 3 2 1

Contents

Introduction

Business forces are eroding static competitive advantages faster than ever. And this is not only true for technology markets, where the pace has just accelerated. It is also true in industries that were considered "mature." Mittal, the steel company, is revolutionizing its industry. And its advantage does not come from amazing new technology, but from a relentless focus on doing business differently. Procter & Gamble has made explicit its compromise with innovation as the only way to remain profitable. This compromise with new technologies and business practices has already meant the resignation of one CEO, but not because he was too slow. Rather, he went too fast.

Innovation has emerged as the only way to sustain competitive advantage over time. Success is not to be found in a technology, in a market position, or in a business model; success resides in an organization's ability to innovate and be ahead of its competitors. This three-volume set is designed to provide the reader with the most up-to-date knowledge on how to be innovative. It addresses this issue from the various perspectives that are needed to have a well-rounded understanding of how to drive innovation in an organization.

The first volume takes a strategy perspective to answer the question of how to design an organization to be competitive in its market space. Innovation is not something that a manager can turn on only when needed. It is not a faucet that can be shut off when we don't need innovation and turned on when we do. Innovation is both a state of mind and a way of life. The first volume explores this idea from different perspectives on strategy.

The second volume looks at innovation from the perspective of the individual. It addresses the question of how to design organizations to enhance creativity. This volume focuses on drivers of creativity at the individual and team levels. Then it moves up a level of analysis and looks at organizational forces that shape this creativity—culture and rewards.

The third volume is about execution. It answers the question of how to get innovation done. The focus of this volume is how to design the management infrastructure to encourage innovation. Using a car race metaphor, the second volume is about the driver; this third one is about the car. The chapters address different tools to enhance innovation, from organizational structures to processes and measures.

The three volumes combine the perspective of large companies and small start-ups. Innovation is not the exclusive territory of one set of organizations. It happens in large companies as well as young ones; it happens in for-profit companies as well as not-for-profit organizations—under the umbrella of social innovation. The three volumes combine these various sources of innovation.

VOLUME 1: DEFINING INNOVATION STRATEGIES

Innovation starts at the top of an organization. It is top management's compromise with innovation that drives it. The first chapter in this volume shows how companies following an innovation strategy have outperformed more conservative ones. The chapter presents evidence from research studies and company stories to illustrate the importance of innovation to success.

Top management's commitment to innovation shows up in many different aspects. The chapters in Volume 1 address the aspects that make an innovative enterprise. The first aspect is the design of the *organization's interfaces with the environment*.

A key finding in both academic research and managerial practice is that innovation is not an individual activity—the popular image of the lone genius coming up with the most amazing ideas in a garage is a gross and dangerous simplification. Innovation—moving ideas into value—is a team effort. Ideas emerge and improve through exposure. The not-invented-here syndrome, where anything from the outside of a limited group is seen as inferior, is one of the most dangerous organizational pathologies. Top management is in charge of encouraging the interaction among people from different departments, bringing in people with different backgrounds, and ensuring the fluidity of ideas from outside the organization. One of the chapters in the first volume provides an interesting story on how innovation has happened in history. After reading this chapter, the reader will see innovation in a different light and understand how personalities, groups, and the environment interacted to deliver some of the most important innovations of the twentieth century.

In this first volume, three chapters cover the importance of the environment to innovation. One of them examines how Silicon Valley is redefining itself to maintain its undisputed leadership as the world's innovation hub. The chapter delineates the dynamism linked to people with different trainings interacting to create. Innovation in Silicon Valley is a team sport, with constant fluidity of ideas and backgrounds. Isolated companies have no room in the Valley. The second chapter takes the perspective of a university—one of the main sources of technological innovation—and its experiences with the corporate world. The chapter provides an interesting discussion on how technology-transfer offices work and the challenges they are facing to become more effective in moving technology breakthroughs to society. The third chapter also looks at the interface of the university and industry—a key link in leveraging the knowledge generated in universities. It presents a study on Engineering Research Centers: an organizational form that the National Science Foundation developed to improve technology commercialization at universities. The chapter details what makes some of these centers more successful.

Another aspect of innovation management that top management is in charge of is *defining the organization's innovation strategy*. Innovation is often confused with freedom. Providing direction and guidelines, setting criteria, and telling people what not to do are seen as ingredients to kill innovation. Much like the lone innovator, the need for unrestricted freedom to innovate is a myth. If top management wants innovation, it needs to set the strategy— decide what not to do and where the company needs to go. The CEO of Logitech—the leading company in computer devices such as mice and keyboards—provides a good example of giving directions and defining what is not within the company's strategy. He describes his company's strategy as "dominating the last inch," the inch that puts a person in contact with technology. So the company is not interested in technology products or in software products; it is interested in technology and software that facilitate the person-machine interaction. Logitech's CEO believes that this is a large enough space.

Three chapters in this first volume address the strategic dimension of innovation management. One of them provides a framework on how to think about innovation strategies. It describes the various levers that top management use to shape strategy. A second one addresses the important distinction between incremental and radical innovations. Incentives, risk aversion, and organizational antibodies lead to an emphasis on incremental innovation— more visible and profitable over the short term, but with the risk of jeopardizing the long term. The need for radical innovation and how to manage radical innovations are issues addressed in these chapters. While too much incremental innovation is dangerous, the opposite is also true. The right amount of innovation and the right mix are unique to every organization and where they are in their development. The third chapter addresses different ways in which management knowledge has thought about innovation strategy—how it has evolved from the idea of strategy as a plan designed by top management and implemented by the organization to the idea of innovation happening throughout the organization with top management being in charge of guiding and structuring these efforts. The evolution of the concept of strategy has led to changes in the way strategy implementation is executed.

Two chapters in the first volume address two important topics related to innovation. The first one presents the idea of social innovation—innovation in social settings, often through not-for-profit organizations. The advances in this topic of innovation have been amazing over the last few years. The world of social organizations has seen a management revolution as donors with deep managerial experience have adopted best practices in commercial companies as well as social organizations. In the academic world, a topic that was hardly taught has become one of the most popular courses in business schools. Stanford Graduate School of Business has launched a Social Innovation Center that publishes a magazine focused on the topic; it also offers several electives to MBAs and executive programs for non-profit organizations' leaders. The chapter addresses this important topic and examines how to adapt what we know about innovation in for-profit companies to social innovation.

The second important topic covered in this initial volume is innovation in start-up firms. The paradox here is that when talking about innovation, some people only think about how to make large firms more innovative, while others believe that only start-ups are innovative. The truth is that innovation happens in both types of organizations. This chapter discusses the evolution of start-up firms. A key transition point for these companies happens when their size is such that professional management tools are needed to implement strategy. The company is not a group of friends who can be managed as a group; it becomes an organization. Entrepreneurs often have a difficult time making this transition, and often they are replaced to bring in a manager. This chapter focuses on this transition point and how successful start-ups make this transition.

VOLUME 2: IMPROVING INNOVATION THROUGH PEOPLE AND CULTURE

The innovation lever addressed in the second volume is the internal environment. The amount of innovation within an organization depends, to a large extent, on top management's ability *to create the right culture and the right setting for people's creativity to thrive*. The volume starts by looking at what makes people creative. The first chapters describe in detail what we know about creativity and how to fully use the creative potential of people.

Creativity at the individual level has been the focus of much recent research. The conclusions from this research provide a complex picture, even more when creativity happens in an organization with different forces acting upon it. The need to transform ideas into useful solutions creates additional tensions in organizations. These tensions require balancing acts and a commitment from top management to let people run with ideas with a fuzzy future. The more novel an idea, the harder it is to visualize where it leads and the more fragile it is. Ideas need a runway to develop and an encouraging environment without premature judgments or negative feelings. They need experiments and prototypes to manage uncertainty. The planning is about how to resolve uncertainty, rather than visualizing the future, which is the practice with which we commonly associate planning.

Creativity is not about creating a perfect state; it is about balancing different forces over time. Positive and negative affective states, extrinsic and intrinsic motivation, autonomy, and guidance are required.

A recurring theme is the importance of the environment beyond individual creativity traits. People who could be considered less creative will outperform creative individuals if they have a supportive environment that the latter do not have. The characteristics of this environment range from leadership to co-workers. A person will be more creative when her supervisor does not micromanage and leaves space for ideas to emerge and mature, when the supervisor provides inspiration and stimulates innovation through, for instance, goals that demand creativity, when this person is fair and supportive in her evaluations. Similarly, co-workers who are creative and value creativity put together an environment where people thrive.

Contrary to common wisdom, creativity requires discipline—not the military discipline that eliminates it, but the discipline of working on it. Creativity does not just happen; people and organizations need to want it to happen. A key component of creativity is openness to experience, interacting with the outside world, with people with different experiences and points of view. Some people have a natural tendency to interact with "weird" people; but most of us prefer the safety of what we know. Discipline is required to overcome these creative blocks. Another component of creativity is to consciously think about these experiences and make the effort to translate them into ideas. Again, our natural tendency is to let these experiences go by, without considering how they can enrich the way we live and work.

Another important ingredient of creativity is self-confidence. Often, we are not creative because we do not believe we can be so. We don't even try to come up with new ways to look at the world. Several personal attitudes are blocks to new ideas, from having doubts about trying to think differently to fear of failing. Failure and creativity come together; actually, failure happens more often than success when risks are taken. In the same way that organizations that penalize failure will kill innovation, fear of failure kills the risk-taking attitude required for creativity.

The initial stage in formally tackling creativity is idea generation. At this stage, there should be no limits to what comes into the process. To do this, people involved have to forget about their self-image and their fear of saying something wrong—what other people are going to think. The richer this initial step, the better the raw material available. It is only as this process progresses that this raw material is processed into feasible ideas.

From individual creativity, the volume progresses into the topic of organizational culture and the social context of innovation. Certain organizations are more innovative than others. Strategy, as described in Volume 1, accounts for part of it. The informal norms and codes of conduct, what is broadly understood as culture, account for another important part. Finally, management infrastructure—the focus of Volume 3—accounts for the rest.

Culture has always fascinated managers and researchers in organizations. A culture that supports innovation is a culture that encourages people to interact with their networks to identify opportunities. It also provides resources and recognition to people who take risks exploring new ideas. It is a culture that recognizes effort and failure—a key ingredient of innovation. More importantly, innovative cultures tend to be strong cultures—cultures that reinforce and live very clear values and objectives. Clear values shift the attention from short-term financial performance to consistency with these values over time.

An innovative culture supports autonomy—where people can experiment—and risk taking. It has bias for action; rather than waiting for things to happen, an innovative culture will support people experimenting and prototyping their ideas. It has a winning mentality, with the objective of leading the market and achieving goals that seemed to be unreachable. It values openness to the world to enrich the idea generation process and values teamwork where ideas are bounced and refined. It is a culture that does not kill dissenting views but rather encourages the different points of view.

But culture goes beyond the organization to the level of nations. Certain nations are more innovative than others. The economic well-being, an appreciation for scientific work, a robust educational system, and the size of the nation all affect the level of innovativeness of a nation.

Finally, the second volume addresses the process of innovation—how to design such a process to enhance individual creativity—and the design of incentives—both social and economic—to support rather than hinder innovation. Creativity may be useless without adequate processes that support and nurture this creativity. Similarly, creativity and innovation can be damaged if incentives are counter-productive. Interestingly, the design of appropriate incentives varies with the type of innovation.

VOLUME 3: DESIGNING STRUCTURE AND SYSTEMS FOR SUPERIOR INNOVATION

The prior volumes deal with strategy and how to create an environment that encourages innovation. The focus of this third volume is how to design the organization and its management systems to support innovation. It addresses the third aspect that top management has to address in creating an innovative company: *designing the structures, processes, and systems that generate ideas, selecting the most promising ones, and transforming them into value.*

The volume also emphasizes the importance of cross-national interaction in getting innovation done. Three chapters address this issue from different perspectives. One of them examines the international component within product development. The second one looks at how venture capital—the money of innovation—has evolved from a regional to an international focus. Today, most venture capital firms' portfolios are diversified geographically with investments in North America, Europe, and Asia. A third chapter devotes its attention to how leading firms are managing R&D across borders. Different models are possible in addressing the need to coordinate knowledge from different parts of the world. But certain models are more adequate given the particular characteristics of the challenges at hand.

Another aspect relevant to the structure and systems of innovative organizations is the design of an appropriate measurement system. "What gets measured gets done" is frequently cited as a management principle, and it also applies to innovation management. But measures should not be used to evaluate performance, as they are sometimes used in other settings; their main role is to supply the information that guides discussion. Only in very specific types of innovation is it advisable to link measures to evaluation. Well-designed measurement systems track the entire innovation process. They provide information about the quality of the raw material for innovation—diversity of people, contact with the external world, and the quality of the ideas—all the way to the value created by innovation. In between, the system measures the balance of the innovation portfolio and the effectiveness of the innovation process.

Three chapters focus on organizing for innovation. One of them provides a balanced perspective between academic research and organizational applications on how to run product development projects. The second looks into the organization of novel ideas—usually harder to develop within an established organization—around the concept of incubators. Both chapters complement each other, providing the tools required to manage incremental and radical innovation. The third chapter presents the results of a research project on the characteristics of innovative firms. The study combines scientific rigor with enlightening examples.

An important issue in innovation management also addressed in this volume is intellectual property—in particular, how new intellectual property emerges from the combination of existing ideas. Innovation is not a blank page but the ability to combine existing ideas in novel ways.

Overall, the three volumes give a complete view of how to make an organization innovative. They balance depth in the state-of-the-art scientific knowledge with state-of-the-art managerial applications. We hope you will enjoy them!

The Case of Honda Accord Wagon Development: A Knowledge Creation Perspective

IKUJIRO NONAKA and VESA PELTOKORPI

For many industries, new product development (NPD) is the most important factor driving organizational success. In industries such as automobiles, biotechnology, consumer and industrial electronics, computer software, and pharmaceuticals, the majority of companies depend on products introduced within the last five years for more than 50 percent of their annual sales (Schilling & Hill, 1998). The increased emphasis on new products has spurred scholars from strategic management, engineering, marketing, and other disciplines to study NPD processes (see, e.g., Brown & Eisenhardt, 1995; Krishnan & Ulrich, 2001 for reviews). While scholars in the positivist NPD literature have successfully identified several antecedents of successful NPD, they are limited to explain "how" and "why" novel products are created because they overlook human values, ideals, and desires.

Instead of considering these subjective dimensions as exogenous to NPD processes, we propose that they are at the core of innovation and knowledge creation. In order to provide a holistic perspective of NPD processes, it is important to take into account both subjective and objective dimensions of NPD and their dialectic interplay in one theoretical framework. In the present chapter, NPD is described through the organizational knowledge creation theory (see e.g., Nonaka, 1991, 1994; Nonaka & Takeuchi, 1995), consisting of a shared context in motion (*ba*), a process model of knowledge conversion (SECI [acronym for Socialization, Externalization, Combination, and Internalization]), and leadership. This model is used to describe cross-leveling interplay between tacit knowledge and explicit knowledge in the development of the seventh generation Honda Accord Wagon that won the Japan Car of the Year Award for 2002–2003.

The rest of this chapter comprises five sections. The first section starts with the motivation for this study and a selective review of NPD literature. Next, it provides a conceptual framework, starting with the shared context in motion (ba), the knowledge creation process (SECI), and the interlinking role of leadership. The second section describes the development of the Honda Accord Wagon. The case, looking inside the "black box" of NPD, is based on interviews and presentations with key managers responsible for developing the Honda Accord Wagon. The third section discusses findings and builds a theoretical discussion. The final sections present managerial implications and a brief conclusion.

MOTIVATION FOR THE STUDY AND CONCEPTUAL FRAMEWORK

Motivation for the Study

Scholars in several disciplines focus on NPD because new products are the nexus of competition in many industries. NPD processes are frequently divided into overlapping concept and development phases (e.g., Clark & Fujimoto, 1991; Schulze & Hoegl, 2006). During the concept phase, product ideas are developed into product specifications, and numerous strategic decisions are made on product features, target markets, competitive positioning, and so on. And during the development phase, the product concept specifications are translated into design plans and the actual technical development work is carried out. NPD literature, which focuses on numerous aspects in these phases, is categorized in the rational plan, communication, and problem-solving streams (Brown & Eisenhardt, 1995). The rational plan research focuses on a wide range of determinants of financial performance, and the communication stream of research concerns the effects of communication on project performance. The problem-solving stream focuses on the effects of the product development team, its suppliers, and leaders of the actual product development process.

Each of these streams has distinctive strengths and weaknesses. Although scholars in the rational plan research have identified several antecedents of successful NPD (e.g., Myers & Marquis, 1969), they are limited in their ability to explain "how" and "why" these processes take place. As NPD is often described as "the sequence of steps of activities that an enterprise employs to conceive, design, and commercialize a product" (Ulrich & Eppinger, 1995), one may create a conception of NPD as a rational and well-planned phenomenon. However, managers engaged in NPD processes would probably agree with us that the creation of product concepts is far from a linear, step-by-step process. Instead, concept creation is blurry, favored by subjective intuitions and ideals. Despite several decades of research, managers still rely on gut feel with respect to concepts that are likely to satisfy the needs and wants of customers.

Scholars focusing on communication in NPD emphasize the importance of communication among project members and with the entities outside the NPD team (see e.g., Katz & Tushman, 1981; Ancona & Caldwell, 1989). These scholars have pointed out the importance of information gatekeepers (people with extensive social networks) to NPD success. Moreover, these scholars have shown that group composition, project leader, and internal and external communication have a positive impact on NPD performance. In contrast to the rational plan research, scholars in the communication view emphasize the importance of organizational context and individual behavior in the effectiveness of NPD processes. Although we agree that communication is important, it alone cannot explain why some products meet the needs and wants of customers. This is partly because the communication perspective overlooks the phenomenon of people acquiring tacit knowledge.

Scholars in the problem-solving stream of research have observed that successful NPD is dependent on a balancing act between relatively autonomous problem solving by the project team, and the discipline of a heavyweight project leader, strong top management, and an overarching product vision (e.g., Imai, Nonaka, & Takeuchi, 1985; Takeuchi & Nonaka, 1986). Through detailed case studies, these scholars provide a microview of the contextual complexity of NPD in several Japanese organizations. It was observed, for example, that different phases of the NPD process in Japanese organizations are loosely linked and overlapping, and that NPD teams are given autonomy during the concept development phase (Imai, Nonaka, & Takeuchi, 1985; Takeuchi & Nonaka, 1986). However, as these studies used the information processing paradigm as an explanatory framework, they were still not able to provide a comprehensive explanation of NPD processes, including human intentionality and values (Nonaka, 2005).

These three streams of research focus on different aspects and further our understanding of NPD to a certain degree. Together, they indicate that NPD is a complex, multifaceted process that includes several phases, communication, technology, project team interdependencies, and so on. The weakness, however, especially with the rational plan and communication perspectives, is that they focus predominately on the objective dimensions of NPD. In these approaches, new products are created from existing knowledge, and organizations are presented as information processing machines. Subjective aspects of embedded but intentional human actors are overlooked. Instead of treating subjective aspects as disturbing "noise," we take into account the subjective and objective dimensions of NPD by drawing from the organizational knowledge creation theory.

Conceptual Framework

The organizational knowledge creation theory, consisting of context (*ba*), a process model (SECI), and leadership, provides a holistic framework to describe NPD processes as knowledge creation. In essence, the management of knowledge creation is about leading and organizing *ba* and their interaction (Nonaka, Toyama, & Konno, 2000).

Shared Context in Motion (*ba*)

Kitaro Nishida (1921) developed the concept of *ba* (which roughly means "place" in Japanese) to discuss the problems associated with meaning creation and the nature of objects and knowing subjects. This philosophical concept originates in Plato's *topos*, Aristotle's *hypokeimenon*, and Lask's field theory. The concept of *ba* has been extended by Nonaka and associates (e.g., Nonaka & Konno, 1998; Nonaka, Toyama, & Konno, 2000; Nonaka, Peltokorpi, & Tomae, 2005), who have used it as the foundation of knowledge creation. *Ba* is defined as "shared context in motion" because it is constantly evolving (Nonaka & Toyama, 2005). In contrast to dualistic theories in which context is located mainly in the human mind (Thompson & Washam, 2004), *ba* emphasizes the role of evolving relationships and the phenomenological notion of intersubjectivity.

Ba is a shared context for emerging relationships, which provide a platform for advancing individual and collective knowledge (Nonaka & Konno, 1998). *Ba* refers not just to a physical space, but also a specific time-space, or the relationships among people in that specific time-space. Well-functioning *ba* needs participants with diverse perspectives and experiences. From the divergent realities that participants bring to the shared context in motion, intersubjectivity is developed and modified through the creation of shared language, symbols, and interactions. In phenomenology, this movement toward shared knowledge is described through triangular roles (Depraz, Varela, & Vermersch, 2003). In pragmatism, George Mead (1934) observed that efficient social interaction was predicated on an individual's capacity to anticipate how others would respond to his or her behavior. Individuals accomplish this by playing the roles of others, and by viewing themselves from other people's perspectives.

Ba exists on various ontological levels. Individuals form the *ba* of teams, which in turn form the *ba* of organizations. And the market environment forms the *ba* for the organization. Interactions in overlapped *ba* enable employees to search, locate, link, and disseminate knowledge within and beyond organizational boundaries. In organizations, middle managers and project leaders connect top managers and lower-level employees, and play important roles in locating knowledge and linking *ba* into larger knowledge-creating systems. The management of these linkages is important in multiteam projects, i.e., large-scale projects consisting of several teams with separate tasks working interdependently on the same overall project. *Ba* requires permeable boundaries to allow linkages among relevant knowledge domains. Linkages among *ba* facilitate rapid flows of knowledge, problem identification, and the propagation of innovation. Senior managers should thus sponsor the creation of loose organizational arrangements around which various *ba* can emerge.

The dynamic configuration of *ba* extends beyond the boundaries of a firm determined by ownership. Viewing a firm as multilayered *ba* makes it possible to synthesize the perspective of a firm as subjective processes and objective structures (Nonaka, Toyama, & Konno, 2000). This means that one needs to examine not only the structure of the firm, but also the meanings created in *ba* and the relationships among *ba*. Although subjectivity is needed to create new knowledge, objectivity is needed to apply that knowledge efficiently. This subjectivity-objectivity synthesis also sheds light on the paradox of structures suited to routine and nonroutine tasks (Thompson, 1967). The formal structures determine interactions in terms of command and information channels. In NPD, project teams can be viewed as structural arrangements that facilitate knowledge creation. However, formal interactions between project teams are a fraction of the interaction needed in knowledge creation. Knowledge emerges and evolves through interactions among organization members and between them and the environment.

Knowledge Creation Process (SECI)

Knowledge is noted to contain a tacit dimension that is personal, hard to externalize, and context specific, and an explicit dimension that is more readily expressed, codified, and thus transferred with relative ease (Polanyi, 1952, 1966). These distinct but interrelated dimensions of knowledge promote the knowledge conversion process, which takes place through the four phases of *socialization* (from tacit knowledge to tacit knowledge) ⇒ *externalization* (from tacit knowledge to explicit knowledge) ⇒ *combination* (from explicit knowledge to explicit knowledge) ⇒ *internalization* (from explicit knowledge to tacit knowledge) (see Nonaka, 1991, 1994, 2005) (Figure 1.1). Some knowledge is lost in the conversion process because not all internalized knowledge can be externalized, and not all externalized knowledge can be codified.

During the socialization phase, individuals acquire tacit knowledge through informal interactions and practice. Socialization occurs when people spend time together, such as when members of an organization share experiences in informal meetings with each other, suppliers, customers, or affiliated firms. A study with ninety-four new development projects indicates that team members who have built a shared understanding of the product idea and its objectives are in a better position to integrate their diverse knowledge bases and to develop more innovative product concepts (Schulze & Hoegl, 2006). In addition, socialization occurs between product developers and customers (Nonaka & Takeuchi, 1995). For example, by observing what customers want, employees are able to develop hypotheses, improving the fit between market needs and the products and services to be introduced.

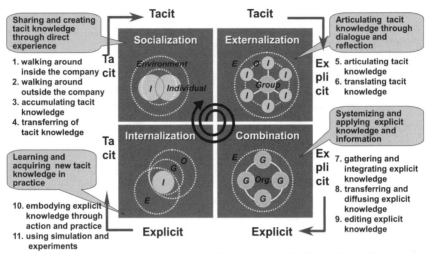

FIGURE 1.1.   SECI Model

The acquired tacit knowledge is of little use unless it is externalized and shared. Exposure to diverse ideas during the externalization phase is important, as every step in the innovation process is proposed to be about someone asking about imaginary possibilities, speculating about what would happen if, as well as reflecting on yet-unrealized and perhaps unrealizable solutions (Rescher, 2003). Instead of deduction, abduction and retroduction are noted to be effective in externalizing deeper layers of knowledge (Lawson, 1997). These methods help people to externalize and synthesize dialectically the contradictions between their tacit knowledge and environment, or contradictions in the tacit knowledge of people (see Nonaka & Toyama, 2005).

During the combination phase, the externalized knowledge is combined, systematized, and presented in a more explicit form, and verified with complementary knowledge within and beyond the organizational boundaries. Novel combinations of explicit knowledge are also noted to create new knowledge. Crawford (1997) argued that the systematic gathering and analysis of knowledge allows the creation of creative and innovative product concepts. In addition, designing solutions that are new combinations of existing ones provides an efficient way of identifying and implementing suitable technical answers to the challenges posed by the new product concept (Schulze & Hoegl, 2006). Organizations can facilitate the collection, editing, synthesizing, and dissemination of explicit knowledge through databases and computer networks (Nonaka, 1994).

Internalization is a phase during which explicit knowledge is converted to individual tacit knowledge. People internalize new knowledge through training, learning-by-doing or reflective practice, simulation, collective discipline, and social interaction. The internalization phase further describes how internalized explicit knowledge becomes a base for routines. The created products, as the tangible end products of knowledge creation processes, produce growth and shareholder value through profitable growth. The new knowledge provides the basis for subsequent spirals of knowledge creation, expanding horizontally and vertically as they move through communities of interaction. The knowledge creation spiral grows in scale as it moves from the cognitive processes of individuals and up the organizational levels.

Leadership

Leadership links the context (*ba*) and the process (SECI) (Nonaka, Toyama, & Konno, 2000; Nonaka, Peltokorpi, & Tomae, 2005). Top management shows the direction for knowledge creation by creating visions, defined as value-driven articulations of an idealistic *praxis* for a social collective (Nonaka, Peltokorpi, & Tomae, 2005). These knowledge-based visions connect the past with the present and future, as the past has meaning only as a projection of the future (Heidegger, 1962). The future is not a determinate logical end: it opens up a cascade of potentials exploited through knowledge creation. Employees cooperate in the achievement of organizational goals because they have understood and internalized those goals (Hedlund, 1994; Kogut & Zander, 1992).

Middle managers bridge top management visions with the chaotic front line reality, and manage and interlink *ba* (Nonaka, Toyama, & Konno, 2000). They internalize visions through interacting with top managers, and play the roles of instructor, coach, mentor, and coordinator to facilitate knowledge creation. It has further been proposed that middle managers provide the care needed in knowledge creation (von Krogh, 1998). Important leadership tools and qualities in managing *ba* include broad social networks and the ability to secure organizational resources (Nonaka, Toyama, & Konno, 2000).

Although control is important in speeding up organizational processes, the most effective dimension of power is rooted in language (Pettigrew, 1977; Alvesson, 1996). More than others, middle managers have the opportunity to give meaning to contextual events, and in doing so contribute to the development of shared norms and values in *ba*. Sharing the context with subordinates enables middle managers both to convey their messages efficiently and to recreate contextual meanings. Pettigrew (1977) describes this as the management of meanings, referring to symbol construction and value use designed to legitimize one's own demands and delegitimize those of others.

In sum, the organizational knowledge creation theory posits that NPD is a contextual phenomenon influenced by human subjectivity. Although products can be created on objective market data, this data is interpreted by subjective individuals. However, knowledge that is not private and subjective is produced through group validation (Rorty, 1979). The SECI process shows how the subjective personal knowledge is socially validated and becomes again the base of new knowledge cycles. Project leaders play important roles in organizing *ba* to motivate employees to share their knowledge, and organizing linkages among *ba* within and beyond the organizational boundaries. In the following sections, this phenomenon will be examined at Honda.

NEW PRODUCT DEVELOPMENT AT HONDA[1]

Six features differentiate the Honda NPD from other Japanese and overseas carmakers. First, NPD teams at Honda are formed for a single project. In most other carmakers, engineers are highly specialized and spread their functional skills across several different products' development. In contrast, NPD teams at Honda are independent, focused units in which engineers concentrate on developing one car. As engineers, not easily transferred between projects, are allowed to work on a single NPD project, Honda is able to make large changes to new models. While many carmakers believe that the simultaneous design of a new engine and a new car is too risky, and introduce new cars with old engines or vice versa, Honda changes an entire engine design from engine blocks with each model change. Honda believes that only by refining, reoptimizing, or redesigning the engine can a coherent match among the body, chassis, and engine be achieved. Only through such coherence is the car's true character realized. In contrast, Toyota and Nissan seldom change the entire design and develop new engines based on previous ones.

Second, the Honda development organization has a matrix structure with fewer layers, managers, and titles than other comparable companies. Functional units in the development organization are subdivided into product groups. Even the engine department includes different groups, each devoted to developing an engine for a specific new product. Because a new team is formed for each NPD project, the development organization resembles an autonomous project team structure. The NPD projects are led by Large Project Leaders (LPL), usually selected from the independent Honda Research Laboratory. Because a new LPL is assigned to every new project, coordination between different models and generations is deemphasized. All NPD projects have three overlapping phases. The P development phase, devoted primarily to concept development, occurs during the first year. During the second year, the D development phase, in which technical solutions are created for the developed concepts, takes place. During this period, blueprints and prototypes are created, and prototype testing is conducted. The last half-year is for manufacturing processes at the headquarters factory.

Third, functional interdependences in the development organization are created by the SED system. The functional units of sales, engineering, and development (SED) collaborate during NPD. While having different functional objectives, they are committed to the bigger vision created through *Tama*

Dashi Kai (brainstorming) and *Wai Gaya* (discussions). At Honda, meetings are often held at resort inns, bars, and other informal places. In the meetings, all participants, regardless of seniority and age, are considered equal, and each participant's opinion has equal weight. The only rule is that criticism should not be made unless supported by constructive proposals. The atmosphere of open, trustful dialogues is one reason that each participant has the confidence to step forward and contribute. In addition to increasing innovation, these methods increase individual responsibility, as lower-level employees who come up with novel ideas do not leave all decision making to managers. To strengthen the feeling of oneness, distinctions between white-collar and blue-collar workers are minimized. All employees wear the same white suits while at work and eat in the same dining halls, regardless of their rank or status.

Fourth, Honda has formalized methods to solve ill-defined problems through three levels of questions (A, A0, and A00). The first level, level A, is a question about specifications. A-level questions can be about product specifications, such as "what should be the desired horsepower for this engine?" There are various ways to answer this question due to contradictions created by fuel efficiency and power, or safety and speed, to decide on the specifications of an engine. Engineers try to solve such contradictions not by finding the optimal balance between contradicting conditions, but by asking a question one level higher. The second level, A0-level questions, are about the concept, such as "what is the concept of this engine?" Engineers reflect on this question and decide on the specifications that are necessary to realize the concept. If the contradictions cannot be solved with the A0-level questions, then the third level, A00-level questions, are asked. The A00-level questions are more existential, such as "what is this engine for?" or "why should we build this car?" All of these questions encourage individuals to think about the fundamentals of their work and the products they create.

Fifth, Honda cars are built on concepts, reputed to make up 80 percent of their new cars. As Honda is committed to develop revolutionary products, this makes the P development phase important. Although Honda, similar to most other carmakers, gathers a lot of marketing data, they treat this data differently. At Honda, marketing data gives only an ex-post view of consumer needs and wants. That is why people seek to go beyond the data to develop products that provide customers with unexpected positive surprises, including the joy of buying, which is part of the Honda corporate philosophy. In order to create superior products, the "Three Reality Principle" is used. First, go to *gemba* (actual place), where phenomena occur. Following this principle, knowledge is acquired by observing how the products are actually used. Employees may stake out parking lots in grocery stores to watch and videotape how customers fit groceries into their cars. This way, they see the imperfections and design cars tailored for customer needs. Next, know the actual situation. This principle emphasizes the knowledge acquisition by touching, seeing, and being in contact with the actual elements, both human and technical. Finally, be realistic. Each individual needs to judge the gained knowledge realistically to solve problems.

Sixth, concepts need to be linked with the joy of buying, the joy of selling, and the joy of creating. There first needs to be the joy of buying that goes beyond customer satisfaction for each person who buys a Honda product. Honda has four steps to create the joy of buying. First, customers must understand the product and its fundamental concept. Second, customers must accept the product and decide to buy it. Third, customers must be completely satisfied with the product. Fourth, the joy of buying is experienced if the Honda products and services exceed the customers' expectations. There should further be the joy of selling. To achieve the joy of selling, what is important is not just the relationship between the customer and products. The products should provide the opportunity for a human relationship with the customers. Employees who sell and service Honda products seek to respond sincerely to customers' needs and wants. When the quality and performance of products are excellent, employees engaged in selling and servicing Honda products are proud to present the company to the customer. Moreover, there needs to be the joy of producing, including manufacturing, production engineering and R&D, and suppliers. Producing high-quality products that exceed the expectations of Honda dealers and customers contributes to this joy.

HONDA ACCORD WAGON DEVELOPMENT

The Accord Wagon development project shows how model changes at Honda are based on new concepts and technology. Each model generation has a new LPL who tries to develop something new and maintain a good tradition. The seventh-generation Honda Accord inherits the same principle of harmony among individuals, cars, and society embedded in every Accord generation since 1991. Despite being the seventh generation, the Accord Wagon was a new vehicle in terms of technology and concepts, and fulfilled the three joys required from each new vehicle because it was selected among ten domestic and international competitors to win the Japan Car of the Year Award for 2002–2003. A sign of the product development strength is that this marked the third consecutive win for Honda (Honda Civic 2000–2001 and Honda Fit 2001–2002).

Large Product Development Leader (LPL)

The Accord Wagon project LPL was Haruo Inoue. He had worked for Honda for thirty-five years. Joining Honda because of his passion for cars, he worked on the interior section in the architectural department for the first ten years. After that he was assigned to several NPD projects. Despite his long career, and the fact that most employees are selected as LPL for the first time in their forties, Inoue had no experience leading an NPD project. For Inoue, already fifty years old, the Accord Wagon project was his last chance to be selected as LPL. Working in the production department, Inoue was finally selected as LPL, perhaps because of his deep commitment to combining the contrasting sedan and wagon concepts in one vehicle.

In contrast to several other carmakers that tend to develop wagons on existing products, Inoue felt that the Accord Wagon should not be a mere extension of the sedan, because those wagons fail to satisfy customer needs and wants. In addition, he understood that imitation of existing products was a source of failure for new products. Finally provided with a chance to lead an NPD project, Inoue was committed to developing a wagon that would provide customers with unexpected positive surprises. He had developed a tacit understanding of what customers could expect from wagons, because he liked the outdoors and drove his wagon to the mountains during the weekends. Taking his bicycle with him, he realized that wagons needed to be fast and easy to drive and contain a large luggage compartment for sports utilities.

The project was officially started in June 2000. Inoue named the project W1, with W signifying the wagon and 1 the top, winning product. The aim of the project was to create the best (number-one) wagon in the world. Inoue had two and half years to develop the seventh-generation Accord Wagon. Similar to other projects, the last year and a half would be devoted to translating the created concepts into design plans and creating the supporting technology to transform the concepts into tangible products. According to Inoue, the first year, during which the new concepts were developed, proved to be the most critical and challenging period in the creation of this award-winning vehicle.

Concept Creation

Accord had long been the top-selling brand at Honda. Unlike NPD teams that have the freedom to design new models, Inoue's task was tricky because he had to simultaneously maintain the old brand image and develop a wagon based on a novel concept. According to Inoue, the P development period was important in determining whether a vehicle would sell or not. If the concept was not strong, then even excellent execution of the latter phases of the project would not matter. That is why NPD teams put a lot of emphasis on the creation of a novel, strong concept. While the W1 team had a lot of marketing data available, they were committed to creating a concept that took into account the needs and wants of customers, and provided something pleasant and surprising beyond the existing needs and wants. Inoue commented that "unless we create something beyond the data, we cannot satisfy our customers. Our products need to be ahead of marketing data." If products are created on the existing marketing data, it is uncertain whether there will be customer demand when they are released to the market.

Following the "Three Reality Principle," the W1 group visited numerous places to observe consumer behavior. For example, during the course of one day, the group members took a morning drive on a highway to a shopping mall in Hachiyochi, on the outskirts of Tokyo. In the parking lot, they watched and videotaped how people were fitting groceries into their wagons. These observations helped them to detect imperfections in existing wagon models and to share ideas about an ideal wagon for mall shopping. In the afternoon, they drove to a popular sports ground in Nagano Prefecture. Once again they observed consumers and discussed how a wagon used for sports can provide joy to customers. In the evening, they drove to an Italian-designed luxury resort hotel located in the mountainous Yamanashi Prefecture.

At the shopping mall, the group members noticed that shopping is often combined with entertainment. The wagon should therefore be easy to maneuver in the parking lot and have a large load capacity. This is because families, in addition to shopping bags, have strollers with them. At the sports ground, the group members noticed that luggage is seasonal, as people use bicycles during summer and skis during winter. Discussions with wagon owners revealed further that people do not want to put their bicycles on the roof because of the insects and the fear of it being stolen while they are shopping. Therefore, regardless of the season, people should be able to fit their sporting goods into the wagon. Observations at the resort hotel showed people using stylish, foreign-made cars. Therefore, for the resort, the wagon should look elegant and provide a refined image of its owner.

In addition to countless observations and interviews, the team conducted focused group interviews in cooperation with the marketing department. People were first given 300 wagon pictures to choose from in five minutes. Most of the people chose a picture combining the contrasting qualities of casual and formal. These people were then asked to describe their ideal wagon type. From these interviews and *waigaya* meetings, a shared image of an ideal wagon and its target customers started to emerge. The wagon should synthesize the contrasting qualities of casual and formal. Target customers would be in their late thirties, people who would enjoy their lives in various scenarios. These people like to work hard and play hard during their free time. They enjoy their jobs, hobbies, and would have an overall high-quality life. The key words for the Accord Wagon concept were elegant and sporty.

The group collaborated intensively with several functional departments during the concept creation phase. The concept was justified during these interaction processes, and alterations were made based on the feedback from various parts of the organization. Concept sharing and the creation of a shared mindset were considered to be vital for the project's success; as Inoue said, "unless we agree on the basic concept at the early phase, we are going to waste time during the latter parts of the project." Inoue believed that a distinctive strength of Honda was the fast creation of a shared concept that helps group members count on each other and various organizational resources until the last stage of the development project.

Concept Breaking

Created concepts are holistic images that have to be broken into separate components. Thus, the purpose of concept breaking is to move from concepts to integrated product characteristics, such as interior and exterior design. Because the created concept embraced various activities of the target customers, the group encountered numerous hurdles. In general, there were two types of wagons on the market: the ones that drove fast and the ones that had a large cargo space. The problem was that fast wagons tended to have small cargo spaces, and vice versa. Like most wagons on the market, the previous Accord Wagon generation was fast but had a small cargo space. Inoue saw no reason to build another fast wagon in an already saturated market. In order to meet the concept, the W1 group had to create a wagon that was both fast and had a large cargo space. This wagon would be formal and casual, fulfilling the various customer needs.

A synthesis of these contrasting goals was more difficult than initially expected. While a new engine could solve the driving dilemma, wagons with large cargo spaces tended to be square and box shaped. It was agreed during the concept creation that exterior design was an important feature of the wagon. Committed to building a wagon with an appealing, streamlined design and a large cargo space, the W1 group started synthesizing the contrasting features through metaphors. While it initially seemed that the synthesis was impossible, Inoue played an important role in guiding dialogues in more fruitful directions. Eventually, the falcon emerged as a guiding image for the exterior design. Like falcons, the wagon should be fast but have a nicely shaped body. That is why the final model had a streamlined design with a wing roof at the end of the wagon to emphasize the falconlike appearance. It explains further why engineers took so much time perfecting the wagon's distinctive headlights, and why the wagon's grille is distinctively V-shaped.

The next task was to align the interior design with the exterior design. In various meetings, the group members had lively discussions on the ideal interior, especially the cargo space (or luggage compartment). During initial meetings, some group members described the cargo space in terms of the number of boxes or pieces of luggage it could hold. Instead of developing a wagon to move cargo, Inoue required that team members stop calling the luggage compartment a cargo space. They should consider the luggage compartment as a place where people put their dreams. This slight shift in focus enabled team members to equate cargo with luggage or dreams. Inoue explained that the difference between cargo and luggage is small but crucial. While luggage can be equated to branded bags, cargo has connotations of cardboard boxes.

Names of even the smallest parts, such as the cargo lamp, were changed to "luggage" to symbolize the dreams of customers.

Instead of developing a tall wagon to increase luggage space, the team decided to alter lower parts of the vehicle. By doing this, the team did not compromise the streamlined design for increased luggage space. In order to develop the wagon's luggage floor to be lower, wider, and longer, the group developed a unique rear trailing arm double wishbone suspension that was small and compact. In addition to providing a larger interior, this new wheel suspension system provided maximum accuracy in defining the wheel movement during driving. The result was precise and predictable handling of the wagon, reduced body movement, and improved braking. This way the wagon provided better driving and a wider and longer load area. In fact, while the exterior design maintained its sporty design, the wagon had the biggest load capacity in its class. Also, the overall interior was extended from the previous Accord Wagon generation.

Like the streamlined exterior, the interior of the luggage compartment should also be appealing. In order to create a spacious feeling in a small space, the development team designers visited a famous old teahouse close to Kyoto. This tearoom is recognized by the Japanese government as a national treasure. Designed by the legendary Senno Rikyu, the tearoom is very small (only two tatami mats), yet its innovative architectural design provides a spacious image because of the special interior design and wood coating. In this small room, all parts, such as windows, were altered to create a spacious atmosphere. Similarly, the interior of the wagon should provide the same atmosphere to the customers. The ideas and concepts acquired in the tearoom were incorporated in the luggage compartment design. In fact, the team looked at every single part and sought to make it consistent with the concept when they designed the wagon. For example, the falcon metaphor is the reason why the long rear window creates a powerful and poised silhouette.

Board Meeting Presentation

At the end of the first year, these concepts were presented in a meeting of board members. If successful, the project would proceed from the P development phase to the D development phase. Although the concept was recognized as representing a dream, it was felt to lack the three joys, especially in providing unexpected pleasant surprises to customers. When board members asked how the concept provides joy to customers, the team members were unable to provide a clear, satisfactory explanation. Instead of criticizing the created concepts, the board members suggested automated rear seats, etc. The purpose of the board meeting presentation was to validate created concepts and refine or reconstruct these concepts if needed. As such, this meeting was a comprehensive, real-time test of the extent to which the developed concept met organizational traditions and justified the product opportunity.

The board evaluation meeting was not successful, and the group was given one week to develop the concept. The group started to reconsider the joys the wagon should provide to customers. They took into account the suggestion of automated rear seats, but felt that it would add more cost than it would provide value to customers. Instead, the wagon should have a power-operated tailgate that opens and closes with a push of a button, and a one-motion rear seat that increases cargo space with just a pull of the seatback lever. The one-motion rear seat provided maximum space with minimum effort. And the power-operated tailgate allowed customers to open and close the rear door during snowy or rainy days when they had luggage in both hands. One week later, these ideas were accepted because they were based on new technology and would provide the needed joys to customers.

Organizing Intangible and Tangible Resources

During the D development phase, the wagon concepts were converted into objective plans and the actual technological development was carried out. This phase, involving larger resource commitments than the concept phase, was characterized by the search for, and implementation of, concrete solutions to meet the demands set out by the product concept. The team faced several more hurdles because the power-operated tailgate and the one-motion rear seat were based on nonexistent technology. Although LPLs have a lot of autonomy, they are not in charge of budgeting. As the resources are in functional departments, LPLs need to have leadership skills to motivate and pull project managers together to support NPD projects.

As mentioned above, products at Honda are developed in networked matrix structures. Because of the matrix structure, in which the horizontal line is the NPD project and the vertical line is the functional department, project leaders maintain affiliations with their functional departments. They lead subgroups, each devoted to developing a part of a specific product, in functional departments. Each project leader has two supervisors: the LPL and his or her divisional leader. In the W1 project, there were twenty project leaders responsible to both Inoue and their divisional leaders. Often, LPLs and divisional leaders have conflicts due to different priorities. For example, LPLs may seek to introduce new technology to new models, which increases costs. In contrast, divisional leaders seek to make maximum profits with minimum investments.

Project leaders, located between LPLs and divisional leaders, are in crucial roles of determining whether projects are successful or not. Their responsibility is to develop the needed technology and make sure that the overall product specifications are met. Occasionally, project leaders have limited commitment to NPD projects. At Honda, the power differences between LPLs and divisional leaders are unclear. As the LPL is not in charge of budgeting, his strength is based on his visions, expertise, passion, personality, and philosophy, and ultimately how much people like him. The LPLs are strong in character but relatively weak in formal power. Thus, an important factor for successful NPD projects is the LPL's ability to motivate project leaders to contribute their knowledge and skills to projects. Inoue was a typical LPL, being charismatic, talkative, and able to persuade project leaders to take part in risky technology development.

Extensive social networks developed during his thirty years at Honda enabled Inoue to motivate two project leaders to develop the needed technology. A project leader from the body section, who had worked as a senior (*kohai*) to Inoue in the architectural department and had learned a great deal during their interactions, started to develop technology for the power-operated tailgate. The project leader was confronted by his divisional leader for participating in this risky project that required extra investments. However, he convinced his supervisor that development of this kind of technology was important. Through his networks, this project leader located an external team working on similar technology, and these teams started to collaborate. During the technological development, various detailed things had to be considered. For example, the tailgate had to be fitted with sensors for safety reasons. If there is an obstruction between the tailgate and the wagon, the tailgate reverses its direction.

The project leader committed to developing completely new technology for the one-motion rear seat had also worked as *kohai* to Inoue, and because of this, the technology development did not meet any formal resistance. More difficult, however, was motivating the limited number of employees to spend extra effort to develop the technology in a limited time period. This project leader motivated his team members by spreading the word across the organization that his project team was engaging in the development of this new technology for the first time in the world. During the technical development, various adjustments, such as rebuilding the rear seat safety belt function, had to be made.

Final Phases of the W1 Project

After the group had tackled these technical problems, the main responsibilities for developing the wagon were shifted to manufacturing and marketing. Testing and improvements were also conducted during this phase. For example, the Formula 1–inspired double wishbone suspension was tested and developed at Suzuka and Mogegi in Japan and Nurburgring in Germany. Faithful to the Honda NPD tradition, the wagon had a new engine that tied the concept into a coherent package. The chassis was designed to provide increased security, especially in terms of front-end collisions. Airbags were used to protect passengers in case of side collisions. The wagon further included the HiDs (Honda Intelligent Driver Support System), helping to reduce the burden on the driver during freeway driving.

After the wagon was released to the public, Inoue started to work as a technical information manager. In order to share the best practices for future projects, he wrote a research paper that was widely circulated at Honda. He emphasized the importance of dreams in concept creation, echoing the corporate philosophy of Soichiro Honda. In addition, Inoue highlighted the importance of creative conflicts during the concept creation, saying that "we are able to synthesize contrasting concepts through frequent constructive conflicts, instead of abandoning one of these concepts." The wagon project is one example of this relentless commitment to creating vehicles based on strong concepts that provide customers with something new and unexpected.

DISCUSSION

The theoretical framework and the case show that NPD processes are far more complex than presented in the rational plan, communication, and problem-solving perspectives. Instead of focusing on one aspect of NPD, the holistic organizational knowledge creation theory posits that NPD processes are dependent on the interaction context (ba), knowledge creation influenced by subjective dreams and values and objective social reality, and leadership (Nonaka, 1991, 1994; Nonaka & Takeuchi, 1995). Through the interactions of subjective tacit knowledge and objective explicit knowledge, new knowledge and products are created. The interaction context (ba) and leadership provide energy and direction to these creative activities.

Instead of transferring market opportunities to product concepts in a linear fashion, as indicated in the positivist accounts of NPD, the case indicates that concepts were created through indwelling and intense social interactions. As the method, the W1 group used the Three Reality Principle. In the beginning, they sought to indwell to the world of customers in various ways. Through observations, informal interactions, and using a wagon for shopping, pursuing hobbies, and going to dinner, group members acquired tacit knowledge. In addition, focused group interviews made it possible to create a more detailed image of the needs and wants of customers. Through these first-hand experiences, the group built an image of a wagon that fulfills the diverse needs of customers. This process was based more on intersubjectivity than deductive thinking or top-down control. Indeed, during *waigaya* meetings, employees share their ideas and discuss them until all participants agree on one thing. This enables employees to perceive a given phenomenon from several different angles and to validate their tacit knowledge. The group had numerous meetings to synthesize the contrasting concepts of a wagon that is fast and has a large cargo capacity. If the group had chosen only one of these concepts, it would have been easier for them to develop the wagon. Instead, they were committed to synthesizing these contradictions through dialogues and metaphors rather than eliminating one of them.

In addition, close involvement of several functional units helped to create a concept based on diverse cross-functional knowledge. The advantage of developing a clear, strong concept during the early phases is that such a concept brings understanding of what to prioritize during the later process phases. At Honda, concepts are created in close collaboration with sales, engineering, and development. The involvement of a large number of people from different functions is beneficial because during the D development period, there is not much time for experimentation and exploration of the concept during the later project phases. This cooperation made it possible to develop a shared understanding of the product concept and reduced conflicts based on misunderstandings. For example, employees could go back to the overarching concepts through A0-level questions when facing complex problems. The case indicates also that intensive social interactions may not be necessary during the later project phases because technical knowledge among project groups were transferred, for example, through drawings.

Although the development of the Accord Wagon can be explained through social interactions of individuals, this explanation is only partial because these individuals are embedded in a social context that influences their thoughts and actions. The corporate culture of Honda is strongly influenced by its founder, Soichiro Honda. The desire to produce innovative products for this charismatic, hands-on leader was uncompromising, and continues to influence organizational activities at Honda. At Honda, people and individual differences are respected. This provides structures for a free and vital corporate culture that encourages creativity. Honda engineers are encouraged to test the boundaries of science as well as their own imaginations. At the same time, they are influenced by the organizational culture because they need to respect other people's ideas and sound theories. Through the synthesis of individual intentionality and structural voluntarism, novel and rational concepts are developed. Unlike most of its competitors, who seek to develop vehicles based on rational future estimates of customer demand, Honda believes more in absolute terms. It is not enough for Honda to develop vehicles based on market analysis—each vehicle has to further provide the joys of buying, selling, and manufacturing. By developing vehicles based on these holistic philosophical ideals, each Honda model is unique, designed to excite, inspire, and perform.

LPLs have an important role in creating a context in which people externalize and combine knowledge in an effective manner. Essentially, LPLs energize and organize *ba* and their interactions. For example, Inoue guided dialogues during concept creation and helped the W1 group to design a wagon inspired by the metaphor of a falcon, stretched aerodynamically in full motion. In several cases, focus on seemingly small details enabled team members to think about the essentials and break the existing mental frames. The role of leadership in the latter part of the project changed from coach to network facilitator and motivator. During the D development phase, Inoue used his extensive social networks to motivate and pull together project managers to finish the project successfully in the given time frame. At Honda, senior managers have intentionally left the formal power of LPLs ambiguous to emphasize leadership based on personal qualities. Similar to other successful LPLs, Inoue's leadership is based on contrasting qualities of determination and humility. He was further highly successful in understanding and synthesizing the contextual micro- and wider organizational demands.

IMPLICATIONS

This study has managerial implications. First, the case indicates the importance of concept creation in the early phases of the NPD process. During the concept creation, LPLs should emphasize the acquisition of knowledge through socialization, such as observations of customer behavior. The senior management, in turn, should allow NPD teams enough time to develop a clear, coherent, and shared concept that guides the NPD processes and reduces conflicts created by misunderstandings. Second, analogies and metaphors can be used to extend mental boundaries to develop novel design solutions. Through the metaphor of the falcon, group members developed a shared image and designed a wagon with a streamlined design and a large cargo capacity. Before this metaphor, group members focused on the existing wagons and were not able to expand their thinking. Third, the case indicates that organizations can create a supportive context that facilitates knowledge creation. At Honda, constructive dialogues during *waigaya* meetings enable people to challenge existing paradigms and share their ideas without being ridiculed. Honda employees say that these meetings help to develop concepts and clear up ambiguous goals. While companies cannot change their cultures overnight, senior managers are able to promote NPD processes by providing project structure and support while leaving enough room for teams to be autonomous, especially during the concept creation phase.

CONCLUSION

This chapter described NPD from the knowledge creation perspective. While scholars have enabled us to understand some common features of successful NPD projects by identifying their antecedents, they often leave knowledge creation as a "black box" because the human-related dimensions are disregarded. It was shown through theoretical framework and case study that subjective human dreams and desires form the basis for successful NPD. Instead of being understood as a linear, sequential process, it is a dialectic phenomenon based on subjective ideas and social interaction processes.

The case indicates that the distinctive strengths of Honda are rooted in the development of strong concepts at the beginning of the project, the "Three Reality Principle" that encourages employees to experience the reality from the customers' point of view, the synthesizing of contrasting entities through *waigaya* meetings, and the seamless cooperation among sales, engineering, and development throughout NPD projects. These processes are based on Soichiro Honda's corporate philosophy that simultaneously embraces individual intentionality and structural voluntarism. The Accord Wagon was therefore largely developed in the Honda Way.

NOTE

1. Honda is one of the youngest of the large global carmakers, tracing its roots back to an auxiliary engine-equipped bicycle in 1948. Honda is currently the world's largest motorcycle manufacturer and Japan's third largest carmaker (after Toyota and Nissan). The business areas are motorcycles, automobiles, financial services, and power products. In fiscal 2005, Honda employed 137,827 employees and used approximately 467.7 billion yen, or 5.5 percent of its sales, on research and development.

REFERENCES

Alvesson, M. (1996). *Communication, power, and organization.* New York: Walter de Gruyter.

Ancona, D. G., & Caldwell, D. F. (1989). Demography and design: Predictors of new product team performance. *Organization Science, 3*(3), 321–341.

Brown, S. L., & Eisenhardt, K. M. (1995). Product development: Past research, present findings, and future directions. *Academy of Management Review, 20,* 343–378.

Clark, K. B., & Fujimoto, T. (1991). *Product development performance: Strategy, organization, and management in the world auto industry.* Cambridge, MA: Harvard Business School Press.

Crawford, M. C. (1997). *New product management* (5th ed.). Chicago: Irwin.

Depraz, N., Varela, F. J., & Vermersch, P. (2003). *On becoming aware: An experiential pragmatics.* Amsterdam: Benjamins Press.

Hedlund, G. (1994). A model of knowledge management and the n-form corporation. *Strategic Management Journal, 15,* 73–91.

Heidegger, M. (1962). *Being and time.* New York: Harper & Row.

Imai, K., Nonaka, I., & Takeuchi, H. (1985). Managing the new product development process: How Japanese companies learn and unlearn. In K. B. Clark, R. H. Hayes, & C. Lorenz (Eds.), *The uneasy alliance.* Cambridge, MA: Harvard Business School Press, 337–381.

Katz, R., & Tushman, M. (1981). An investigation into the managerial roles and career paths of gatekeepers and project supervisors in a major R&D faculty. *Administrative Science Quarterly, 27,* 103–110.

Kogut, B., & Zander, U. (1992). Knowledge of the firm, combinative capabilities, and the replication of technology. *Organization Science, 3,* 383–397.

Krishnan, V., & Ulrich, K. T. (2001). Product development decisions: A review of the literature. *Management Science, 47*(1), 1–21.

Lawson, T. (1997). *Economics and reality.* New York: Routledge.

Mead, G. H. (1934). *Mind, self and society.* Chicago: University of Chicago Press.

Myers, S., & Marquis, D. G. (1969). *Successful industrial innovation*. Washington, DC: National Science Foundation.

Nishida, K. (1921). *An inquiry into the good*. New Haven, CT: Yale University Press.

Nonaka, I. (1991). The knowledge creating company. *Harvard Business Review, 69,* 96–104.

Nonaka, I. (1994). A dynamic theory of organizational knowledge creation. *Organization Science, 5*(1), 14–37.

Nonaka, I. (2005). Managing organizational knowledge: Theoretical and methodological foundations. In K. G. Smith & M. A. Hitt (Eds.), *Great minds in management: The process of theory development*. New York: Oxford University Press, 373–393.

Nonaka, I., & Konno, N. (1998). The concept of "ba": Building a foundation for knowledge creation. *California Management Review, 40* (3), 1–15.

Nonaka, I., Peltokorpi, V., & Tomae, H. (2005). Strategic knowledge creation: The case of Hamamatsu Photonics. *International Journal of Technology Management, 30*(3/4), 248–264.

Nonaka, I., & Takeuchi, H. (1995). *The knowledge-creating company*. New York: Oxford University Press.

Nonaka, I., & Toyama, R. (2005). The theory of the knowledge-creating firm: Subjectivity, objectivity and synthesis. *Industrial and Corporate Change, 14* (3), 419–436.

Nonaka. I, Toyama, R., & Konno, N. (2000). SECI, ba, and leadership: A unified model of dynamic knowledge creation. *Long Range Planning, 33,* 1–31.

Pettigrew, A. M. (1977). Strategy formulation as a political process. *International Studies of Management and Organization, 7*(2), 78–87.

Polanyi, M. (1952). *Personal knowledge*. Chicago: University of Chicago Press.

Polanyi, M. (1966). *The tacit dimension*. London: Routledge & Kegan Paul.

Rescher, N. (2003). *Epistemology: On the scope and limits of knowledge*. Albany, NY: SUNY Press.

Rorty, R. (1979). *Philosophy and the mirror of nature*. Princeton, NJ: Princeton University Press.

Schilling, M. A., & Hill, C. W. L. (1998). Managing the new product development process: Strategic imperatives. *Academy of Management Executive, 12*(3), 67–81.

Schulze, A., & Hoegl, M. (2006). Knowledge creation in new product development projects. *Journal of Management, 32,* 1–27.

Takeuchi, H., & Nonaka, I. (1986). The new product development game. *Harvard Business Review*, January–February, 137–146.

Thompson, D. J. (1967). *Organizations in action*. New York: McGraw-Hill.

Thompson, M., & Walsham, G. (2004). Placing knowledge management in context. *Journal of Management Studies, 41*(5), 725–747.

Ulrich, K. T., & Eppinger, S. D. (1995). *Product design and development*. London: McGraw-Hill.

Von Krogh, G. (1998). Care in knowledge creation. *California Management Review, 40*(3), 133–154.

2

Funding Innovation through Venture Capital: A Global Perspective

MARTIN HAEMMIG

Venture capital is about commercializing innovation, often resulting either from entrepreneurs who leave their larger corporation or from researchers ending their academic career to move on to industry. They are driven by an idea to build their own product or service through their own company that either gets acquired (M&A) or gets publicly listed (IPO) on a stock exchange. It is important to understand that venture capital is not financing the fundamental research of the "R" side of R&D but rather the "D" element, advanced product development. The IPO is a means of raising large sums of capital for a company to expand its business, and it represents the most lucrative exit mechanism for its investors, who take major risks and demand healthy returns as compensation. On the other hand, a trade sale (M&A) by a larger company represents the most common exit alternative for the VC-backed companies.

Since 2001, about 85 to 95 percent of venture-financed companies in the United States, Israel, and Europe have focused on technology-related products and services, while the balance have gone into pure service or retail-related businesses. In Asia, on the other hand, there is often a different twist to it. India is focusing heavily on business outsourcing and software programming, as well as contracted development work or trials in the pharmaceutical and biotech sectors. Apart from semiconductor-driven technology, China, on the other hand, is currently focusing its venture capital investments more on applications or business model innovation opportunities that are highly

Venture-Backed Companies Outperform in Job and Revenue Generation in Ten Industry Sectors

The Global Insight study shows that venture-backed companies fared better in job creation and revenue growth than their U.S. private company peers in ten separate industries. Even in sectors that suffered net job losses, such as computer hardware and semiconductors, venture-backed companies were less affected. Not only did they grow faster than their national industry counterparts, but the sectors with higher concentrations of VC financing experienced higher employment growth differentials. The best example is the computer software industry, where venture-backed firms employed 88 percent of all computer software workers. Also, venture-backed software firms saw their revenues grow by 31 percent, compared with an overall 5 percent growth rate for the industry as a whole.

Venture Capital Impacts Companies in All Fifty States

From 1970 to 2003, venture capitalists invested $338.5 billion dollars into more than 21,600 U.S. companies. States where venture capital investment has been the strongest in the last three decades, such as California, Texas, and Massachusetts, have produced the most jobs and revenues for the country. Several states that are not necessarily known for the highest levels of

TABLE 2.1. National versus Venture Capital Employment and Sales Growth, 2000–2003

	Job Growth		Revenue Growth	
Sectors	National Firms	VC-backed Co.	National Firms	VC-backed Co.
Biotechnology	5%	23%	22%	28%
Business/Financial	−1%	4%	11%	11%
Communications	−18%	5%	−7%	2%
Computer Hardware	−14%	−1%	−2%	12%
Computer Software	−8%	17%	5%	31%
Healthcare Products	−2%	16%	6%	9%
Healthcare Services	9%	10%	25%	26%
Industrial/Energy	−9%	1%	0.2%	6%
Retailing & Media	−1%	12%	9%	20%
Semiconductors & Electronic	−26%	−10%	−21%	−16%
TOTAL	**−2.3%**	**6.5%**	**6.5%**	**11.6%**

Source: Global Insight Inc., 2004

TABLE 2.2. National Jobs at Originally Venture-Backed Companies in 2003; Top Fifteen States

Rank	State	Jobs 2003	Cumulative VC Investment 1970–2003 ($bn)
1	California	2,470,942	$ 140.1
2	Texas	899,173	$ 20.5
3	Massachusetts	712,329	$ 35.5
4	Pennsylvania	604,045	$ 9.5
5	Georgia	551,439	$ 7.2
6	Tennessee	543,018	$ 2.3
7	New York	470,527	$ 18.4
8	Washington	399,863	$ 9.6
9	Virginia	333,199	$ 8.6
10	New Jersey	310,925	$ 10.1
11	Florida	309,717	$ 8.2
12	Minnesota	287,984	$ 4.3
13	Illinois	235,941	$ 7.4
14	Ohio	195,180	$ 3.2
15	Connecticut	189,692	$ 5.5

Source: Global Insight Inc., 2004 [Total VC investment 1970–2003]

venture investing, but where a venture-backed market leader resides, have made significant contributions to the national economy as well. Examples include Washington (headquarters to Microsoft and Costco); Tennessee (headquarters to Federal Express); and Georgia (headquarters to Home Depot).

Venture Capital's Business Cycle

Venture capital is a cyclical business, subject not only to internal dynamics but also to the influence of external economic forces and to fluctuations in financial markets. Indeed, the data show that ventured firms increased their size and share in the economy over the last three years, despite the dot-com bust and high-tech equipment sales downturn. Venture-supported firms showed more continued solid progress.

VC-Backed Companies Top Contributors to R&D

In addition to jobs and revenues, venture-supported companies, often in conjunction with academic institutions, are performing a greater share of total

TABLE 2.3. National Revenues at Venture-Backed Companies in 2003; Top Fifteen States

Rank	State	Revenues 2003 ($bn)	Cumulative VC Investment 1970 – 2003 ($bn)
1	California	$ 437.8	$ 140.1
2	Texas	$ 188.1	$ 20.5
3	Massachusetts	$ 107.4	$ 35.5
4	Washington	$ 101.5	$ 9.6
5	Pennsylvania	$ 94.4	$ 9.5
6	Georgia	$ 91.5	$ 7.2
7	New York	$ 80.2	$ 18.4
8	Virginia	$ 63.9	$ 8.6
9	Florida	$ 60.6	$ 8.2
10	Tennessee	$ 60.3	$ 2.3
11	Minnesota	$ 56.9	$ 4.3
12	New Jersey	$ 49.6	$ 10.1
13	Connecticut	$ 48.9	$ 5.5
14	Illinois	$ 34.4	$ 7,4
15	North Carolina	$ 26.9	$ 5.8

Source: Global Insight Inc., PwC, TVE, NVCA MoneyTree Survey, 2004

U.S. research and development (R&D). Small companies backed by venture capital were particularly active. According to data from the National Science Foundation, the dollar value of small company R&D rose from $4.4 billion in 1984 to an estimated $40.1 billion in 2003, a ninefold increase. The share of American R&D done by companies with fewer than 500 employees rose from 5.9 percent in 1984 to 20.7 percent in 2003. Not only do these small companies fuel innovation on their own, but they also "feed" larger R&D firms with a steady stream of idea generation, according to the study. Of the top fifty American firms in R&D spending, forty-one were either originally venture-backed or were major acquirers of VC-created companies.

U.S. Venture Capital Dominates Globally

A dominant share of the entire world's total VC dollars, an estimated 72 percent, is invested in U.S. companies. That is second only to Israel when adjusted for the relative size of the economies of the two countries. In spite of its wealth, the U.S. has been able to maintain a high rate of economic growth due to the recurrence of new high-tech investment opportunities. The

American venture capital industry supports more than 40 percent of the companies entering the public market via IPOs.

As a worldwide leader in venture capital investments, the United States is setting the pace for innovation, research and development, and entrepreneurship. It is one of very few countries that have a continuum of VC investors, which helps diversify risk and ensure a steady flow of quality deals, providing excellent opportunities to grow the American economy.

THE VENTURE CAPITAL INDUSTRY

An Overview

According to America's National Venture Capital Association (NVCA), venture capital is money provided by professionals who invest alongside with management in young and rapidly growing companies that have the potential to develop into significant economic contributors. Venture capital is an important source of equity for start-up companies.

Professionally managed venture capital firms generally are private partnerships or closely held corporations funded by private and public pension funds, endowment funds, foundations, corporations, wealthy individuals, foreign investors, and the venture capitalists themselves.

Venture capitalists generally:

- Finance new and rapidly growing companies;
- Purchase equity securities;
- Assist in the development of new products or services;
- Add value to the company through active participation;
- Take higher risks with the expectation of higher rewards;
- Have a long-term orientation.

When considering an investment, venture capitalists carefully screen the technical and business merits of the proposed company. They only invest in a small percentage of the businesses they review (typically 0.5–1.0 percent), companies with a long-term perspective. Going forward, they actively work with the company's management by contributing their experience and business savvy gained from helping other companies with similar growth challenges.

Venture capitalists mitigate the risk of venture investing by developing a portfolio of young companies in a single venture fund. Many times they will coinvest with other professional venture capital firms, called syndiation. In addition, many venture partnership will manage multiple funds simultaneously. For decades, venture capitalists have nurtured the growth of America's high technology and entrepreneurial communities, resulting in significant job creation, economic growth, and international competitiveness. Companies such as Digital Equipment Corporation, Apple, Federal Express, Compaq,

Sun Microsystems, Intel, Microsoft, and Genentech are famous examples of companies that received venture capital early in their development.

Adding Value by Venture Capitalists

A large research effort undertaken by PriceWaterhouseCoopers before, during, and after the dot-com bubble on 351 technology companies in the United States (162), United Kingdom (87), and Continental Europe/Israel (102) provides a comparison in the added value services received by entrepreneurial venture-backed companies from their investors.

The answers provided by the fast-growth companies conclude that the average American venture capital firm outperforms the U.K. and Europeans/Israelis in every single item. The only exception was found in "Real Estate Assistance," where the British VCs show a slightly stronger support than their American counterparts, although this service is not really relevant. Unfortunately, the dataset does not sufficiently distinguish the Israeli VC firms from their European counterparts, since the result would likely favor the Israelis, given their well-known track record in terms of exits (IPO and M&A). Figure 2.1 shows the different services provided by the venture investors.

The recent scarcity of exit opportunities (IPO and M&A) has forced the VC firms to hold their existing portfolio firms for longer periods, which means managing these companies has moved to center stage. A report by KPMG Corporate Finance Group in 2003 reveals that monitoring managing and supporting the existing portfolio accounts for an average of over 40 percent of the VC firms' resources, with many firms way above this figure, particularly in early stage technology sectors.

Private Equity Investing

Venture capital investing has grown from a small investment pool in the 1960s and early 1970s to a mainstream asset class that is a viable and significant part of the institutional and corporate investment portfolio. Most investors refer to venture investing (VC) and buyout investing (LBO) as "private

TABLE 2.4. Added Value Provided by Venture Capitalists

(1) Customer introduction	(7) Engineering and product development
(2) Strategic alliance introduction	(8) Real estate assistance
(3) Portfolio company alliance	(9) Strategy development
(4) Recruitment and hiring	(10) Technology
(5) Marketing and PR	(11) Other
(6) Financial management	

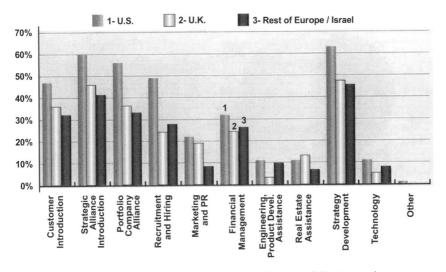

FIGURE 2.1. Added Value by Venture Capitalists to Their Portfolio Companies

Source: PwC: Paths-to-Value study from 1998 to 2001, updated 2002–2003

equity investing." This term sometimes gets confusing, since some financiers use the term "private equity" to refer only to buyout fund investing (LBO). In any case, an institutional investor will allocate about 2 to 5 percent of its institutional portfolio for investment in alternative assets, such as the private equity asset class (VC and LBO) as part of their overall asset allocation. Currently, over 50 percent of U.S. investments in the private equity asset class come from institutional public and private pension funds, with the balance provided by endowments, foundations, insurance companies, banks, individuals, and other entities who seek to diversify their portfolios and generate superior returns with these investments.

What Is a Venture Capitalist?

The typical person-on-the-street depiction of a venture capitalist is that of a wealthy financier who wants to fund start-up companies. The perception is that a person who develops a brand-new change-the-world invention needs capital; thus, if they can't get capital from a bank or from their own pockets, they enlist the help of a venture capitalist.

In truth, venture capital and buyout firms are pools of capital, typically organized as limited partnerships that invest in companies that represent the opportunity for a high rate of return within three to seven years. The venture capitalist may look at several hundred investment opportunities before investing in only a few selected companies with favorable investment opportunities. Far from being simply passive financiers, venture capitalists foster growth

in companies through their involvement in the management, strategic marketing, and planning of their investee companies. They are entrepreneurs first
and financiers second. The direct influence of success they have on these
high-growth companies is far more significant than that of any investor in
public companies.

Even individuals may be venture capitalists. In the early days of venture
capital investment, in the 1950s and 1960s, individual investors were the ar-
chetypal venture investors. While this type of individual investment did not
totally disappear, the modern venture firm emerged as the dominant venture
investment vehicle. However, in the last few years, individuals have again
become a potent and increasingly larger part of the early-stage start-up venture life cycle. These "angel investors" will mentor a company, especially in its
very early stages, and provide needed capital and expertise to help develop
companies. Angel investors may either be wealthy people with management
expertise or retired business professionals who seek the opportunity for first-
hand business development.

Investment Focus

Venture capitalists may be generalist or specialist investors, depending on
their investment strategy. Venture capitalists can be generalists, investing in various industry sectors, various geographic locations, or various stages of a company's life. Alternatively, they may be specialists in one or two industry sectors,
or may seek to invest in only a localized geographic area and in certain stages.

Not all venture capitalists invest in very young start-ups. While VC firms will
invest in companies that are in their initial start-up modes, venture capitalists
will also invest in companies at various stages of the business life cycle. A venture capitalist may invest before there is a real product or company organized
(so-called "seed investing"), or may provide capital to a start-up company in its
first or second stages of development, known as "early-stage investing." Also, the
venture capitalist may provide needed financing to help a company grow
beyond a critical mass to become more successful ("expansion stage financing").

The venture capitalist may invest in a company throughout the company's
life cycle, and therefore some funds focus on later-stage investing by providing financing to help the company grow to a critical mass in order to attract
public financing through a public stock offering (IPO). Alternatively, the venture capitalist may help the company facilitate a merger or acquisition (M&A)
with another company by providing liquidity and exit for the company's
founders and its investors.

At the other end of the spectrum, some venture funds specialize in the acquisition, turnaround, or recapitalization of public and private companies that
represent favorable investment opportunities.

There are venture funds that will be broadly diversified and will invest in
companies in various industry sectors as diverse as semiconductors, software,

retailing, and restaurants, and others that may be specialists in only one technology.

While high-technology investment makes up most of the venture investing in the U.S., and the venture industry gets a lot of attention for its high-technology investments, venture capitalists also invest in companies such as construction, industrial products, business services, etc. Several firms specialize in retail company investment, and others focus on investing only in "socially responsible" start-up endeavors.

Venture capital firms come in various sizes, from small seed specialist firms of only a few million dollars under management to firms with over a billion dollars in invested capital around the world. The common denominator in all of these types of venture investing is that the venture capitalist is not a passive investor, but has an active and vested interest in guiding, leading, and growing the companies they have invested in. They seek to add value through their experience and network from investing in tens and hundreds of companies.

Some venture firms are successful by creating synergies between the various portfolio companies they have invested in; for example, one company that has a great software product, but does not have adequate distribution technology, may be paired with another company or its management in the venture portfolio that has better distribution technology.

Length of Investment

Venture capitalists will help companies grow, but they eventually seek to exit the investment in three to seven years. An early-stage investment make take up to ten years to mature, while a later-stage investment may only take a few years, so the appetite for the investment life cycle must be congruent with the limited partnership's appetite for liquidity. The venture investment is neither a short-term nor a liquid investment, but an investment that must be made with careful diligence and expertise.

Types of Firms

There are several types of venture capital firms, but most mainstream firms invest their capital through funds organized as limited partnerships in which the venture capital firm serves as the general partner. The most common type of venture firm is an independent venture firm that has no affiliations with any other financial institution. These are called "private independent firms." Venture firms may also be affiliates or subsidiaries of a commercial bank, investment bank, or insurance company and may make investments on behalf of outside investors or the parent firm's clients. Still other firms may be subsidiaries of nonfinancial, industrial corporations making investments on behalf of the parent itself. These latter firms are typically called "direct investors" or "corporate venture investors."

Other organizations may include government-affiliated investment programs that help start-up companies either through state, local, or federal programs. One common vehicle is the Small Business Investment Company, or SBIC, program administered by the Small Business Administration, in which a venture capital firm may augment its own funds with federal funds and leverage its investment in qualified investee companies.

While the predominant form of organization is the limited partnership, in recent years the tax code in the U.S. and other countries has allowed the formation of Limited Liability Partnerships (LLPs) or Limited Liability Companies (LLCs) as alternative forms of organization. However, the limited partnership is still the predominant organizational form. The advantages and disadvantages of each have to do with liability, taxation issues, and management responsibility.

The venture capital firm will organize its partnership as a pooled fund; that is, a fund made up of the general partner and the investors or limited partners. These funds are typically organized as fixed life partnerships, usually having a life of ten years. Each fund is capitalized by commitments of capital from the limited partners. Once the partnership has reached its target size, the partnership is closed to further investment from new investors or even existing investors so the fund has a fixed capital pool from which to make its investments.

Like a mutual fund company, a venture capital firm may have more than one fund in existence. A venture firm may raise another fund a few years after closing the first fund in order to continue to invest in companies and to provide more opportunities for existing and new investors.

It is not uncommon to see a successful firm raise six or seven funds consecutively over the span of ten to fifteen years. Each fund is managed separately and has its own investors or limited partners and its own general partners. These funds' investment strategy may be similar to other funds in the firm. However, the firm may have one fund with a specific focus and another with a different focus and yet another with a broadly diversified portfolio. This depends on the strategy and focus of the venture firm itself.

Corporate Venturing

One form of investing that was popular in the 1980s, and has become trendy again, is corporate venturing. This is usually called "direct investing" in portfolio companies by venture capital programs or subsidiaries of nonfinancial corporations. These investment vehicles seek to find qualified investment opportunities that are congruent with the parent company's strategic technology or that provide synergy or cost savings.

These corporate venturing programs may be loosely organized programs affiliated with existing business development programs or may be self-contained entities with a strategic charter and mission to make investments congruent with the parent's strategic mission. Some venture firms specialize in advising, consulting, and managing a corporation's venturing program.

The typical distinction between corporate venturing and other types of venture investment vehicles is that corporate venturing is usually performed with corporate strategic objectives in mind, while other venture investment vehicles typically have investment return or financial objectives as their primary goal. This may be a generalization, as corporate venture programs are not immune to financial considerations, but the distinction can be made.

The other distinction of corporate venture programs is that they usually invest the parent's capital, while other venture investment vehicles invest outside investors' capital.

The Most Commonly Practiced Investment Vehicle—Limited Partnership

This is the dominant investment structure used in the U.S., Europe, Israel, and a majority of countries in the Asia-Pacific region, though Taiwan, as well as some percentage of Japan and Korea, uses other vehicles. There are still countries, including Switzerland and China, that don't permit the LP structure yet, although it is only a matter of time to get the regulations changed.

The venture capital firm acts as general partner (GP) of the limited partnership, responsible for managing the fund, while institutions and other investors become limited partners (LP). Returns to investors and the private equity firm are defined in the partnership agreement, called PPM—Private Placement Memorandum. This will typically involve annual "management fees" (2–3 percent), and a share in capital gain of the fund called "carried interest" (15–25 percent), provided it has reached a threshold, often called "hurdle-rate" (typically around 10 percent IRR since the fund's inception). Advantages and disadvantages affect both the private equity manager (PEM) and the private equity investor (PEI).

Advantage of limited partnerships. First, the limited partnership is tax-transparent, meaning that income and capital gains flow through the partnership untaxed. Returns are taxed in the hands of the end investors according to their own specific tax regime, which is particularly important to tax-exempt pension fund investors. Second, considerable flexibility surrounds the structure and terms of each limited partnership, enabling private equity managers to tailor each partnership to the particular needs of the fund. Third, each limited partnership has a fixed life (typically ten years). Capital gains (carried interest) are shared between the limited partner (LP) and investors and the general partner (GP), the fund manager. This gives the latter strong incentives to invest for absolute growth over a defined period, to the benefit of the former.

Disadvantage of limited partnerships. Limited partnerships are not publicly tradable. Interest may change hands in the secondary market, but there is no ready access to liquidity or a market price.

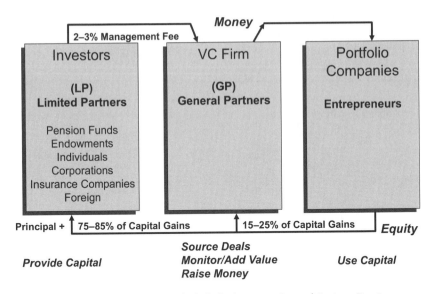

FIGURE 2.2. Financial Flows in Typical Limited Partner-General Partner Structure
Source: Chris Rust, Sequoia, 2001

VENTURE GLOBAL CAPITAL MARKET

Venture Capital Investment Marked the Beginning of a New Cycle in 2004

For the first year since 2000, many global areas saw a slight increase in the amount invested in venture capital. Across the United States, Europe, and Israel, an aggregate $25.7 billion was invested in 3,222 deals (Ernst & Young/ VentureOne).

In the U.S., investment increased 8 percent to $20.4 billion, while in Israel investment increased 27 percent to $0.7 billion (investment in Israeli companies based both in and outside of Israel increased 25 percent to $1.2 billion). In Europe, venture capital investment, which declined 30 percent from 2002 to 2003, stabilized in 2004 at $4.5 billion.

If 2004 was the beginning of a new cycle, then the trends we are beginning to see provide an indication of the types of companies that investors are betting on to form the successes of the future, the money that is being raised to fuel future investment, and the geographical distribution of global investment.

Initial Round Investment Makes a Comeback—Investing in the Future

An up-tick in 2004 of first round funding—companies receiving their first venture capital investment—for the first time since 2000—supports the view

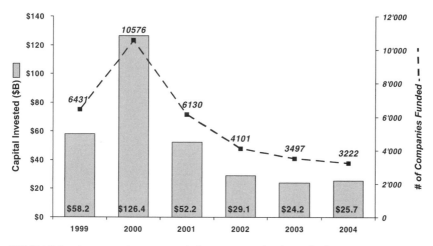

FIGURE 2.3. Aggregate Venture Capital Investment in the United States, Europe, and Israel (1999–2004)
Source: VentureOne-VentureSource database, Zero2IPO, 2005

TABLE 2.5. Total Venture Capital Financing in the United States (USA) and Europe (EU) in 2004 (in $)

2004 Share	Health Care		Info-Technology		Product/Services		Other	
	USA	EU	USA	EU	USA	EU	USA	EU
Total Investment in %	32%	43%	55%	44%	11%	8%	2%	5%
by $-amount	$6.7bn	$1.9bn	$11.6bn	$1.9bn	$2.3bn	$0.4bn	$0.4bn	$0.2bn

Source: VentureOne-VentureSource database, 2005

that the VC industry is entering a new venture capital cycle. Venture capitalists were back in the market for new investments in 2004.

In the United States, initial round investment increased 10 percent by number of deals and 17 percent by amount invested to $4.1 billion invested in 661 deals. Initial rounds were also a bright spot for Europe in 2004, where the amount of capital invested in these rounds increased by 42 percent to $1.3 billion, despite seeing the number of initial round investments decrease by 7 percent to 335 rounds.

Initial financings are the company creation rounds, indicating where the industry is placing its long-term bets. Different industries in the United States and Europe were important for initial financings in 2004. In the United States, software, consumer and business services, and biopharmaceuticals led initial financings. In Europe, biopharmaceuticals, software, and communications were

TABLE 2.6. **Investing in the Future: Initial Financing in United States (USA) and Europe (EU) in 2004 (by rounds)**

2004 Share	Health Care		Information Technology		Product/Services		Other	
	USA	EU	USA	EU	USA	EU	USA	EU
Initial VC Investments (1st round)	23% (#144)	26% (#73)	56% (#344)	48% (#132)	14% (#89)	16% (#45)	7% (#43)	10% (#27)
Biopharmaceuticals	10%	16%						
Health CareServices	2%	1%						
Medical Devices	10%	8%						
Medical IS	2%	2%						
Communications			8%	10%				
Electronics			5%	7%				
Information Services			6%	1%				
Semiconductors			7%	4%				
Software			29%	25%				
Retail					1%	3%		
Services					11%	7%		
Products					2%	6%		
Others							7%	10%

Source: VentureOne-VentureSource database, 2005

in the forefront. Their technologies and services will enter the market in the next two to four years and are expected to reach some recognizable penetration in the coming four to six years, the time the company either gets acquired or goes public through an IPO.

Global Venture Capital Investments—A Shift toward Asia Is Emerging

The United States still invests around two-thirds of all venture capital around the world, about $20 billion of the $30 billion invested globally. The second block of countries receiving investments between $1 billion and $1.5 billion are Canada, United Kingdom, China, and Israel. The biggest growth encountered in 2004 was in Israel, China, and India, a trend that is expected to continue in the coming years. China saw a temporary plateau in 2005,

TABLE 2.7. Global Venture Investment Ranking 2004 ($30bn)

Rank	Country	Investment ($bn)	Deals (No)
1	United States	$20.4	2067
	> Bay Area	$7.1	638
	> New England	$2.5	255
	> So. California	$2.0	174
	> New York City	$1.5	146
	> Texas	$1.0	108
	> Washington St.	$0.8	85
	> Potomac	$0.7	82
2	Canada	$1.5	589
3	United Kingdom	$1.4	286
4	China (PRC)	$1.3	253
5	Israel	$1.2	179
6	France	$0.8	194
7	Germany	$0.7	125
8	India	$0.6	47
9	Sweden	$0.4	134
10	Switzerland	$0.2	29
11	Denmark	$0.2	61

Source: VentureOne-VentureSource database, Canada VC Association, Zero2 IPO, 2005

since a relevant regulation was enacted in January that took most of the year to see its amendment pass. The recent capital that is being raised to fuel future investments will see the shift in geographical distribution of global investment, with Asia emerging even stronger and, although still far apart from the United States, challenging old Europe.

Exit Opportunities for Venture-Backed Companies—China Is on the Map

According to Ernst & Young/VentureOne, the United States realized sixty-seven venture-backed IPOs in 2004, raising a total of $5 billion, up from just twenty-two IPOs raising $1.4 billion in 2003. Healthcare companies dominated America's exits, with thirty-nine IPOs raising $2.1 billion. Bio-pharmaceutical companies accounted for the majority of these, with medical devices also accounting for a sizable number. The predominance of liquidity opportunities for healthcare companies has perhaps spurred the recent increases in investment into this industry group. From 2003 to 2004, the

TABLE 2.8. Global Venture-Backed Tech-Investments and Exits (IPO and M&A) in 2004

2004	USA	Europe	Israel	Asia
VC Investments ($30bn)	69%	14%	5%	12% *all Asia*
IPO (value realized)	74.3%	14.0%	3.6% *in USA*	8.1% *China only*
M&A (value realized)	85%	12%	3.6% *in USA*	1% *China only*

Source: Ernst & Young/VentureOne-VentureSource database, Zero2IPO, 2004

dollars invested in healthcare companies in the U.S. increased by 11 percent to reach $6.6 billion.

In 2004 there were also higher value exits through M&A in the United States, as improving stock markets provided companies with more valuable currency to buy start-ups. In 2004 there were 376 venture-backed M&As with $22.6 billion paid, up from 339 with $12.5 billion paid in 2003. The median amount paid in an M&A rose from $19 million to $22 million.

In Europe, thirty-four venture-backed companies completed IPOs, raising $932 million, up from only nine IPOs raising $167 million in 2003. IT rather than healthcare accounted for the majority of IPOs in Europe, with seventeen exits raising $476 million. Communications and networking companies accounted for the majority of IPOs in the IT group in Europe. M&A activity grew slightly as well, going from 141 in 2002 to 147 in 2004. Software, with sixty-one transactions, was the main driver of European M&A activity.

Zero2IPO in China reports that there was significant growth in venture-backed exits in China as well, with twenty-four venture-backed companies raising $4.3 billion. Four of the top ten global technology IPOs in 2004 were Chinese, all listed on the NYSE or NASDAQ–SMIC (NYSE: SMI); Shanda (NASDAQ: SNDA); Job51 (NASDAQ: JOBS); and CTrip.com (NASDAQ: CTRP). Trade sales (M&A) represented nearly half of all exits, while IPOs represented nearly 70 percent of the total exit amount.

THE GLOBALIZATION OF VENTURE CAPITAL

The global economy has fueled the growth of entrepreneurship and created investment opportunities almost everywhere in the world. Entrepreneurs continue to develop innovations that create new markets and businesses. These companies increasingly need to be global in scale in order to successfully capture market share and build out to a sustainable business that pays solid returns to investors.

Global Technology Demand Drives International Start-Ups and Their VC Firms

Competition drives both small and large corporations toward efficiency in any aspect of the business. Technology is one relevant factor that can assist these firms in either remaining or emerging as leaders in their global environment. The pressure from shareholders on their returns forces these players to focus increasingly on their core business, speeding up time to market with new products or services, and thus to search for external technologies to complement their internal R&D efforts. This provides huge opportunities for start-ups to provide some missing product or service pieces, which help these larger firms stay competitive in their offerings.

This demand spurs increasingly a circle that includes larger corporations, start-up companies, their venture capital firms, and fund investors. It is this environment that requires international VC firms to provide their expertise of building companies and their global network to enable start-ups to go international. The added value by international VCs helps build faster and more globally exposed start-up companies that lead to bigger and more competitive firms and thus potentially higher returns for VC funds, if executed properly.

Global Venture Capital Investment Flows in 2004—U.S., Europe, Israel, Asia

Foreign "direct investments" to local portfolio firms and investments made outside the domestic market can be significant. American based VC firms invest 87 percent domestically and 13 percent in foreign countries. Europe's VCs invest 75 percent in their region, while an additional 25 percent goes overseas. Israel's VCs invest 86 percent in Israeli and/or Israel-related start-ups. Asian VCs invest 74 percent in their region, while 26 percent is directed to overseas companies, mainly to the United States to tap into higher return investments and to learn the trade through coinvestments. Asian VCs and multinational tech firms look increasingly to Israel in order to access technology.

On the other hand, American venture-backed companies receive an additional 8 percent on top by foreign VC firms. Europe's VC-backed entrepreneurial companies obtain an additional 47 percent (mainly from the U.S.) on top of their EU-based VC firms, while Israeli companies obtain 120 percent and Asian companies 52 percent above their domestic VC funding. In summary, about $5 billion of the $30 billion in 2004 was invested outside their geographical region, not including the intra-Europe and intra-Asian deals.

A study carried out (by Ernst & Young/VentureOne/Martin Haemmig) late in 2004 into cross-border investment found that several European venture capitalists are investing more frequently in the United States than in Europe, indicating that the European venture capital industry is more globalized than previously thought. In 2004, European VCs invested in 200 rounds in the United States, and just 140 rounds cross-border in Europe through the first three quarters of

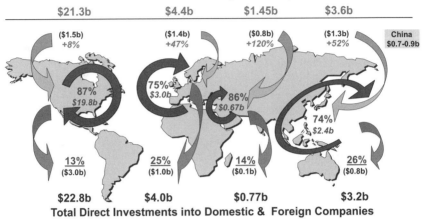

FIGURE 2.4. Global Direct Investment Flow into Innovative Companies in 2004 ($30.7 bn)
Source: VentureXpert/Venture Economics, IVA, EVCA, Zero2IPO, 2005 (Martin Haemmig)

2004. The United Kingdom and Germany were the biggest investors in the United States. American venture capitalists reciprocated with numerous investments in European companies, with a preference for the United Kingdom and France. This trans-Atlantic exchange indicates that venture capital is becoming a much more global phenomenon than previously thought and contradicts the conventional wisdom of a few years back that venture capitalists would not invest in a company farther away than a two-hour drive. Although early-stage venturing requires local support and hand holding, venture capitalists are willing to move to global places where opportunities emerge, even if it means setting up an office or collaborating with local partners.

RATIONALE FOR VENTURE CAPITAL FUNDING

Venture capital investments have reached global attention with the dot-com craze in 1999–2000, where investment peaked $100 billion in the United States and about $120 billion globally. The 2002–2004 timeframe has still seen healthy annual investment levels of about $30–35 billion across the globe, which is higher than any level prior to 1998. Although this volume represents only the combined R&D expenditure of the largest eight U.S. technology corporation levels (Ford, GM, Pfizer, IBM, Microsoft, Motorola, Cisco, and Intel), the economic impact of the very small start-up companies is substantial. Each year, about 2,000–2,500 companies receive formal venture investments in the United States in the post-bubble era, about 1,000–1,500 in Europe, 400–600 in Israel and 500–1,000 in Asia.

Most of these emerging start-up companies focus on products, solutions, enabling technologies, and services, where the market is either too small for the big global players or where these young and dynamic entities are simply faster in the market than their larger counterparts. Depending on the liquidity of capital markets, the young firms either go public within four to seven years from their inception (about 20–45 percent of the pool in the 1990s and only 2–5 percent between 2001 and 2005 had IPOs), while the balance gets acquired typically by larger firms. It is noteworthy that a substantial portion of these high-risk investments experienced bankruptcy early in their life cycle.

Time to market and the rapid development of new technologies, as well as the competitive environment, force large and medium-sized tech-based companies to lay out their technology road maps, focusing on their core competencies, and complement the missing elements by reaching out to start-up companies in order to fill the gaps to the final product or solution offering.

The mobility of (1) technology, (2) capital, and (3) people has spurred substantial cross-border investments because emerging innovations developed in smaller countries have to be commercialized into larger markets to justify their huge investments. On the other hand, the future success of many countries will depend strongly upon the integration and liquidity of their venture capital market and the inventiveness and management of their high-tech industries.

The technology boom in the 1990s and the recent availability of modern telecommunication and the Internet for ease and low-cost global reach enabled many of the technologically excluded countries to become technological adopters. Israel, Taiwan, South Korea, and Singapore have graduated in the last decade from this group to join the top-rank innovators, while China and India begin to make strong inroads in the post-dot-com era. As of today, it is not about developing new technology in China but rather the use of known core components for applications that are rapidly scalable with some twist to protect the imbedded intellectual property, while India's focus has been more on the business outsourcing side and on software.

Virtually all nations proclaim allegiance to global markets, but a more intractable division is taking hold, this time based on technology. A small part of the globe, accounting for some 15 percent of the earth's population, provides nearly all of the world's technology innovations. A second part, involving perhaps half of the world's population, is able to adopt these technologies in production and consumption. The remaining part, covering around a third of the world's population, is technologically disconnected, neither innovating at home nor adopting foreign technologies (*The Economist*, 2000). New communication technologies will blur these boundaries, while venture capital has proven its relevant impact on nations' economic growth through the creation of innovative solutions that serve a real need in the market.

THE FUTURE OF VENTURE CAPITAL IN THE GLOBAL INNOVATION ARENA

The venture capital world has changed and is undergoing a significant period of transition characterized by increasing globalization, a focus on capital efficiency, and the return of the Internet.

As competitive pressures make the capital efficiencies offered by the pool of lower-cost talent in regions such as China, India, and Eastern Europe impossible to ignore, and as the growing consumer markets of the Far East—especially China—present increased opportunities, the need to go global today arrives much earlier in the life cycle of most venture-backed company. The globalization of venture-backed companies, growing markets and technology development outside the mature hotbeds, and the innovation being conducted by and for markets like China and India that will ultimately be taken global are the forces driving the globalization of the venture capital industry. These trends will create many more examples of venture-backed companies structured to have R&D centers in China, India, Israel, Russia, and the United States, manufacturing facilities in China, India, Eastern Europe, and Vietnam, and management headquartered near the main customer markets—and operating as true global companies from day one.

Globalization of Venture Capital Will Continue in the Future

Many companies today need to be global from the outset in order to access top talent wherever it is found, realize production efficiencies, and tap the most promising markets. Equally, innovation is no longer the sole province of the established hotbeds; whether in China, India, or another one of the emerging technology hotbeds, innovation is now global. These factors are in turn driving venture capitalists to become global as well, in order to help their portfolio companies to access foreign markets and source talent and to find the best deals wherever they arise. In this context, a key question exists: if we are at the beginning of a new cycle, what regions will drive global growth in venture capital?

There is no doubt that the United States will continue to receive the largest amount of venture investment in the foreseeable future. The outlook for Europe is not so certain, as the area has not yet seen the same increases in investment as in the United States. Given the lesser presence of venture capitalists in Europe, some companies have chosen to hold an initial public offering on a market such as the alternative investment market (e.g., AIM in London) to raise capital, rather than taking on venture capital financing. This is most common in markets such as Russia, where the venture capital industry is less developed. Investment trends in Europe have historically lagged behind the United States by two quarters, and given this, the same upswing in venture capital investment seen in the United States and Israel may well occur in 2005 and beyond.

Further evidence for the globalization of the technology industry as a whole comes from the World Economic Forum's recently released annual technology rankings. The report ranks countries based on their ability to exploit global information and communications technology. The United States moved from first to fifth place in the report in 2005, indicating that the environment for technology is improving outside of the United States—something likely to continue. Singapore, Iceland, Finland, and Denmark were ranked in positions one to four in the report. Although the United States remains the major market into which technology is sold, and is still ranked first for "business readiness" by the WEF survey, these statistics provide interesting food for thought.

Emerging Markets Are Gearing Up—China, India, Russia, Brazil, and Mexico

Venture capitalists are increasingly looking to China and other emerging markets such as India for new opportunities. China and India in particular exhibit many signs of entrepreneurial potential, as Silicon Valley did in the 1970s—signs such as a large base of engineering talent, technological innovation, a large customer base, and access to capital. At any venture capital conference attended these days, it is hard to avoid a session on "your China strategy." Many investors clocked up the air miles recently as they traveled to China and India to pursue market opportunities, whether to help portfolio companies expand into new markets, expand their networks, or explore investment opportunities.

Asia overall has seen a rise in the number of VC funds raised, investments made, and exits realized. Funds investing in this region are now both domestic and foreign. In Asia, a cycle began after the financial crisis of 1997 that is now coming to a close for private equity funds. Returns have been good, making fundraising easier and providing proof that venture capital can work in Asia. To a large degree, the 1997 financial crisis in Asia destroyed traditional ways of doing business based on old family wealth, thus providing an opening for venture capital and private equity.

Other interesting places for future venture capital investments are Russia, Brazil, and Mexico, which all operate below the radar screen of most venture capital firms today. Multinational technology firms with sales and marketing activities in these emerging markets have already identified opportunities and have their venture capital units scouting for potential deals. The former vice president at Intel Capital, Claude Leglise, views the three countries through his recent experiences (Ernst & Young Global VC Report, 2005).

Russia has two things that are attractive from our perspective. Like in China, the consumption of computers and communication devices is growing very rapidly in Russia; so is its domestic market—it's probably the fastest-growing country in Europe between the Atlantic and the Urals. The other attractive feature is Russian science. A lot of extremely exciting technology has been designed in Russia. But this is not news—that's why companies like Boeing have had operations there for a long time, and that's why Intel has a lot of people over there to design algorithms.

The thesis in Russia is that venture capitalists or multinationals will find mechanisms to take the inventions out of the academy, the institute, and turn them into businesses. The challenges are many, and they are actually more complex than in China. But the first corporate venture capital units—e.g., Intel, IBM, etc.—starting with their investment activity a couple of years ago, have already had some good results from it.

Brazil and Mexico have an altogether different flavor related to the development of telecommunications and the development of computer systems in those countries. Brazil was protected from the outside world for many years and developed a unique competency in banking software, in part to manage the hyperinflation they experienced. Intel, for example, found some interesting investment ideas there. Their main theme has been the construction of communication networks in those countries. In Mexico, for example, Intel Capital focused on enabling infrastructure when compared with Russia or China.

Global Investment Focus by the VC Firms around the World, 2005–2010

A survey in spring 2005—initiated by NVCA, the American National Venture Capital Association and Deloitte & Touche LLP—of 545 venture capital firms around the world measured attitudes and intentions regarding investment regions and industry sectors in the timeframe until 2010. The recent trend of venture capital firms to go global continues. American venture capitalists are following the entrepreneurs, no matter where they are around the world.

This is even true for the most local focused Silicon Valley top-brand VC firms, such as Sequoia, Kleiner Perkins, Mayfield, NEA, Bessemer, Doll Capital Management, Venrock, RedPoint, etc., since they have either invested in local Chinese VC firms or are setting up their own offices in China or India. These two Asian destinations are named as top global targets in emerging markets, since entrepreneurialism is embedded in their culture and the growth, combined with its associated opportunities, will be there over the next decade.

The United States remains the top investment target for domestic and most foreign VC firms. All of the American VC firms indicated they will continue their investing activity in the United States. Not less than 16 percent of foreign firms indicated that they expect to even increase investing activity in the United States over the next five years. Combined, 65 percent of all VCs surveyed worldwide indicated plans to invest in the United States over the next five years. With a wide range of quality deals, experienced local investors, and a solid IPO market, the United States is seen by VCs as a mature, proven marketplace.

American VC firms. About 20 percent of U.S.-based VC respondents plan to increase their global investment activity over the next five years, up from 11 percent currently investing abroad. Forty-two percent plan to invest abroad only with other investors that have a local presence; 39 percent plan to develop strategic alliances with experienced foreign-based venture capital firms; and 30 percent plan to open satellite offices in select regions globally. The U.S. VCs indicated that they expect to maintain their U.S. investment presence, both in terms of physical presence and investment levels. According to American VCs, the countries of greatest investment interest over the next five years are China (20 percent), India (18 percent), Canada/Mexico (13 percent), Continental Europe (13 percent), Israel (12 percent), and the United Kingdom (11 percent).

Canadian VC firms. Of Canadian VC respondents, 29 percent plan to increase investment activity in the United States over the next five years. Currently, 48 percent are investing in the United States, with 67 percent planning to invest in the United States over five years. All Canadian VCs plan to continue investing in Canada.

Israeli VC firms. The United States and Israel are their top two destinations for investment, with 19 percent indicating plans to increase investment in the United States. Currently, 44 percent are investing in the United States, which is expected to increase to 56 percent investment over the next five years. Forty-three percent are currently focusing their investment plans on Israel, and the same number plans to invest in Israel over the next five years.

European VC firms. For Continental European VCs, 19 percent indicated they will increase their foreign investment focus, and 43 percent indicated they plan to increase their investment in the United States over the next five years. Eighty-five percent indicated plans to continue their current geographic investment focus on Europe. While the United States is the primary foreign market where European VCs plan to invest now and over the next five years, they also consider minor investment in China (14 percent), India (10 percent), Australia (8 percent), Israel (8 percent), Canada/Mexico (6 percent), and Taiwan (4 percent).

Asian/Taiwanese VC firms. Asia-Pacific VC respondents (of which 84 percent are based in Taiwan) indicated that the United States is their primary non-APAC destination for investment. In fact, 40 percent of all APAC VC firms indicated plans to invest in the United States over the next five years, up from 31 percent of those currently investing in the United States. Taiwan is the primary investment target for 77 percent of the respondents.

Survey sample (NVCA and Deloitte & Touche). A total of 545 responses was collected from general partners with assets under management ranging from less than $100 million to greater than $1 billion. The survey was conducted between February and April 2005. Of the total number of respondents, 257 were based in the Americas, 141 in EMEA, and 147 in APAC.

STRUCTURAL CHANGES IN THE GLOBAL INDUSTRY IMPACTS
VENTURE CAPITAL

During the bubble era, it was all about disruptive business models that promised to change the landscape of business in record time. With the downturn, the prevailing point of view shifted 180 degrees. Investors basically told entrepreneurs to settle down, get real, get valuable, and be frugal. As we go into the second half of the decade with a modest growth market, the disruptive part of the portfolio regains importance, but there is also a retained interest in continuous innovation. Start-ups also have the option of becoming scouts at the head of the army finding the most promising direction. Looking at the venture equation, however, scouts have to realize that their multiples will not be as high, although their risk-adjusted returns could be quite attractive. Venture capitalists investing in scouts have to rethink their expectations related to exits, liquidity, and valuations. In many ways, we are back to the future of the 1980s and early 1990s, an environment that requires much more capital-efficient models.

From High-End Technology Lead-Users Directly to Consumer Markets

That said, there is a new way disruptive innovation is getting introduced into the economy, and that is through consumer markets first. This represents a huge new trend. Formerly, technology was introduced to the top of the market—government and high-end labs—and trickled down from there, crossing the chasm into the enterprise and then into the tornado of the consumer.

Many of the business models today are all bits and no atoms and are being born for scalability directly into the tornado of consumers. They initially look like fads, so it is hard to tell which ones will become a market. A few will stand alone at the end of the day, with many being incorporated into bigger models. Netscape was the first company born directly into the tornado. Google, eBay, and Yahoo! were other followers. In the new consumer markets, masses of people are marketing to each other—it's not vendor driven.

It's also producing a new style of entrepreneurial venture. The old model was based on harnessing deep science to market development, in order to produce complex systems for the enterprise. The new style involves capturing the imagination of a community—"cool" is key. Figuring out what's cool is not something that Silicon Valley veteran VC investors are good at. The investors who can will become a big part of the new venture landscape. This is where Chinese, Indian, and Korean entrepreneurs, who understand their local consumer markets, are likely to get a fair share of the "lifestyle" segments. Mobile technologies and the Internet are the driving vehicles behind it, and the emerging markets in Asia are likely to leapfrog the western countries with their legacy systems. In addition, the direct consumer markets in China and India seem to have an unlimited reservoir of buyers that is just starting to open up.

According to the NVCA and Deloitte & Touche survey in 2005, venture capitalists worldwide are planning to increase their investments slightly from 2005 to 2010 into companies targeting consumer business directly. About 19 percent of all VCs surveyed said they are currently focusing on consumer business companies, with that number moving to 21 percent over the next five years. Venture capital is opportunistic, and many of these subtle shifts in industry focus reflect a natural evolution of the market. The VC industry moved from hardware to software in the 1990s; it is now moving from corporate buyers to consumer buyers. The interest in consumer business reflects the recent boom in products that people use every day, such as cell phones and MP3 players, with the highest growth rates in Asia.

New Technologies Can Drive the Next Venture Capital Cycle

Previous venture capital cycles were driven by major technologies, whether semiconductors, PCs, the Internet, or communications. According to Geoffrey Moore (E&Y Global VC Report, 2005), nanotechnology and biotechnology are two key technologies for the new venture capital cycle. Nanotech is actually an attribute of many markets, while biotech is a genuinely new venture vein. The intersection of biotech and informatics is going to be huge—people fundamentally want to live, and live longer.

The second wave of the Internet is also extremely important. Earth is wiring itself a new nervous system, which has important implications for the way we work, driving globalization through offshoring and outsourcing. Competition will be fiercer. This second wave creates a target-rich opportunity for infrastructure ventures, especially in security and storage. There will be scaling opportunities in semiconductors related to application-specific processors. Routers, switches, RFID, sensors—all of these technologies will become increasingly important as machine-to-machine communications take off. Everything on the planet will to have an IP address. The economic and business impact of machines talking to each other will dwarf the impact of automation.

"Fortune 100" companies are stuck in inertial patterns where IT is an extension of legacy systems. There are, in effect, technological sea lanes out of which they can move only with great difficulty. It will be up to entrepreneurs and multitiered public and private capital sources to tackle the innovations that will change the way business works. The scarce ingredient in this equation is the entrepreneur, someone who can see an opportunity, apply risk capital within a time horizon that provides appropriate returns to investors, and make it happen in the world.

Geoffrey Moore argues that America's unique ability is to make markets out of nothing. Their culture has a unique perspective on failure. For Americans, the experience of failure can actually be an asset, as they just learn from it and get back into the game. In other countries, if you make one mistake, you're out—there is an aversion to entrepreneurship built in. Silicon Valley is a highly sophisticated community of venture capitalists, entrepreneurs, market development professionals, and consultants and will continue to be central to company creation and innovation.

The Internet makes it possible to work more collaboratively and break down the distinction between here and there with countries like India and China. Originally it was all about America; now it is less so. The emergence of new innovation centers just means that the American venture capitalists and entrepreneurs have the opportunity for mature participation in larger networks, at the expense of managing more complexity. This could prove to be a strength of Europeans, who have years of experience in collaborating cross-border because their small and medium enterprises (SME) had to seek markets outside their territory to gain the critical mass for their niche applications.

According to the NVCA and Deloitte & Touche survey in 2005, venture capitalists worldwide are planning to stay in the current industry sectors, however, some adjustments are expected from 2005 to 2010. From their current investments in biopharmaceuticals at 32 percent, they plan to decrease it slightly to 29 percent over the next five years. Currently, ITC technology is the lead focus for 51 percent of the VCs' investments. This is expected to remain relatively steady at 48 percent over the next five years. Technology comprises software, communications/networking, information services, semiconductors, electronics, and hardware.

Technology is at the heart of American and Israeli entrepreneurs and venture capitalists. This is what they have been doing for years and what they feel comfortable with. It is therefore very likely that they may become key technology providers for other emerging countries, where that local talent will develop applications for their massive home markets. Time will tell how soon China and India will develop their own leading technology based on their own standards. The first signs are already up, particularly in the telecommunication and mobile sectors.

Renewable Energy and Environmental Protection Provide New Opportunities

According to the NVCA and Deloitte & Touche survey in 2005, venture capitalists worldwide are planning to increase their investments from 2005 to 2010 into companies operating in the energy/environment sector. About 12 percent of all VCs surveyed said they are currently focusing on investments in energy/environment, with that figure jumping to 21 percent over the next five years. The increased interest in energy/environment reflects the opportunities the VC industry sees in developing cost-effective energy sources.

Small Company Contribution to R&D in the United States Is Significant

American research and development (R&D) is the envy of the world. Academic and government-sponsored research centers often contribute to the new ideas that make ventured companies work. Indeed, R&D is the staple of the venture capital industry, and small firms are playing a larger role in this activity.

The Global Insight Inc. 2004 survey found that venture capital-financed companies, when adjusted for size, spend over twice as much on R&D as non-VC-backed firms. In particular, small firms in the venture-dominated information technology and medical-related sectors are major contributors to these trends. The share of American R&D performed by firms with fewer than 500 employees rose from 5.9 percent in 1984 to an estimated 20.7 percent in 2003. The dollar value of small company R&D rose from $4.4 billion in 1984 to an estimated $40.1 billion in 2003, a ninefold increase.

The increased penetration of small company research is most striking in the biotechnology sector. The small company share of biotech research has expanded massively from some 3 percent in 1984 to nearly 40 percent in 2003, while the share of the large companies shrank from 31 percent in 1984 to 18 percent in 2003.

Even when small VC-financed companies grow to be among the biggest public companies in their industry, they remain leaders in R&D. Many of the technology companies founded during the earlier days of venture capital in the U.S. some 20 to 30 years ago, have quickly grown from small private companies to among the largest in the country.

Of the top firms in America's R&D spending, many were either venture financed themselves, such as Microsoft, Cisco, and Intel, or were major acquirers of start-up companies, like Johnson & Johnson and Pfizer.

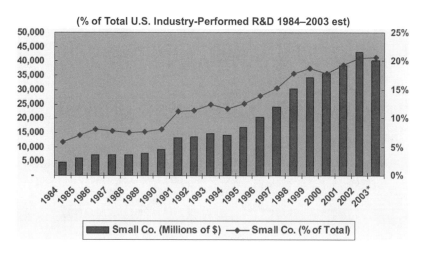

FIGURE 2.5. Small Company Contribution to R&D in the United States
Source: NSF, R&D in Industry: 1991–2003 (Global Insights, Inc. & NVCA, 2004)

TABLE 2.9.   Top 20 R&D-Spending Companies, 2001 (United States)

Rank	Company	R&D Spending
1	Ford Motor Company	$7.4 B
2	General Motors	$6.2 B
3	Pfizer, Inc	$4.8 B
4	IBM	$4.6 B
5	Microsoft	$4.4 B
6	Motorola	$4.3 B
7	Cisco Systems	$3.9 B
8	Intel	$3.8 B
9	Johnson & Johnson	$3.6 B
10	Lucent Technologies	$3.5 B
11	Hewlett-Packard	$2.6 B
12	Merck & Company	$2.5 B
13	Bristol-Myers Squibb	$2.3 B
14	Eli Lilly and Company	$2.2 B
15	Pharmacia	$2.2 B
16	Sun Microsystems	$2.0 B
17	General Electric	$2.0 B
18	Boeing	$1.9 B
19	Wyeth	$1.9 B
20	Procter & Gamble	$1.8 B

Source: NFS, R&D in Industry: 1991–2003 (Global Insights, Inc. & NVCA, 2005)

CONCLUSION

Venture capital addresses the funding needs of entrepreneurial companies that generally do not have the size, assets, and operating histories necessary to obtain capital from more traditional sources, such as public markets and banks.

Far from being simply passive financiers, venture capitalists foster growth in companies through their hands-on involvement in the management, strategic marketing, and planning of their portfolio companies. Venture capitalists invest alongside management and employees through equity financing and the practice of using stock option plans to motivate all workers. They are entrepreneurs first and financiers second.

As equity owners and board members, venture capitalists succeed when the portfolio company succeeds. Successful venture capitalists will readily point out that many of their most successful companies ended up with a business or product model that was quite different from the original business plan. This morphing of a business from a fledgling start-up to a successful company is the key role of the venture capitalist.

Venture capital firms generally are private partnerships or closely held corporations funded by private and public pension funds, endowment funds, foundations, corporations, wealthy individuals, foreign investors, and the venture capitalists themselves.

When an investment is made, a percentage of ownership in the company is given to the venture fund in exchange for the capital provided. The expectation is that at least some of the investments will prove to be extremely profitable, even if others eventually fail. Typical exits for successful investments include sale to public markets through an initial public offering (IPO) or acquisition by a larger company (M&A).

Although the venture capital industry has become much more visible in the past few years, it has been building companies for several decades. From 1970 through 2003, the industry invested $338.5 billion in 26,494 companies.

Venture capital is a cyclical business, subject not only to internal dynamics, but to the influence of external economic sources and to fluctuations in financial markets. Indeed, the 2000–2003 data (Global Insight, 2004) show that ventured firms increased their size and share in the economy over the last three years, despite the dot-com bust and high-tech equipment sales downturn. Venture-supported firms showed continued solid progress.

The major change in venture capital since the start of the new millennium is the globalization of this industry. The key drivers are the "mobility" of (1) technology, (2) capital, and (3) people, which has spurred substantial cross-border investments, because emerging innovations developed in smaller countries have to be commercialized in larger markets to justify their huge investments. On the other hand, the future success of any country will depend strongly upon the integration and liquidity of its venture capital market and the inventiveness and management of its hi-tech industries.

What started in the United States about 50 years ago is becoming mainstream even in emerging markets, impacting significantly markets, businesses, job creation, and the competitiveness of nations. Emerging markets will shift from pure manufacturing to innovation and knowledge-based industries, creating challenges and opportunities to mature countries and established multinational firms. In essence, the venture capital industry is an interesting lead indicator of where technology and markets may shift in the next few years, and multinational companies are well advised to keep it on the "watch list."

REFERENCES

Chesbrough, Henry. 2003. *Open Innovation: The New Imperative for Creating and Profiting from Technology.* Boston: Harvard Business School Press.

CVCRI – China Venture Capital Research Institute. *China Venture Capital Yearbook 2005.* www.cvcri.com.

Deloitte & Touche LLC – Global Venture Capital Survey 2005. *Future Venture Capital Investments by Regions and Industry.* Commissioned Research by NVCA.

Ernst & Young – Venture Capital Advisory Group. Renewal and New Frontiers. *Global Private Equity: Venture Capital Insights Report 2004–2005.* 2005.

Ernst & Young – Venture Capital Advisory Group 2005. Creating a Technology Hotbed in China. *Lessons learned from Silicon Valley and Israel.* Shanghai, 04-2005.

Global Insight Inc. 2004. Renewal and New Frontiers. *Venture Capital Benefits to the U.S. Economy.* Commissioned Research by NVCA.

Haemmig, Martin, CeTIM – Center for Technology and Innovation Management. *International Venture Capital Investments.* ISBN 7-309-04384-4, Fudan Press/China, 2005.

Haemmig, Martin, CeTIM – Center for Technology and Innovation Management. *Private Equity Investments.* ISBN 3-409-12296-6, Gabler and Financial Times/Germany, 2003.

Haemmig, Martin, CeTIM – Center for Technology and Innovation Management. *The Globalization of Venture Capital.* ISBN 3-258-06565-9, Haupt/Switzerland, 2002.

Moore, Geoffrey – Author and Venture Partner at Mohr Davidow Ventures. *Crossing The Chasm.* ISBN 0066620023, 1999.

Moore, Geoffrey – Author and Venture Partner at Mohr Davidow Ventures. *Inside the Tornado.* ISBN 0887308244, 1999.

NVCA – National Venture Capital Association, 11-2005. www.nvca.org.

PriceWaterhouseCoopers – Paths-to-Value. *Added Value Study of Venture Capitalists in United States, Europe and Israel.* 2003.

Venture Economics – a Thomson Financials company. VentureXpert: Database for Venture Capital in United States, Europe, Israel and Asia. www.ventureeconomics. com.

VentureOne, a DowJones company. VentureSource: Database for Venture Capital in United States, Europe and Israel. www.ventureone.com.

Zero2IPO – China Venture Capital Research Center. *China Venture Capital Annual Statistical Report 2004.* www.zero2ipo.com.cn/en.

3

Drivers and Measures of Innovation Success

MARC J. EPSTEIN

C orporate CEOs often complain that their organizations are too bureaucratic to drive the kind of innovation that is necessary to compete. They develop a strategy and tell Wall Street that they will lead in
innovations, and then they don't deliver. Why not?

Though CEOs want more breakthrough innovation, they get very little. The
vast majority of new product developments are incremental improvements or
line extensions based on existing technologies, markets, or products. Only 5
percent are considered breakthroughs by the companies. Why don't they get
more breakthroughs? Most often, managers say that it's really expensive and
they don't know how to do it. And then there are barriers to innovations set
up by the same companies that say they want it. Corporations establish incentives that encourage meeting budget and avoiding risk. This encourages managers to invest in safe products—not a big chance of a big loss, but also little
chance of a big profit.

In some companies, the measurements are a big part of the problem.
Though companies are not using as many metrics that are linked to innovation strategy as they could, some are using metrics that are downright counterproductive. Some companies use number of products launched as a metric

This chapter draws heavily on material discussed on pages 143–178 of *Making Innovation Work:
How to Manage It, Measure It, and Profit from It* by Tony Davila, Marc J. Epstein, and Robert Shelton (Philadelphia: Wharton School Publishing, 2006).

to evaluate and reward their innovativeness. But what behavior does that motivate? Product development managers report that to meet their targets and get their rewards, they focus on developing many small product improvements rather than spending the time or money on potential breakthroughs.

In other companies, the organizational structure is the barrier to new developments. In some companies, R&D managers come up with some powerful ideas, but the existing business units do not want to sell the product since they do not see them within their core product mix or their capabilities. In many companies, the new product ideas are generated in the marketing departments of the business units and contract with the new product development and R&D groups for the development. But then there is often no incentive for breakthrough developments in R&D and no money for scanning or exploring new possible breakthroughs.

What is needed is a carefully designed system that encourages innovation and a structured process to guide the development. The systems and controls produce greater innovation than just leaving the process to be free and hoping that ideas will self-generate.

CEOs say that they need to propel their companies to needed growth, and in most large companies, spending on research and development of between $1 billion and $5 billion is not unusual. Since they can't seem to develop it, some companies have given up and opted to outsource much of their innovation needs. Others remain frustrated by a large expenditure that never seems to pay off.

Senior managers also complain that they do not have the leading indicators of performance to react sooner on innovation gaps and thus do not perform well in the ideation, selection, or execution phases of innovation. They can only evaluate success at the end of the process, which is usually too late. Even when innovation is indicated as an important goal of the company, the performance measurement systems are often poor and do not provide the incentives and guidance to motivate the creativity, flexibility, and innovation that are desperately needed.

This chapter provides a description of both the drivers and measures of innovation success. It describes the actions that managers can take to facilitate increased organizational innovation and performance and a selection of a broad set of measures of innovation success. The components include what to do (strategy), who needs to be involved (leadership), how to organize the company for innovation (structure), and how to operationalize and implement innovation in organizations (systems).

THE INNOVATION CONTRIBUTION MODEL

This framework and analysis to measure the effectiveness of benefits (payoffs) of an investment in innovation, R&D, or new product development, either generally or in an individual innovation project specifically, includes a careful analysis of the causal relationships and the impact of potential managerial

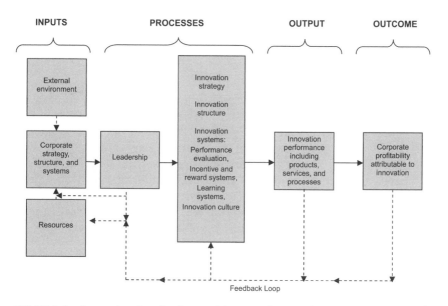

FIGURE 3.1. Innovation Contribution Model: Antecedents and Consequences of Investments in Innovation

actions in innovation on long-term corporate profitability.[1] It also includes an extensive listing of potential measures of inputs, processes, outputs, and outcomes. As companies consider beginning or broadening innovation activities, a clearer understanding of the benefits and costs is critical. This chapter provides the objectives, drivers, and measures of innovation success.

This dynamic model (Figure 3.1) focuses on the key factors for corporate success in innovation. It includes the critical inputs and processes that lead to success in innovation (output), and that ultimately lead to a contribution to overall corporate profitability (outcome). It also describes how a company that lacks significant innovation can become a company that uses innovation properly to significantly enhance its corporate profitability.

A company's existing strategy, structure, and systems represent important inputs to the model, leading to processes through which a strong leader can transform all three to achieve innovation success. The processes begin with leadership in the formulation and implementation of a successful innovation project. Leadership starts with a commitment by the CEO and other senior managers to consider the appropriate role for innovation in an organization. The CEO should facilitate a dialogue within the company on the changes necessary for the appropriate innovation effort. The CEO, along with other key executives, must examine the role of innovation in the company's industry, ascertain its current position with respect to its competitors, and determine an appropriate level of investment.

Next, proven guidelines for innovation strategies permit the company to build on its position. Though these strategies do represent some different options, successful innovation operations will likely incorporate all of them into its activities.

Appropriate systems must be implemented to ensure the successful integration of innovation. Corporate culture, performance and operational measures, compensation systems, and learning systems must all be considered unique challenges. With the appropriate systems and inputs in place, companies are able to reap the outputs associated with innovation performance, including customer acquisition, customer loyalty, R&D performance, and value capture.

Finally, the outcomes detailed in the model are not vague goals. This chapter provides a detailed approach to measuring the payoffs of innovation investments, to better understand the causal relationships and which specific actions lead to improved profitability, in addition to better evaluation of the outcomes.

Many researchers and managers have recognized the need to identify and measure the impacts of corporate actions and to provide a better analysis of the return on investment (ROI) of innovation investments. However, the appropriate metrics have not been well developed. The framework presented here provides the necessary specificity to articulate the causal relationships that lead to innovation success and related measures. In this way, both general managers and innovation professionals can more effectively evaluate the success of innovation and the potential and actual payoffs of innovation investments. The causal linkage analysis illustrates the importance of leadership, strategy, structure, and systems and highlights the specific managerial actions that lead to success.

To assess the payoffs of innovation investments, companies must implement systems that evaluate the impact of innovation projects on financial performance and the trade-offs that must be made among competing organizational constraints and barriers to implementation. These systems assist senior executives as they develop an innovation strategy and allocate corporate resources to support that strategy. The systems also assist innovation managers as they evaluate the trade-offs and decide which projects provide the largest net benefit to both short-term financial performance and the long-term success of the firm. The careful identification and measurement of the payoffs also permits innovation managers to demonstrate the impact on corporate profitability and value creation. It also provides information for better corporate resource allocation decisions in the CEO's and CFO's offices, based on a better understanding of the ROI—including a fuller understanding of the benefits and costs of innovation. Hence, to implement their innovation strategy, companies are faced with a significant challenge: to quantify the link between corporate actions in innovation and corporate financial performance.

Indeed, only by making the "business case" for innovation expenditures can managers truly integrate innovation impacts into their business strategies.

Yet many companies have failed to develop the appropriate innovation projects. Instead, they have often acted because they had a feeling that it was the right thing to do or because their competitors were making similar moves in innovation investments. However, projects put into place for these reasons alone are vulnerable to cost overruns and poor ROI, changes in senior management, or shifting corporate or consumer priorities.

To present a clear business case for innovation projects, senior managers need to identify the metrics of innovation performance and how that performance impacts overall long-term corporate profitability. This increased attention to the thorough identification and measurement of the metrics of innovation is echoed in many measurement frameworks and strategic management systems. Frameworks such as the balanced scorecard and shareholder value analysis focus on the causal relationships and linkages within organizations and the actions managers can implement to improve both customer and corporate profitability and drive increased value.[2] However, substantial work is required to establish the relationships that relate specifically to innovation strategies. Undeniably, the identification and measurement of the impact of innovation strategies are particularly difficult as they are usually linked to long time horizons, a high level of uncertainty, and impacts that are often difficult to quantify. But this analysis is important to improve resource allocation, decision making, and profitability.

In recent years, companies have placed increasing importance on the development of performance metrics to better measure and manage innovation performance. Although the need for performance measures for innovation has been identified, adequate work has not been done in proposing a large number of specific metrics. Innovation analysis has typically been operating without adequate measures that permit an effective evaluation of innovation benefits, success, or value. This lack of sufficient performance metrics has meant a lack of both actual and perceived accountability for firm innovation operations to various stakeholders.

This problem is compounded as senior managers consider the high costs typically associated with innovation and the seemingly small percentage of innovation projects that succeed. Sometimes the projects are flawed, but often the measures of success are also flawed. It is absolutely essential to develop the appropriate metrics in order to succeed in innovation.

Many decisions related to the operations of the company significantly affect the success of all innovation projects, including decisions related to leadership, strategy, structure, and systems. As they are essential to superior innovation performance, the key success factors that are the determinants of innovation success become the foundation for rigorous performance evaluation systems for innovation.

The main model describes the inputs, processes, outputs, and outcomes of innovation activities (Table 3.1). These are further articulated as innovation objectives within the innovation causal model of performance. Corporations

TABLE 3.1. Innovation Contribution Model: Innovation Objectives

Outcomes	Long-term Corporate Profitability
Outputs	Customer acquisition
	Customer loyalty
	R&D performance
	Value capture
Processes	Leadership: Commitment and focus on innovation projects
	Innovation strategy: Coherent and aligned strategy
	Innovation structure: Integration of innovation into business model; balanced innovation networks inside and outside of organization
	Innovation systems: Appropriate processes for effective innovation implementation
Inputs	Adequate capital and people
	Corporate Structure: Appropriate organizational structure
	Corporate Strategy: Alignment with type of products offered, customers served, and competitive positioning
	Corporate Systems: Suitable training and processes
	External environment: Adapted to external forces

must make important choices regarding the formulation and implementation of innovation strategies in relation to the overall external environment and corporate resources, strategy, structure, and systems (inputs). Other factors, such as leadership and innovation strategy, innovation structure, and innovation systems (processes), also significantly affect the performance and success of innovation projects. The consequences and success of the company's actions on these inputs and processes impact various outputs, including customer acquisition, customer loyalty, R&D performance, and value capture. If the strategy formulation and implementation are successful, these outputs should ultimately be seen in improved overall corporate profitability (outcome).

After carefully identifying the specific innovation objectives, the drivers of success must be defined. These help specify more precisely the keys to innovation success and the actions that managers can take to improve corporate profitability. The use of various management control levers and performance measurement and management systems are a part of the implementation of innovation strategies. The objectives, the drivers, and the metrics related to innovation success should be part of a clear articulation of the causal relationships leading from the inputs to the processes and then flowing to the desired outputs and outcomes. It is important to identify and communicate the causal

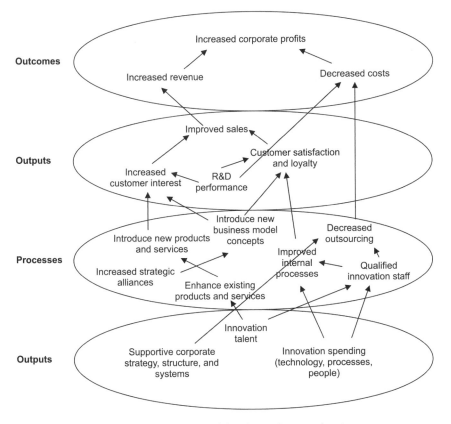

FIGURE 3.2. Innovation Contribution Model: Drivers of Innovation Success

links throughout the organization to guide the formulation and implementation of innovation strategies. The causal linkage map of drivers (Figure 3.2) is useful to ensure that all necessary actions are taken to achieve success, that unnecessary actions are not taken, and that all employees understand their critical roles in innovation and organizational success.

INPUTS: EXTERNAL ENVIRONMENT, CORPORATE RESOURCES, STRATEGIES, STRUCTURES, AND SYSTEMS

As discussed earlier, in the past many companies made decisions related to innovation where the focus was on competition rather than the potential benefits of the innovation project. In the current business climate, with increased focus on corporate accountability and efficiency, it has become increasingly important to provide a quantitative estimate of the costs of an innovation project in comparison to the benefits likely to accrue. When considering innovation, it is crucial that senior managers fully evaluate the external environment and the resources, strategies, structures, and systems already present in the company to determine a project's fit and its likelihood of success.

External Environment

Though many inputs to innovation success are controllable by corporate managers, some inputs constrain many corporate activities, require significant corporate adaptation, and influence success. The external environment may include changes to the business environment, the economy, technological developments, competitors, suppliers, and customer needs. Even though companies may have coherent strategies, structures, and systems and adequate corporate capital and labor resources for innovation success, changes in the external environment can be an important input that will significantly impact corporate decisions.

Corporate Resources

The critical corporate resources within any organization are its people and capital. In determining whether a corporation has the capabilities and resources to support new or expanded innovation, it is necessary to look at the people and capital that currently exist in the corporation. Are the company's employees highly motivated and trained? Do they have the skills necessary for success? Such questions convey the conduciveness of a company's employees and organization to the changes and challenges that accompany an escalation in focus on innovation. From a capital perspective, if a firm is already financially constrained, it may have difficulty allocating sufficient funds for major innovation projects. The availability of financial resources is also dependent on the commitment of the senior management to new or expanded innovation efforts. Without adequate financial resources, these ventures cannot succeed. Thus, corporate resources are a critical input for innovation success.

Corporate Strategies

The development of innovation strategies must fit within an overall corporate strategy. One of the purposes of strategy is to clarify what efforts are within the bounds of the company's playing field and therefore should be pursued. By clarifying these boundaries, the company focuses creativity and energizes action. Thus, though the model is dynamic and corporate strategy may be altered by the development of innovation, the corporate strategy remains an important input to the formulation and implementation of innovation strategy. Companies make very different choices depending on geographical diversity, product type, product mix, customer type, level of service, and pricing. These choices not only impact corporate strategy, but also significantly affect innovation strategy.

Corporate Structures

An organization's corporate structure plays a major role in determining the organization of innovation operations within it. Whether a company has a large number of strategic business units or networks across a wide geographical area with many different languages will influence many innovation decisions. Whether the company is more or less decentralized with independent business units and whether the organizational structure is arranged by geography, by product type, by customer type, by channel, or with a matrix will influence the choice of innovation strategy and implementation. These structures become inputs to the innovation strategy, structure, systems, and leadership necessary for innovation success.

Corporate Systems

An organization's corporate systems are critical elements in driving innovation success. Through the development and implementation of effective corporate systems, innovation breakthroughs can be facilitated. Companies need systems in place that provide proper motivation, incentives, and rewards to encourage the type of risk taking that can lead to advances in innovation. Managers need to create an environment where taking increased risks on breakthrough innovations is recognized as likely to produce more failures and where the short-term focus on productivity must be balanced with a long-term perspective. The corporate systems implemented set a direction for the actions that specifically relate to both innovation systems and innovation performance and their impact on corporate financial performance.[3]

PROCESSES: LEADERSHIP, INNOVATION STRATEGIES, STRUCTURES, AND SYSTEMS

Once the viability of innovation efforts is determined, by evaluating the inputs available in an organization, senior managers who are planning and developing innovation programs can focus on the processes that drive superior innovation performance and connect the inputs to innovation success. Process measures are vital during execution because they can signal the need to change course or alter the execution. Four main processes are critical for innovation success: leadership, innovation strategy, innovation structure, and innovation systems. The managers' effective use of these processes will determine the outputs and outcomes.

Leadership

A company's leadership must be both knowledgeable about innovation and committed to the innovation venture for it to succeed. Senior managers must provide full support to innovation initiatives and communicate that support throughout the company. If a company cannot secure strong enough public support of innovation programs at the senior management level, then even though an innovation program may be undertaken properly at the R&D level, it is unlikely to reach its potential. This leadership and managerial commitment is critical to mobilize the employees and set an innovation culture.[4]

Innovation Strategy

Innovation success is dependent on a well-formulated and well-executed innovation strategy. The strategy must be consistent with corporate strategy and innovation structure and systems. Its alignment with these other inputs and processes is critical to success. The company's choice of which ideas to select and execute, the customer profile, and the product and service capabilities the firm already has are just some of the factors that will affect the innovation strategy. These and the other strategic choices will then impact the company's success in customer acquisition, customer loyalty, supply chain optimization, and value capture.[5]

Innovation Structure

Choices about how a company decides to design and implement its innovation structure are key process issues the companies must address in relation to its innovation efforts. Factors critical for this decision, such as the appropriate level of outsourcing, the relationships the company wants to develop with partners, the existing organizational structure, and the desired innovation sourcing network, affect the ultimate outcome of the innovation effort on overall corporate profitability.[6]

Innovation Systems

To ensure that highly qualified employees and proper processes are in place to meet a company's stakeholders' needs, senior managers must develop and implement appropriate formal and informal systems for innovation. Innovation system issues such as measurement, incentives, and learning are all part of the processes pertinent to innovation. The effects of senior managers putting systems in place to best meet their employees', customers', partners', and other stakeholders' needs extend far beyond items such as lower costs and more timely customer service systems, to heightened productivity and greater sales. The systems can move the company toward decreasing overall organizational costs and increasing company revenues, with an ultimate goal of increased corporate profitability.[7]

MEASURING INNOVATION SUCCESS

Appropriate measures of innovation payoffs are essential to monitoring the key performance drivers (inputs and processes) and assessing whether an innovation effort is achieving its stated objectives (outputs) and thus contributing to the long-term success of the corporation (outcomes). Companies often waste resources on projects or do not invest when they should because they are unable to effectively evaluate the potential payoffs of innovation investments.

Measuring returns on innovation projects can be a daunting challenge. Predicting customer behavior is difficult, and many financial benefits of innovation projects are seen as difficult to measure. Further, the very nature of change in an innovative environment is such that precise measurements are often difficult.

Many senior managers have come to believe that further investment in innovation is an imperative that is required to maintain or develop a competitive position. They often make expenditures without completing a rigorous analysis. However, today's more stringent economic environment has caused many senior managers to question the payoffs of innovation investments before making resource allocation decisions and are demanding more carefully specified ROI calculations.

As companies assess the choice of appropriate measures to evaluate innovation investments, numerous potential issues arise. Since the choices are different for each company, substantial customization is necessary. Senior managers should consider six initial questions that can lead to the development of appropriate measures for innovation:

- What measurement systems are currently in place and being used within the organization?
- What are the important criteria to the company and its constituencies and stakeholders?
- What does the company specifically expect to accomplish with this innovation investment?
- What is the anticipated timeframe associated with this innovation investment?
- Who are the parties involved in implementing this innovation investment, and who will be affected by the results?
- What critical processes are associated with the successful execution of the innovation project?

To address these questions, it is imperative that companies not only specifically tailor their innovation measurement approach but also use multiple measures to fully analyze their situations. Different measurement criteria are important for companies that have different strategies or may be in a different stage of their life cycle or their innovation development. The multiple measures will typically include both financial and nonfinancial measures that are leading and lagging indicators of performance. They may be used in a balanced scorecard or other approach and can be developed specifically for innovation or as a part of an overall corporate performance measurement system.[8] Companies can also use a weighted scoring system to evaluate investments related to overall innovation, a specific project, or business strategy.

There are many obstacles to implementing a successful measurement system, whether a lack of focus, a low priority, or just the difficulty of it. It is the responsibility of senior managers to evaluate the innovation efforts and decide on the right measures for their organization and ensure that the measures are captured and responded to properly. To obtain adequate resources for innovation and to effectively manage innovation, the payoffs of investments in innovation must be calculated and integrated into management decision-making systems for both operational and capital investment decisions.

DEVELOPING APPROPRIATE METRICS

To closely monitor the cause-and-effect relationships evidenced in the innovation causal linkage model, appropriate metrics must be developed. These metrics must be consistent with and support the objectives and drivers and key success factors already defined. The selected metrics will likely include a combination of input, processes, output, and outcome metrics to effectively measure performance (see Table 3.2). It is important to measure innovation performance at each of the stages and dimensions to gain a clear picture of successes and failures and the specific managerial actions that can drive improved performance. Senior managers involved in the innovation decision-making process should develop metrics appropriate to the strategy and objectives of the innovation investment, the company, and its stakeholders. During the measure selection process, it is useful for the involved individuals to choose just a few measures, so that senior managers involved in the innovation process are focused on the critical performance indicators.

The list of metrics presented here is not meant to be a comprehensive set of innovation performance measures. Rather, it is a selection and example of some metrics that may be appropriate. Managers must select those that most closely fit their strategy and adapt or develop others. There is no rule for the right number of metrics to include in a measurement system; however, including too many tends to distract managers from pursuing a focused strategy. Generally, a complete measurement system includes perhaps three to six measures for each element being evaluated and no more than twenty measures in total.

For each key success factor, a specific target should be identified and results should be measured against these targets. These results should be widely communicated among not only those senior managers directly involved in innovation but also other individuals within the organization upon whom the investment in innovation will have an impact. Any innovation measurement system will have little impact if the results are not fully

TABLE 3.2. Innovation Contribution Model: Metrics for Inputs, Processes, Outputs, and Outcomes

Inputs	Metrics
Corporate strategy	• Competitive position within industry • Cost, development time, delivery time, quantity, and price of products and services offered • Number, complexity and size of competitors, customers, partners, and suppliers
Corporate structure	• Dollars of resources available • Number of strategic business units (SBUs) • Geographic diversity of production and sales • Level of empowerment to SBU and functional managers
Corporate systems	• Customer and employee satisfaction and retention rate • Product and process quality score • Investment in training
Resources	• Dollars available for innovation investment • Skills assessment of existing employees • Quality assessment of current company technology and processes
External environment	• Assessment of competitor innovation investments • Assessment of customer needs • Assessment of supplier needs and capabilities

Processes	Metrics
Leadership	• Time dedicated to innovation • Budget percent allocated to innovation efforts • Performance percentage linked to innovation success • Objectives for innovation efforts clearly communicated to senior managers and employees
Create and execute appropriate innovation strategies	• Number, cost, price, and perception of new products and services offered from innovation projects • Perception of brand • Profitability of innovation operations
Design and institute proper innovation structure	• Level of innovation integration across business units and functions • Mix of innovation sources • Percentage of innovation projects outsourced • Number of strategic alliances

TABLE 3.2. (CONTINUED)

Inputs	Metrics
Develop and implement appropriate innovation systems	• Number and quality of employee innovation skills and knowledge • Percentage of performance measures and rewards aligned and linked to innovation activities • Amount and quality of customer data acquired related to innovation • Investment in training, workshops, and conferences

Outputs	Metrics
Customer acquisition	• New customers gained through innovation • Number of customers through existing products/services who buy new products/services • Number of new customers of new products/services who go on to buy existing products/services • Market share
Customer loyalty	• Frequency of repeat customers • Average annual sales per customer • Customer satisfaction with innovation activities • Percentage of customer attrition • Ratio of new visitors to repeat visitors
R&D Performance	• Number and quality of ideas generated • Success of ideas passing through selection and execution processes • Free time allowances for R&D employees • R&D staff turnover
Value capture	• Cost and price of products and services offered to customers • Average of prices paid by customers • Number of new products and service lines introduced • Profitability of innovation operations • Revenues generated through innovation efforts (total revenue, innovation revenue, revenue per innovation customer) • Customer profitability

Outcome	Metrics
Long-term corporate profitability	• Stock price • Income growth • Sales growth due to innovation • EVA

discussed. Results should be monitored regularly and used to identify areas of weakness, address the plans and systems in place, and establish new initiatives to improve deficiencies.

The measures chosen should be quantifiable, in either absolute or percentage terms, as well as complete and controllable. They should be complete in that the measure sums up in one number the contribution of all elements of performance that matter; for example, profitability is a summary measure of revenue generation and cost control. They should be controllable in that employees in the organization can actually influence improvement in the factor measured.

Some of the metrics shown here are evaluations of overall firm performance. Others are indicators of innovation performance that are derived through an aggregation of measures of individual business units and functions. It is important to evaluate the performance of both overall innovation performance and the specific aspects of innovation that lead to revenue enhancement or cost savings to determine the success of various operations and the corrective action that can be taken to make improvements.

The measures should be of use to both senior and middle managers in the business units and functions. Thus, they must be disaggregated so each unit can examine its contribution to the achievement of the company's innovation strategy. These analyses ensure that each unit is making a contribution to the innovation effort and improving corporate profitability. Additionally, these metrics can be used to provide a gap analysis that enables managers to determine what other inputs or processes are required to meet the company's innovation objectives.

Different tools and techniques are available to measure the different aspects of innovation performance. For example, customer surveys are powerful tools to help companies better understand the benefit of innovation investments for increasing revenue or decreasing costs related to their customers, thus providing valuable information regarding opportunities to improve overall profitability. Internally, surveys, focus groups, and other techniques are increasingly being used to measure and monitor employee, personnel, and stakeholder reactions and provide feedback.

Once metrics have been developed, data on these indicators must be collected and statistical analysis, such as multiple regressions, should be performed to analyze and test the validity of the customized innovation measurement system and causal relationships hypothesized by the company. As companies evaluate the initial measurement system's performance, they will typically add metrics and drop others because of a lack of evidence of a strong relationship. It is here that a final measurement system emerges, and the focus then shifts to applying the model to support improved decision making.

The Balanced Scorecard

Performance evaluation systems give companies the vital feedback necessary for evaluating innovation strategy and overall innovation performance.

These systems can be the basis for constant improvement within the organization. The balanced scorecard is particularly useful as a performance evaluation system and even more valuable as an interactive strategic management system. Increasingly, companies have used this tool to aid in both the evaluation of performance and the implementation of strategy. This tool can be useful when applied to an organization's innovation efforts in particular.[9]

Organizations must assess the success of both the formulation and the implementation of innovation strategy. They must then evaluate innovation performance and adapt future strategies accordingly. The right set of performance measures should include both leading and lagging indicators. It should include both financial and nonfinancial metrics, should be linked to strategy, and should include a combination of input, process, output, and outcome measures.

The balanced scorecard focuses on better understanding the causal relationships and linkages within organizations and the levers that can be pulled to improve corporate performance. It relies on a better understanding of the drivers of value to aid managers in making decisions to improve corporate performance, specifically, innovation performance. The traditional model contains four dimensions that relate to the core values of the company: financial, customer, internal business processes, and learning and growth.

The *financial dimension* focuses on the shareholders' interests and shows the link between strategic objectives and financial impacts. Metrics associated with this dimension must demonstrate whether strategy has succeeded financially. The *customer dimension* focuses on measures that reflect how the company is creating customer value through its strategy and actions. The *internal business processes dimension* comprises measures that indicate how well a company performs on its key internal systems and processes. The *learning and growth perspective* stresses measures of how well the company is preparing to meet the challenges of the future through its organizational and human assets.

The four perspectives of the balanced scorecard connect through chains of cause and effect—learning and growth actions impact internal business process outcomes, internal business process actions impact both customer and financial outcomes, and improved customer value leads to stronger financial performance. Overall, these factors link together and reinforce each other, jointly contributing to driving and measuring the accomplishment of innovation strategy and value creation through innovation.

Table 3.3 portrays one possible set of balanced scorecard measures for a company to evaluate innovation performance. It is important to note that this is simply another, potentially quite useful, way of looking at the metrics suggested above for evaluation of innovation and overall corporate performance. Again, the list of measures below is to demonstrate that innovation can be measured and to provide an example of potential measures—recognizing that only a small number should be selected for a useful balanced scorecard.

TABLE 3.3. A Balanced Scorecard for Innovation

Objective	Measures

Financial Perspective

Long-term corporate profitability	• Stock price • Income growth • Sales growth due to innovation • EVA

Customer Perspective

Customer acquisition	• New customers gained through innovation • Number of customers through existing products/services who buy new products/services • Number of new customers of new products/services who go on to buy existing products/services
Customer loyalty	• Frequency of repeat customers • Average annual sales per customer • Customer satisfaction with innovation activities • Percentage of customer attrition • Ratio of new visitors to repeat visitors
Value capture	• Cost and price of products and services offered to customers • Average of prices paid by customers • Number of new products and service lines introduced • Profitability of innovation operations • Revenues generated through innovation efforts (total revenue, innovation revenue, revenue per innovation customer) • Customer profitability

Internal Business Perspective

Commitment and focus on innovation	• Time dedicated to innovation • Budget percent allocated to innovation efforts • Performance percentage linked to innovation success • Objectives for innovation efforts clearly communicated to senior managers and employees
Coherent and aligned innovation strategy	• Number, cost, price, and perception of new products offered from innovation projects • Number, cost, price, and perception of new services offered from innovation projects • Perception of brand • Profitability of innovation operations

TABLE 3.3. (CONTINUED)

Objective	Measures
Balanced innovation networks inside and outside of organization	• Level of innovation integration across business units and functions • Mix of innovation sources • Percentage of innovation projects outsourced • Number of strategic alliances
Appropriate processes for effective innovation implementation	• Number and quality of employee innovation skills and knowledge • Percentage of performance measures and rewards aligned and linked to innovation activities • Amount and quality of customer data acquired related to innovation
Corporate strategy aligned with type of products offered, customer served, and competitive positioning	• Competitive position within industry • Cost, development time, delivery time, quantity, and price of products and services offered • Number, complexity and size of competitors, customers, partners, and suppliers
Appropriate corporate organization structure	• Dollars of resources available • Number of strategic business unites (SBUs) • Geographic diversity of production and sales • Level of empowerment to SBU and functional managers
Adapted to external forces	• Assessment of competitor innovation investments • Assessment of customer needs • Assessment of supplier needs and capabilities
Learning and Growth Perspective	
Adequate capital and people	• Dollars available for innovation investment • Skills assessment of existing employees • Quality assessment of current company technology and processes
Suitable training and processes	• Customer and employee satisfaction and retention rate • Product and process quality score • Investment in training
R&D performance	• Number and quality of ideas generated • Success of ideas passing through selection and execution processes • Free time allowances for R&D employees

OUTPUTS AND OUTCOMES: OVERALL FIRM AND INNOVATION-SPECIFIC PERFORMANCE

If the innovation initiatives are well designed and executed and the model of causal relationships properly specified, the identified inputs and processes should lead to improved performance. Outputs describe quality, quantity, and timeliness, whereas outcomes describe value creation. Improved innovation performance should include increasing the success of the innovation process (outputs) and ultimately improving corporate performance either through increased revenues or decreased costs (outcomes). To properly evaluate innovation performance, input, process, output, and outcome measures are all necessary and should be clearly linked in a causal relationship.

These performance indicators empower senior managers with the information to evaluate whether the innovation program is achieving its stated objectives and contributing to overall corporate profitability. Outcome measures capture how the innovation effort translated the outputs into value for the company and the net amount of the value contribution. Since the goals relate to increasing corporate profits, not just improving customer satisfaction, both output and outcome measures are necessary.

A weak performance on the output metrics should signal a need to examine the inputs and processes and determine whether they have been misspecified or just poorly executed. It also can provide an opportunity to identify potential benefits to organizational effectiveness and profitability from innovation that may have been overlooked. This is an opportunity to examine how well innovation programs are contributing to corporate profits and should unveil specific opportunities, directions for improvements, and standards of performance. The innovation measurement system should highlight the specific contributions of the innovation activities, in addition to providing valuable feedback that can lead to future innovation program and corporate improvements.

Results from the innovation evaluation and measurement process should be widely communicated throughout the organization. In a well-executed innovation venture, many units of the company will have some involvement in the innovation effort. The evaluation and measurement of the innovation effort will have little impact if the results are not disseminated throughout the organization to the many disparate areas that both affect and are affected by it. Results should be monitored regularly and used to identify areas of weakness, challenge the plans and systems in place, and present new initiatives to improve deficiencies.

Outputs: Customer Acquisition, Customer Loyalty, Supply Chain Optimization, and Value Creation

R&D performance. In order to be successful at innovation, superior performance from a company's R&D department is critical. This begins with the idea generation process. The effectiveness of internal innovation efforts can be measured to give the organization a sense of whether it is devoting sufficient resources to these efforts and if they are successful. A company can quantify the number of efforts as well as their effectiveness as measured by satisfaction and effectiveness surveys. R&D performance will drive not only potential cost savings but also customer acquisition, and increased customer satisfaction and loyalty, which will translate into improved sales and revenue.

Customer acquisition. Providing new company products and services as a result of innovation creates the potential for acquiring new customers. Companies that produce more innovation products and services will pique new customer interest, which can be translated into improved sales and increased revenue. The innovation activities and innovation leadership, strategy, structure, and systems should permit an increase in new customer acquisition as a powerful potential output.

Customer loyalty. Customer loyalty can be seen through both repeat customers and increased overall customer satisfaction levels. The common business truism that it is less costly to make additional sales to existing customers than to develop sales through new customers is certainly applicable to innovation. Innovation activities can provide an important opportunity to improve customer service levels and relationships leading to increased customer loyalty and repeat purchases.

Value capture. Capturing additional value is at the core of company objectives. In today's economy, customers can easily compare products and services across a range of competing companies. Thus, it is critical for each company to be able to differentiate itself from its competitors, for the benefit of its customers as well as itself. Through innovation, companies can offer customers superior products and services for a competitive price. Additionally, value measures should take into account not only the expected benefits from the current innovation effort but also future benefits associated with the capabilities developed. The opportunities for the creation and capturing of value for the company and its various stakeholders are significant.

Outcomes: Increased Revenues and Decreased Costs Lead to Improved Profitability

One important lesson from past innovation experience is that developing more products and other outputs of innovation activity is not enough. For innovation investments to be of value, the intermediate outputs must eventually pay off in increased corporate profits. Viewed simply, increased profitability can only be achieved through improving revenue or decreasing costs. To evaluate the payoffs of innovation investments and better allocate corporate resources, senior managers must be clear about the ultimate goal and develop ways to measure success. Further, if innovation managers want to obtain additional resources for innovation investments, the ultimate effect on corporate profitability must be measured and the payoffs and ROI be clearly calculated.

CONCLUSION

Management control researchers have long proposed that by aligning strategy, structure, and systems, organizational performance should improve. This proposition is at the heart of management control and performance measurement. But, though there has been substantial research, little conclusive evidence exists to guide managers in the implementation of strategy.

To adequately guide resource allocation decisions, managers need to know the likely payoffs of alternative corporate actions. Thus, the identification and measurement of the causal relationships in organizations is necessary to test the efficacy of management structure and system designs and the new approaches that have been developed for the implementation of strategy and the measurement of performance. This is critical both for improving the effectiveness of managerial practices and for academic research to test the most basic tenets of management control and performance measurement.[10]

In order to compete effectively, corporations must be able to innovate. They must have the appropriate resources available and effectively align the resources with the strategies and structures that will best encourage and achieve innovation success. However, not only is innovation needed, managers must also know how to measure the success of their innovation projects. Measurement is fundamental and critical to improving and sustaining innovation projects. The model that has been discussed is a practical tool that managers can use to assess the need for innovation and measure the outcomes of their innovation investments.

NOTES

1. For further information on causal relationships, see Marc J. Epstein and Robert A. Westbrook, "Linking Actions to Profits in Strategic Decision-making," *MIT Sloan Management Review*, Spring (2001): 39–49; and Robert S. Kaplan and David P. Norton, *Strategy Maps: Converting Intangible Assets into Tangible Outcomes* (Boston: Harvard Business School Press, 2003).

2. Marc J. Epstein and Jean-Francois Manzoni, "Implementing Corporate Strategy: from Tableaux de Bord to Balanced Scorecard," *European Management Journal*, April (1998): 190–203.

3. See Robert Simons, "Control in the Age of Empowerment," *Harvard Business Review* 73 (2) (1995): 80–89.

4. See Michael L. Tushman and Charles A. O'Reilly, *Winning through Innovation: A Practical Guide to Leading Organizational Change and Renewal* (Boston: Harvard Business School Press, 1997).

5. For some important ideas on innovation strategy, see Gary Hamel, *Leading the Revolution* (Boston: Harvard Business School Press, 2000); Chan Kim and Renee Mauborgne, *Blue Ocean Strategy: How to Create Uncontested Market Space and Make Competition Irrelevant* (Boston: Harvard Business School Press, 2005); and Clayton M.

Christensen, *The Innovator's Dilemma: When New Technologies Cause Great Firms to Fail* (Boston: Harvard Business School Press, 1997).

6. For discussions on structure, see Henry Chesbrough, *Open Innovation: The New Imperative for Creating and Profiting from Technology* (Boston: Harvard Business School Press, 2003) and Robert Simons, *Levers of Organizational Design: How Managers Use Accountability Systems for Greater Performance and Commitment* (Boston: Harvard Business School Press, 2005).

7. See Kathleen M. Eisenhardt and Charles Galunic, "Co-evolving: At Last a Way to Make Synergies Work," *Harvard Business Review*, January-February (2000): 91–101; Robert G. Cooper, *Winning at New Products: Accelerating the Process from Idea to Launch* (2nd ed.) (Reading, MA: Perseus Books, 1993); and Robert Simons, *Levers of Control: How Managers Use Innovative Control Systems to Drive Strategic Renewal* (Boston: Harvard Business School Press, 1995).

8. Marc J. Epstein, P. Kumar, and R. Westbrook, "The Drivers of Customer and Corporate Profitability: Modeling, Measuring, and Managing the Causal Relationships," *Advances in Management Accounting* 9 (2000): 43–72.

9. See Robert S. Kaplan and David P. Norton, "The Balanced Scorecard-Measures That Drive Performances," *Harvard Business Review* (1992): 71–79; and Robert S. Kaplan and David P. Norton, *The Strategy-focused Organization: How Balanced Scorecard Companies Thrive in the New Business Environment* (Boston: Harvard Business School Press, 2000).

10. Marc J. Epstein, "Measuring the Payoffs of Corporate Actions: The Use of Financial and Non-financial Indicators," in *Performance Measurement and Management Control: A Compendium of Research*, Marc J. Epstein and Jean-Francois Manzoni (eds.) (Oxford: Elsevier Science, 2002).

_____ 4 _____

Moving from Creation to Value

JULIE H. HERTENSTEIN and MARJORIE B. PLATT

T here has been much discussion in the new product development (NPD) and innovation literature about how to create value for a firm. The research has focused on organizational resources, structures, systems, and processes associated with superior new product performance (Cooper, 1996; Hertenstein & Platt, 2001; Mizik & Jacobson, 2003). Creating value is only one leg of the stool, however. Once a firm produces a product that can create value for the firm and provide value for its customers, it needs to capture the value of its new product by building barriers to forestall competition to enable the firm to effectively extract profits (Mizik & Jacobson, 2003). Further, the company needs to preserve value by efficiently managing resources associated with value creation and appropriation. Thus, there are three legs to the stool supporting profitable NPD efforts, moving a firm from the idea generation to realized value for firm owners: value creation, value appropriation, and value preservation. We argue that each is required to ensure that the firm achieves financial success from its NPD activities.

VALUE CREATION

Impact of Major Functions on New Product Success

Hertenstein and Platt (2001) provide a comprehensive review of NPD literature focused on factors associated with new product success. They highlight the effects of resources, processes, and strategy on new product outcomes. The factors that have been found to be most important in influencing new product outcomes are technology and marketing resources, including the personnel, their skills and expertise, the proficiency of their performance, and the timing of their participation. Typically, research has shown that increases in technology and marketing resources are associated with greater success in new product outcomes (Calantone & di Benedetto, 1988; Calantone, Schmidt, & Song, 1996; Cooper, 1982; Cooper & Kleinschmidt, 1987; Maidique & Zirger, 1984; Montoya-Weiss & Calantone, 1994; Zirger & Maidique, 1990).

Financial resources—specifically, financial personnel, skills, and expertise—may also influence new product success. The impact of financial resources on new product success tends to focus on the use and impact of "upfront" business analysis, which may include such things as forecasting costs and sales, calculating discounted cash flow or return on investment analyses, or conducting a detailed profitability analysis or review of product, marketing, and distribution costs (Cooper & Kleinschmidt, 1986, 1987; Montoya-Weiss & Calantone, 1994). Most studies report that some early financial analysis is related to new product success. However, less is known about the relationship between financial resources (including financial personnel, their skills, expertise, proficiency, and the timing of their participation) and new product success, and more research is required (Hertenstein & Platt, 2001).

Stage-gate Process to Structure NPD Resources

Resources or skills alone will not ensure a successful new product. A well-designed, repeatable NPD process is also necessary to achieve new product success (Cooper & Edgett, 1996; Cooper & Kleinschmidt, 1995; Rochford & Rudelius, 1997). As these studies indicate, a well-documented process not only ensures that critical tasks and analyses will be performed, thereby increasing the likelihood of new product success, but it also enables senior management to assess process effectiveness, which can lead to continuous process improvements.

Cooper (1983) first advanced the idea of an NPD process with clearly defined stages and management decisions, called "stage-gate decisions," following every stage.[1] Cooper and colleagues (Cooper & Edgett, 1996; Cooper & Kleinschmidt, 1995) characterize a high-quality NPD process as one that is complete, focuses on quality execution, emphasizes upfront homework, is flexible, forms a sharp, early definition of the product before development, and involves tough go/kill decision points. Senior managers use a well-structured process to control product development with periodic reviews to kill projects if certain criteria or milestones are not met (Cooper, 1993). Griffin (1997) reports that 52 percent to 69 percent of sampled manufacturing firms use some type of stage-gate NPD process.

Just as key upfront homework is critical to new product success, so is early involvement of key personnel in the NPD process. Early involvement of marketing personnel in the NPD process yielded substantial returns to new product success (Hise, O'Neal, Parasuraman, & McNeal, 1990). Researchers have also found that early involvement of other key players in NPD results in greater success, including production personnel (Fitzgerald, 1997a, b; Larson, 1988), component suppliers (Fitzgerald, 1997a, b; Harbour, 1991), and procurement engineers (Carbone, 1996; Minahan, 1998). Hertenstein and Platt (2001) argue that including a representative from the finance function early in the NPD process is most likely associated with more successful new product outcomes.

Team Structure

One powerful way that firms can control NPD outcomes is through the structure and specific membership of NPD teams (Takeuchi & Nonaka, 1986). In particular, Takeuchi and Nonaka point out that separate, functional teams handing off work in a sequential process are not as effective as an integrated team approach for NPD. Now, most NPD projects are conducted by multidisciplinary, multifunctional teams headed by a project leader and typically staffed by personnel from R&D, engineering, manufacturing or operations, marketing, and sales. Some companies include members of the finance function, purchasing, and industrial design, as well as representative customers or suppliers on their NPD teams.

Empirical research has shown that effectively integrating the R&D and marketing functions increases the chance of new product success (Griffin & Hauser, 1992; Hise, et al., 1990; Kahn & McDonough, 1997; Pinto & Pinto, 1990; Song, Neeley, & Zhao, 1996; Song & Parry, 1997a, b; Souder & Chakrabarti, 1978). For example, Hise et al. (1990) found strong evidence that collaboration between marketing and R&D functional units during the design phase of NPD was a key correlate with new product success. Larson (1988) further demonstrates that many benefits accrue to teams in which members are cross trained in each other's responsibilities, including shorter cycle times, achievement of critical cost and time targets, and increased likelihood the new product will meet customer needs. Thus, it was not just the magnitude of investment of key resources that led to success, but the timing of the activities and the degree of cooperation.

Information Sharing within the NPD Team

Extending the notion that integration and collaboration among the key players, R&D and marketing, are necessary for new product success, several studies have focused specifically on information transfer and sharing among functional areas represented on NPD teams. Moenaert and Souder (1990) offer a model containing factors that induce and inhibit effective information exchange. Rochford and Rudelius (1992) report that a surprising number of functional areas do not contribute or use information from other team members in many parts of the NPD stage-gate process. Yet sharing information among functional areas has a positive impact on new product success. Nobeoka and Cusumano (1997) look beyond sharing of information within a given NPD team. They examined 210 projects in the automobile industry from 1980 to 1991, finding that sharing or leveraging the technology in product platforms among multiple projects is important for sales growth.

One means of efficient information sharing is an information system capable of recording, storing, and accessing information across projects as well as functions. Accounting information is just one type of information needed for complete integration of projects. Companies also need technical, marketing, distribution and customer service information in order to evaluate a project in a comprehensive manner, using a balanced score card (Kaplan & Norton, 1996) or a similar approach. Creating a comprehensive, integrated, accessible information system is clearly a challenge for firms who want to ensure that they are creating value.

VALUE APPROPRIATION

The factors that have been found to affect new product outcomes and thereby create value for a firm—functional resources, multifunctional teams, a documented, repeatable new product development process—are necessary but not sufficient to consistently produce commercially viable, profitable products. Indeed, Mizik and Jacobson (2003) indicate that creating value is but a first step for the firm to undertake in order to realize that value. Once value has been created through innovating, producing, and delivering products to market, the firm must be able to "restrict competitive forces so as to be able to appropriate some of the value it has created in the form of profit" (Mizik & Jacobson, 2003, p. 63). They argue that firms that create value but are unable to protect it are vulnerable to losing the value they have created and having it claimed by competitors.

Marketing Efforts to Capture Value

Many aspects of marketing are aimed at appropriating value, including advertising, reputation and brand effects, and customer switching costs. Mizik and Jacobson (2003) cite examples of firms able to capture considerable value from their innovations (DuPont with Teflon, Microsoft with Windows) as well as those that did not profit from their innovations (EMI Ltd. with the CT scanner).

Value appropriation affects not only the amount of the advantage that a firm is able to capture, but the length of time that the advantage persists (Mizik and Jacobson, 2003). An example of a firm being first to market with a new technology, but missing the long-term opportunity to profit from its innovation, is Creative Technology Ltd. In 2000, this Singapore company was the first to market an MP3 player with a tiny hard drive that could store hundreds of hours of music. In fact, Creative Technology introduced this MP3 player, called the Creative Nomad, two years prior to Apple's iPod. Creative Technology did not understand how to market their innovative product effectively and allowed Apple to make the iPod a market sensation. As of 2004, Apple's annual iPod sales were ten times that of the Creative Nomad (Prystay, 2004), and Apple had effectively appropriated much of the value of Creative's MP3 innovation.

In addition to the significant contribution to value appropriation supplied by the marketing function, others can enable a firm to capture value as well. For example, firms whose products are characterized by effective industrial design are shown to appropriate more value—that is, they perform better on numerous measures of financial performance including stock market returns (Hertenstein, Platt, & Veryzer, 2005). Further, effective industrial design has been shown to have a persistent effect (Hertenstein, Platt, & Veryzer, 2005)—like brand—that may extend the time the advantage persists.

Getting to Market Quickly

Another factor that influences whether a firm appropriates the value it has created is time-to-market. A firm that creates value through its product development and manufacturing efforts but fails to get the product to market in a timely fashion risks having that value appropriated by a competitor who beats it to market. There is some evidence that getting products to market in a timely way increases value through greater increases in sales (Nobeoka & Cusumano, 1997) or shorter breakeven time (Ali, Krapfel, & LaBahn, 1995).

Further, there is considerable evidence about how to speed up new product introduction. Using a cross-functional, dedicated, accountable team with a strong leader and top management support is considered a key driver of project timeliness (Cooper & Kleinschmidt, 1994; Mabert, Muth, & Schmenner, 1992). A second key driver is solid upfront or predevelopment homework, which includes such tasks as initial screening, preliminary technical and market assessments, detailed market studies, and detailed business and financial analysis (Ali et al., 1995; Cooper & Kleinschmidt, 1994). According to Cooper and Kleinschmidt (1994), "Projects where the team and leader spent more time and effort on the up-front homework ... *actually saved time later!*" (emphasis in original, p. 387).

Another key driver of fast-paced product development is having a customer-focused, market-oriented new product effort (Cooper & Kleinschmidt, 1994). Other factors that have been identified as important to speeding up product development include rapid design transfer strategy (Nobeoka & Cusumano, 1997), recognized organizational commitment and top management support (Mabert, Muth, & Schmenner, 1992) and technical proficiency, market attractiveness, product definition, and launch quality (Cooper & Kleinschmidt, 1994). Kessler and Chakrabarti (1999) point out that different factors influence the speed of radical innovation projects and incremental projects. Moreover, some factors that speed up radical innovation (e.g., concept clarity, presence of many champions, co-located teams) were found to slow down incremental innovation.

The Relationship between Time-to-Market and Financial Performance

However, the relationship between timeliness and financial performance is not always as strong as we might expect it to be. This may be due, in part, to some of the hidden costs associated with accelerated product development. When the emphasis is on reducing time-to-market, teams may focus on low-profit, trivial innovation versus breakthrough innovation; they may skip steps in the development process where they would acquire necessary technical and market information; or they may overlook the need to develop a special sales force, distribution channel, or standby plan for problems during launch (Crawford, 1992).

Furthermore, the relationship between timeliness and financial performance may not be evident due to limitations in the data available to analyze this relationship. Griffin (1993) points out numerous difficulties in measuring how long product development takes. First, there are no baseline measures from which to form comparisons if you are evaluating techniques that might reduce product development time. Further, there are problems in defining product development time. For example, if it is defined as "the cycle time from conception to production," does conception occur when the need for a product change is identified or when the solution to the need is posited? Firms identify conception both ways, which adds noise to the analysis. Finally, Griffin (1993) indicates that the cost and profit data necessary to analyze this relationship are not readily available, which also limits researchers' ability to demonstrate a relationship. Thus, the ability to thoughtfully and credibly examine the relationship between product development time and financial performance demands careful definition of time, and carefully defined measures of product outcomes, including profitability, because, as Griffin (1993) indicates, "Producing product flops faster than the firm did before will not help you stay in business" (p. 118).

VALUE PRESERVATION

While others have focused on value creation and value appropriation (Mizik & Jacobson, 2003), we believe it is also important to focus on a third element, value preservation. Whereas value creation is largely about making the right product, value preservation is about making the product right.

Even when a company has created value by creating an innovation that meets customer needs and has appropriated that value by guarding its innovation and preventing it from escaping into the hands of a competitor, the company will not fully realize the value created if it does not preserve the value throughout the product lifetime. Fundamentally, the value the company ultimately realizes from its innovation is the difference between its revenues, and its costs, where costs represent the resources consumed for the innovation. By carefully managing and controlling the resources associated with the product, value is preserved. Resources must be broadly conceived, including, for example, resources or costs associated with development, capital investment, packaging, distribution, advertising, selling, and customer service, as well as manufacturing or product costs.

Ways to Preserve Value

Some approaches require companies to exercise a long-range perspective on value preservation. Designing product platforms to support entire product families is one such approach (Meyer, Tertzakian, & Utterback, 1997). "A product family is defined as a set of products that share common technology and address a related set of market applications ... [t]he technological foundation of the product family [is defined] as the product platform" (Meyer, Tertzakian, & Utterback, 1997). The product platform allows the firm to leverage the initial development costs when creating derivative products. This is the case because the incremental development cost for a follow-on product is considerably less (and may require less time) than would be required for a standalone product. Further, the product platform approach may also enable the firm to reduce product costs due to the use of common parts that reduce inventory carrying costs and provide the potential for volume discounts. (Davila & Wouters, 2004; Meyer, Tertzakian, & Utterback, 1997; Robertson & Ulrich, 1998)

Other approaches to preserving value and controlling product cost early in the NPD process begin with upfront analysis, which includes not only preliminary assessment of the market and technology but also financial analysis that provides a preliminary estimate of the potential value of the opportunity, as discussed above. Rochford and Rudelius (1992) indicate that 75 percent of companies performed a preliminary financial analysis. The results of the preliminary financial analysis provide a baseline to evaluate whether the anticipated value is being preserved as the project progresses.

Related to this preliminary financial analysis is often the establishment of a target cost. Target costing helps companies to attain adequate margins, hence preserving the value realized by the company (Boer & Ettlie, 1999). This is especially relevant in industries where the market effectively controls the price. In the automotive industry, where customers hold established expectations about product characteristics and price levels in various market segments, there are numerous examples of target costing (Albright, 1998; Monden & Hamada, 1991). Target costing begins with determining a target price, then subtracting an acceptable target profit to determine the target cost. The calculation is straight-forward; the challenge is how to achieve the target cost. Further, target costing can help designers to consider costs over the product's life cycle through the establishment of "moving targets" for price and product cost (Schmelze, Geier, & Buttross, 1996).

A heavy emphasis on target costing may not be appropriate in all product development efforts. Davila and Wouters (2004) indicate that when factors such as technology, time-to-market, or customer needs are more pressing than competing on cost, firms may use alternative practices to manage costs during product development. They find that these alternative practices—parallel cost management teams, modular design for cost, cost management strategies, and cost policies—facilitate cost management around, rather than inside, the product development project. This enables companies to successfully manage costs and preserve value without disrupting the product development team's focus on technology innovation, time minimization, and addressing customer needs.

Finally, measures are carefully monitored not only throughout the product development process, but through product launch and commercialization to ensure ongoing value preservation. Several studies report consistent findings regarding the specific measures used to assess new product performance (Hertenstein & Platt, 1997; Hultink & Robben, 1995; Mahajan & Wind, 1992; Page, 1993). Table 4.1 contains the various metrics included in the four studies. While most of these studies reported measures most frequently used, Hertenstein and Platt (1997) reported measures most emphasized during product development. The performance measures consistently found to be used by firms monitoring new product performance include profit, revenue, market share, ROI, and customer-related measures such as meeting customer needs or customer satisfaction. Interestingly, among the most frequently used or emphasized metrics are several traditional financial measures that speak to value preservation, such as profit, profit margins, and ROI.

Further, there is evidence that not only are these performance measures monitored, but if it is found that the firm is failing to preserve value, corrective action is taken. For example, Hertenstein and Platt (2000) found that when product cost exceeded target cost at the end of new product development, 36 percent of firms indicated that they delayed product launch in order to reduce the product cost, and 29 percent indicated that they killed the product altogether, while only 23 percent proceeded to launch the product while hoping that manufacturing could reduce the cost.

Confirming Value Post Product Launch

Related to a company's use of performance measurement as an effective control mechanism to preserve value *during* new product development is the use of post-launch audits to confirm the value of project as a whole and preserve value well *after launch*.

TABLE 4.1. Performance Measures Used to Control New Product Development

	Mahajan and Wind (1992)	Page (1993)	Hultink and Robben (1995)	Hertenstein and Platt (1997)
Financial Measures				
Sales revenue		X	X	X
Sales growth		X		
Profit	X	X	X	
Profit margin		X	X	
Product cost				X
ROI	X	X	X	
Payback	X			
Net present value (NPV)	X			
Market-related Measures				
Sales unit volume	X	X	X	
Market share	X	X	X	
Customer satisfaction		X	X	X
Time-to-market				X
Product-related Measures				
Product quality			X	
Product performance			X	

Descriptions of the stages within a firm's new product development process often include a final-stage post-launch audit and review. (Cooper, 1983, 1996). Further, some researchers contend that post-audit reviews are critical for companies engaged in innovative new product development (Chiesa, Coughlan, & Voss, 1996) and that only through "post-mortems" can companies effectively transfer knowledge across projects and thereby gain a competitive advantage in deployment of technology and design (Thomke & Fujimoto, 2000). Thomke and Fujimoto (2000) argue that project post-mortems are an effective way to achieve project-to-project knowledge transfer. Project post-mortems contain "detailed records of a project's history and include information on specific product and process problems discovered at various stages of development" (p. 134). Typically, the post-mortems also account for people, product, and scheduling issues. This information can be instrumental in carrying forward knowledge from past projects to current projects, thus creating a direct link between early problem solving in a current project (front-loading) and knowledge of past problems and their solutions. Further, they provide evidence from a field study showing that the ability to solve problems early in a project's development led to enhanced development performance, measured in terms of development time, development cost, and prototype reductions.

The post-mortems described above focus primarily on information needed to develop a high-quality product more rapidly and effectively. They do not focus on gathering and recording data on product cost, revenue, and related project development costs post launch so that a comprehensive profit analysis can be undertaken. Further, many firms do not conduct post-launch financial analysis (Cooper & Kleinschmidt, 1986).

As we have seen, there is a need throughout the NPD process for accurate, timely, multidimensional information. An approach analogous to the balanced scorecard (Kaplan & Norton, 1996) may be useful because a variety of information is necessary to assess NPD performance—ranging from the efficiency of the NPD process (development costs, time-to-market) to the efficiency of the manufacturing process (product cost) to financial performance (profits, return on investment) to customer measures (customer satisfaction, customer loyalty) to product measures (quality, product performance).

We want to focus on an important subset of this information: financial performance measures. Mahajan and Wind (1992) report that 70 percent of firms indicate that they conduct the business/financial analysis activity during product development in all cases, and that 55 percent of the firms indicate that this activity is of critical importance. In fact, they find that this activity is more frequently done in all cases, and is more often rated as of critical importance than any other product development activity except the development of the product itself (which 79 percent of firms report is done in all cases, and 71 percent report is of critical importance). Hertenstein and Platt (1997) found that key financial measures ranked up with the key nonfinancial measures in terms of the actual importance placed on those measures during product development. Further, Davila (2000) indicates that better cost information during product development is positively associated with better financial performance of the product. Financial expertise, in the form of financial members of the product development team, is also viewed as making a valuable contribution to the product development effort (Hertenstein & Platt, 2000; Mabert, Muth, & Schmenner, 1992).

Nonetheless, there is evidence that financial analysis is not done as frequently as might be surmised or emphasized as much as it should be. Hertenstein and Platt (1997) found that key product development personnel believed that even more importance should be placed on financial measures than was actually being placed on them during product development. There also seems to be a large drop in the proportion of companies that report conducting financial analysis early in the product development process versus those who report doing it later. For example, Cooper and Kleinschmidt (1986) report that 62.9 percent of companies conduct upfront business/financial analysis as compared to 34.5 percent who report conducting precommercialization financial analysis. Rochford and Rudelius (1992) report similar findings in that 75 percent of firms performed a preliminary financial analysis, but fewer than one in ten performed a precommercialization financial analysis after market testing. One reason for this might be the lack of participation by financial personnel in product development teams, especially the lack of participation throughout the entire product development process.

But another obstacle is the lack of financial information relevant to innovation and new product development maintained in the typical accounting system. Many researchers attempting to study factors that make product development more or less effective have reported that companies simply do not retain the necessary data, or do not retain it in a form amenable to analysis. In examining various approaches for accelerating new product development, Nijssen, Arbouw, and Commandeur (1995) argue that "respondents [may] not have adequate data available to improve on their own companies' NPD. This is based on limited response and missing values" (p.106). They go on to note the need for much more data to evaluate.

Meyer et al. (1997) report that "historical costs and sales revenue were not maintained on a yearly basis for individual products" (p. 96) and "we were unable to gather manufacturing engineering costs, retooling costs, or market introduction costs on a consistent basis" (p. 97). In discussing how to evaluate the effectiveness of product platforms, they indicate that the starting point is information on platform and product engineering costs as well as product sales, but note that "[r]esearchers may be surprised at how few firms have a grasp on these fundamental data" (p. 106). They further indicate that the ideal set of data for product development would include manufacturing engineering, retooling, and market introductions costs: "We were unable to gather these data in the company studied. We believe that such a lack of integration between information systems in engineering, manufacturing and marketing is not atypical in industry" (p. 107).

Griffin (1993) also indicates that cost and profit data necessary to analyze the relationship between product development time and product performance are not readily available: "Corporate accounting systems provide data for external reporting, not for managing new product development" (p. 118). She argues that the best measures of product success would be a combination of market share, profitability, and customer satisfaction data, but finds that "corporate accounting systems are not set up to provide this [profitability] data" by individual product—or discrete improvements to products—and that "obtaining profitability data will require changing the accounting system—a large expense" (p. 118).

However, if the data are not available, then not only can the researchers not analyze the data, but the companies do not have the data necessary to analyze for themselves the effects of their decisions.

Need for Accounting Information System to Support Innovation

We have established that senior managers use performance measures to control the new product development process as they make go/kill decisions at critical stages within the process. Yet it is clear that companies do not typically engage in post-audit reviews, despite evidence that this information can provide powerful tools to transfer important knowledge to other ongoing NPD projects, thereby saving significant time and development costs.

We need to capture information or knowledge from NPD projects not only to evaluate the performance of those projects as they evolve, but also to share that information with future NPD teams. This can be done by creating information systems that document learning and record important financial data to enable managers to assess the full costs associated with projects and thus a more representative measure of product profitability.

In essence, we propose that companies adjust their accounting information system to capture the full stream of costs related to the development and launch of a new product and to enable managers to compare budgeted estimates to actual results. In both cases, we are suggesting that firms create an information system that captures data from projects or new products, making the individual project or product the unit of analysis.

This would require the firm's accounting information system to capture and identify costs associated with a new product occurring over a long period of time, starting with idea generation, extending through product development, manufacturing, marketing, launch, distribution, and, finally, customer service. In doing so, companies can assess profitability by product in a comprehensive way, including all costs related to a particular product throughout the value chain. Not doing so can skew product-specific profit metrics. What is typically done now is to expense R&D costs, product development costs, and marketing costs in the period they are incurred. They become part of the fiscal year results, but are not attached to projects or products with which they are associated. When managers want to determine the performance of a particular product, it is virtually impossible to recapture costs incurred in earlier periods because costs that have been expensed are no longer readily available, and further, the data are not recorded in ways that associate them with specific products. Further, as Griffin (1993) points out, information is often aggregated by product line or brand, and hence data on individual products are unavailable for management consideration. The cost data in manufacturing, in addition, must be of sufficient granularity and reliably traced to specific products to distinguish which products actually incur which costs. According to Kaplan and Cooper (1998), when accurate cost data are provided, not only can the performance of existing products be better assessed, but the financial performance of future products can be improved as well, "Many companies now use their Stage III ABC (activity-based costing) systems primarily to provide better information to product engineers and designers to help lower the total manufacturing costs of new products" (p. 203). Anderson and Sedatole (1998) also express concern that product design decisions need to be based on the "costs, capabilities, or the experience of the firm in producing related products using similar production methods" and not on "rules of thumb that reflect conventional wisdom of the engineering professions and historical costs in an industry" (p. 223–4).

To fully assess the return on investment earned by a product requires a full understanding of and accounting for the investments in the product. Often, investment is taken to mean capital investment, that is, investment in fixed assets. But with new products, there are major investments in research, product engineering, industrial design, customer research, marketing, and others. To limit the performance measures to those associated only with capital investment is to obscure reality, and leaves managers questioning whether they are, in fact, earning a return on their investments in activities like industrial design (Hertenstein, Platt, & Veryzer, 2005, p. 5).

Another important feature of a newly configured information system would be the ability to connect cost estimates made during the development process to actual results. Estimates of many costs associated with the development of the product and the cost of the product itself are typically made during the process. An effective information system is required to enable managers to easily compare estimates (or budgets) to actual results. For example, target product costs are typically estimated during the NPD process. Target costs are often used to make go/kill decisions at critical junctures in the process. After a product is successfully launched, comparing target cost estimates to actual product costs realized during manufacturing could help new product managers determine whether their target cost modeling process is effective.

CONCLUSION

Firms engage in three critical activities in order to realize value from new product development efforts: value creation, value appropriation, and value preservation. All three are necessary to ensure that profits from new, innovative products will be achieved throughout the life of the product. During value creation, a firm marshals all relevant resources within the NPD process to produce a commercially viable product. Once a new product is launched, a firm must take steps to ensure that competitors do not appropriate the profits from its new product. Techniques such as effective marketing, advertising, and timing of product launch may be used to establish barriers to entry, thereby decreasing the probability that others will capture the market. Value preservation requires a firm to control activities throughout the NPD process and after product launch to ensure that profits will be realized during the life of the product. Good management control requires an information system containing both financial and nonfinancial metrics that will support analysis that informs decision making. Prior research has documented the failings of current accounting information systems to support project, product, product-line or brand analysis. This critical resource needs further attention so that firms can learn from past mistakes or successes and thereby improve the probability that new products will succeed in the market.

NOTE

1. The number of stages presented has varied from five (Poolton & Barclay, 1998) to thirteen (Cooper & Kleinschmidt, 1986).

REFERENCES

Albright, T. (1998). The use of target costing in developing the Mercedes Benz M-Class. *International Journal of Strategic Cost Management, 1*(2), 13–23.

Ali, A., Krapfel, Jr., R., & LaBahn, D. (1995). Product innovativeness and entry strategy: Impact on cycle time and break-even time. *Journal of Product Innovation Management, 12*, 54–69.

Anderson, S. W., & Sedatole, K. (1998). Designing quality into products: The use of accounting data in new product development. *Accounting Horizons, 12*(3), 213–233.

Boer, G. & Ettlie, J. E. (1999). Target costing can boost your bottom line. *Strategic Finance, 81*(1), 49–51.

Calantone, R. J., & di Benedetto, C. A. (1988). An integrative model of the new product development process: An empirical validation. *Journal of Product Innovation Management, 5*, 201–215.

Calantone, R. J., Schmidt, J., & Song, X. M. (1996). Controllable factors of new product success: A cross-national comparison. *Marketing Science, 15*(4), 341–358.

Carbone, J. (1996). A buyer's place is in the design lab. *Purchasing, March 6*, 59–64.

Chiesa, V., Coughlan, P., & Voss, C. A. (1996) Development of a technical innovation audit. *Journal of Product Innovation Management, 13*, 105–136.

Cooper, R. G. (1982). New product success in industrial firms. *Industrial Marketing Management, 11*, 215–223.

Cooper, R. G. (1983). A process model for industrial new product development. *IEEE Transactions on Engineering Management, 30*(1), 2–11.

Cooper, R. G. (1993). *Winning at new products: Accelerating the process from idea to launch* (2nd ed.). Reading, MA: Addison Wesley.

Cooper, R. G. (1996). Overhauling the new product process. *Industrial Marketing Management, 25*, 465–482.

Cooper, R. G., & Edgett, S. J. (1996). Critical success factors for new financial services. *Marketing Management, Fall*, 26–37.

Cooper, R. G., & Kleinschmidt, E. J. (1986). An investigation into the new product process: Steps, deficiencies, and impact. *Journal of Product Innovation Management, 3*, 71–85.

Cooper, R. G., & Kleinschmidt, E. J. (1987). New products: What separates winners from losers? *Journal of Product Innovation Management, 4*, 169–184.

Cooper, R. G., & Kleinschmidt, E. J. (1994). Determinants of timeliness in product development. *Journal of Product Innovation Management, 11*, 381–396.

Cooper, R. G., & Kleinschmidt, E. J. (1995). Benchmarking firms' new product performance & practices. *Engineering Management Review, Fall*, 112–120.

Crawford, M. C. (1992). The hidden costs of accelerated product development. *Journal of Product Innovation Management, 9*, 188–199.

Davila, T. (2000). An empirical study on the drivers of management control systems' design in new product development. *Accounting, Organizations and Society, 25*, 383–409.

Davila, T. & Wouters, M. (2004). Designing cost-competitive technolocy products through cost management. *Accounting Horizons, 18*(1), 13–26.

Fitzgerald, K. R., (1997a). Cost tops all design concerns. *Purchasing, April 3*, 64.

Fitzgerald, K. R. (1997b). Purchasing at Harley links supply with design. *Purchasing, February 13*, 56–57.

Griffin, A. (1993). Metrics for measuring product development cycle time. *Journal of Product Innovation Management, 10*, 112–125.

Griffin, A. (1997). PDMA research on new product development practices: Updating trends and benchmarking best practices. *Journal of Product Innovation Management, 14*, 429–458.

Griffin, A., & Hauser, J. R. (1992). Patterns of communication among marketing, engineering and manufacturing—A comparison between two new product teams. *Management Science, 38*, 360–373.

Harbour, J. (1991). Time and money. *Automotive Industries, December*, 9.

Hertenstein, J. H., & Platt, M. B. (1997). Developing a strategic design culture, *Design Management Journal, 8*(2), 10–19.

Hertenstein, J. H., & Platt, M. B. (2000). Profiles of strategic alignment: The role of cost information in new product development. *Design Management Journal Academic Review 1*, 8–24.

Hertenstein, J. H., & Platt, M. B. (2001) Creative accounting? Wanted for new product development. *Advances in Management Accounting, 10*, 29–75.

Hertenstein, J. H., Platt, M. B., & Veryzer, R. W. (2005) The impact of industrial design effectiveness on corporate financial performance. *Journal of Product Innovation Management, 22* (1), 3–21.

Hise, R. T., O'Neal, L., Parasuraman, A., & McNeal, J. U. (1990). Marketing/R&D interaction in new product development: Implications for new product success rates. *Journal of Product Innovation Management, 7*, 142–155.

Hultink, J., & Robben, H. S. J. (1995). Measuring new product success: The difference that time perspective makes. *Journal of Product Innovation Management, 12*, 392–405.

Kahn, K. B., & McDonough, III, E. F. (1997). An empirical study of the relationships among co-location, integration, performance and satisfaction. *Journal of Product Innovation Management, 14*, 161–178.

Kaplan, R. S., & Cooper, R. (1998). *Cost & effect.* Boston: Harvard Business School Press.

Kaplan, R. S., & Norton, D. P. (1996). *The balanced scorecard.* Boston: Harvard Business School Press.

Kessler, E. H. & Chakrabarti, A. K. (1999) Speeding up the pace of new product development. *Journal of Product Innovation Management, 16*, 231–247.

Larson, C. (1988). Team tactics can cut product development costs. *Journal of Business Strategy, September/October*, 22–25.

Mabert, V. A., Muth, J. F., & Schmenner, R. W. (1992). Collapsing new product development times: Six case studies. *Journal of Product Innovation Management, 9,* 200–212.

Mahajan, V., & Wind, J. (1992) New product models: Practice, shortcomings and desired improvements. *Journal of Product Innovation Management, 9,* 128–139.

Maidique, M. A., & Zirger, B. J. (1984). A study of success and failure in product innovation: The case of the U.S. electronics industry. *IEEE Transactions on Engineering Management, 31*(4), 192–203.

Meyer, M. H., Tertzakian, P., & Utterback, J. M. (1997). Metrics for managing research and development in the context of the product family. *Management Science, 43*(1), 88–111.

Minahan, R. (1998). Is this the future of purchasing? *Purchasing, March 12,* 42–47.

Mizik, N., & Jacobson, R. (2003). Trading off between value creation and value appropriation: The financial implications of shifts in strategic emphasis. *Journal of Marketing, 67,* 63–76.

Moenaert, R. K., & Souder, W. E. (1990). An information transfer model for integrating marketing and R&D personnel in new product development projects. *Journal of Product Innovation Management, 7,* 91–107.

Monden, Y., & Hamada, K. (1991). Target costing and kaizen costing in Japanese automobile companies. *Journal of Management Accounting Research, 3,* 16–34.

Montoya-Weiss, M. M., & Calantone, R. (1994). Determinants of new product performance: A review and meta-analysis. *Journal of Product Innovation Management, 11,* 397–417.

Nijssen, E. J., Arbouw, A. R. L., & Commandeur, H. R. (1995). Accelerating new product development: A preliminary empirical test of a hierarchy of implementation. *Journal of Product Innovation Management, 12,* 99–109.

Nobeoka, K., & Cusumano, M. A. (1997). Multiproject strategy and sales growth: The benefits of rapid design transfer in new product development. *Strategic Management Journal, 18*(3), 169–186.

Page, A. L. (1993). Assessing new product development practices and performance: Establishing crucial norms. *Journal of Product Innovation Management, 10,* 273–290.

Pinto, M. B., & Pinto, J. K. (1990). Project team communication and cross-functional cooperation in new program development. *Journal of Product Innovation Management, 7,* 200–121.

Poolton, J., & Barclay, I. (1998). New product development from past research to future applications. *Industrial Marketing Management, 27,* 197–212.

Prystay, C. (2004). When being first doesn't make you no. 1. *The Wall Street Journal, August 12.*

Robertson, D., & Ulrich, K. (1998). Planning for product platforms. *Sloan Management Review 39* (4): 19–31.

Rochford, L., & Rudelius, W. (1992). How involving more functional areas within a firm affects the new product process. *Journal of Product Innovation Management, 9,* 287–299.

Rochford, L., & Rudelius, W. (1997). New product development process: Stages and success in the medical products industry. *Industrial Marketing Management, 26,* 67–84.

Schmelze, G., Geier, R., & Buttross, T. E. (1996). Target costing at ITT Automotive, *Management Accounting, December,* 26–30.

Song, X. M., Neeley, S. M., & Zhao, Y. (1996). Managing R&D-marketing integration in the new product development process. *Industrial Marketing Management, 25,* 545–553.

Song, X. M., & Parry, M. E. (1997a). A cross-national comparative study of new product development processes: Japan and the United States. *Journal of Marketing, 61,* 1–18.

Song, X. M., & Parry, M. E. (1997b). The determinants of Japanese new product successes. *Journal of Marketing Research, 34,* 64–75.

Souder, W. E., & Chakrabarti, A. K. (1978). The R&D/marketing interface: Results from an empirical study of innovation projects. *IEEE Transactions on Engineering Management, 25,* 88–93.

Takeuchi, H., & Nonaka, I. (1986). The new new product development game. *Harvard Business Review, January–February,* 137–146.

Thomke, S. & Fujimoto, T. (2000). The effect of "front-loading" problem-solving and product development performance. *Journal of Product Innovation Management, 17,* 128–142.

Zirger, B. J., & Maidique, M. A. (1990). A model of new product development: An empirical test. *Management Science, 36,* 867–883.

5

Variations on a Theme: The Reinvention and Renewal of Intellectual Property

RALPH MAURER

C reativity is largely a repackaging, or recombination, of old ideas. From Claude Levi-Strauss's concept of bricolage[1] to Andrew Hargadon and Robert Sutton's[2] exploration of knowledge brokering, scholars have emphasized how creativity is best understood as the ability to create novel, useful combinations of existing things. These existing things can be ideas, technologies, products, services, themes, and other elements. Creativity is exercised in the selection of existing elements, the particular "combinatorial" strategies employed, and in the novel elements added to the mix of existing things.

Creative recombination is especially evident in the production of new versions of existing intellectual property. Roman Polanski's 2005 movie version of *Oliver Twist*, Volkswagen's 1997 retooling of the Beetle, and Microsoft's latest version of the Office software suite are all old properties that have been shaped and reshaped into new and updated incarnations. These new versions of existing intellectual property are recombinations of existing things, but they vary substantially in their degree of similarity to the original intellectual property. Sometimes the new version is an effort at renewal—an incremental recombination, as in most new model year revisions of existing car brands. Sometimes it is an effort at reinvention—a radical recombination, as in DJ Danger Mouse's remixing of both the Beatles' White Album and rapper Jay-Z's Black Album into the popular, but not quite legal, Grey Album, in which Paul

McCartney's singing is digitally laid on top of Jay-Z's beats. In all cases, however, threads of the original property are recombined into the new version.

This chapter explores the creative challenges inherent to renewing or reinventing intellectual property, particularly with regard to creative choices about what should stay the same and what should be different about the new version. I argue that a useful but oft-overlooked way to grapple with these challenges is to focus on what is (to borrow Stuart Albert and David Whetten's phrase) "core, central, and enduring" about the original intellectual property.[3] The best way to discover these core, central, and enduring elements is to examine the relationships that exist between the audience for an intellectual property and the property itself. I will use a combination of theory and case studies to demonstrate these points, all of which lead to the "overarching" message that creative decisions cannot be separated from the complex emotional attachments that surround so many creative properties.

DEFINITIONS, CONDITIONS, AND THEORY

Derivative Works, Reinvention, and Renewal: Some Definitions

Both renewed and reinvented properties are derived from an original piece of intellectual property. Not surprisingly, attorneys concerned with intellectual property issues refer to them as "derivative works." This term works well as shorthand for "new versions of existing product, services, brands and other intellectual properties."

Derivative works run the gamut from periodic tinkering with a proven formula to near total overhauls. They vary in both their degree of similarity and their degree of difference to the creative work(s) on which they are based. Given that there is a continuum of possibilities, these changes can be roughly aligned between the ideal types of renewal and reinvention. Pure renewal would be an incremental change to the original work that updates the work but retains all of the major identifiable features. The bicycle company Trek, for instance, has made slight changes every year to its original OCLV (Optimum Carbon Low Void) road bicycle frames since they were introduced in the early 1990s. One year they added a stiffer fork and headtube for better handling. The next year they changed the carbon fiber lay-up to reduce weight a bit. Even to a bicycle aficionado, the changes were incremental; the frame was renewed but largely stayed the same.[4] Pure reinvention would be a radical change to the original work that fundamentally alters and reframes it, only retaining a few features that link it back to the original work. The BBC's (British Broadcasting Corporation) 2005 reintroduction of the *Doctor Who* television series after a sixteen-year hiatus, for instance, bore little aesthetic resemblance to the old show. The multi-episode arcs and low-budget effects of the original were changed to self-contained hour-long stories with strong production values and pop music soundtracks. Most derivative works rest somewhere in between pure renewal and reinvention, but it is useful to classify them as one or the other.

When Do Renewal and Reinvention Happen?

Renewal is a regular, necessary activity for many creative firms, particularly those that produce consumer products. Yearly product cycles, changing fashions and preferences, rapidly evolving technologies and quickly shifting markets necessitate near-constant alterations to existing works in some markets. Palm has little choice but to periodically update the Treo PDA/phone hybrid due to technology changes and evolving consumer use patterns.[5] Intuit must update their Quicken financial planning software because of annual changes in the tax code, new investment categories (such as the Roth IRA created in 2000), and consumer expectation so that this year's version of the software will be different enough from last year's to warrant purchase. This pressure to update is also true for more culturally oriented goods produced in serial form, such as television shows, comic books, and series of novels. As seasons progress, characters must be tinkered with, plots must be refined, and visual and audio elements must keep pace with current trends and innovations. "Change or die" is often the mantra in these industries, and the pressure to maintain a sense of progress (even if that progress is difficult to measure) is intense.[6]

As opposed to the tinkering and upkeep of renewal, reinvention of existing works is usually aimed at resuscitation. Reinvention usually occurs in one of three conditions: in times of crisis (big or small), when the work remains the same for long periods, or after a work is absent from the public eye for a long period. The first, a *crisis*, often takes the form of eroding market share, stagnant product lines, or extreme customer pressure. Reinvention here is aimed at resurrecting something that has "dipped" considerably in the audience's collective opinion. An example of this occurred at the beginning of the television show *The Practice*'s final season (2003–2004), when, in the face of shrinking ratings, half the cast was fired, a new lead was brought on (James Spader), and, at the end of the season, the show was spun off completely into *Boston Legal* in the fall of 2004.[7] The most popular elements of *The Practice*'s last season were kept (including Spader), but the show was otherwise transformed.

The second condition, reinvention of a *long unchanged work*, can provide an opportunity for a firm to change its public image or to resuscitate a once great, but now tired work. This is different from a crisis in that there is not necessarily pressure on the firm to reinvent. The impetus for reinvention in this condition often originates in the creative minds of those tasked with overseeing the original creative work. This has occurred many times in the publication history of DC Comics. In 1986 and again in 2005, DC created mini-series (*Crisis on Infinite Earths* and *Infinite Crisis*) that completely altered the shape of the shared universe inhabited by DC's characters. This involved recharacterizations, major thematic shifts in the stories, and even changes to the history and origins of major characters (e.g., Superman, Wonder Woman, Batman) across the entire line of comic books.

Finally, reinvention of works that have undergone *long periods of absence* is often done in order to evoke nostalgia for a popular old work. DaimlerChrysler's 2006 model-year reintroduction of the Dodge Charger in conjunction with the *Dukes of Hazzard* movie illustrates this creative strategy. The car's release was an attempt to capitalize on nostalgia for the 1968 version of the car's prominent role in the old *Dukes of Hazzard* TV show. The new vehicle bore little resemblance to the old, jettisoning the old two-door format and the low, extended body design. The use of the Charger name and the timing of the car's release, however, were meant to evoke affection for the classic version of the car.[8]

The chart above outlines the two general types of derivative works (renewal and reinvention), reasons why firms make these changes, and some common mistakes associated with each reason for change. Notice that the mistakes listed in the chart are all audience related. This is because of the absolutely central role audiences play in the successful production of derivative works, an argument that the next section presents in more detail.

The Social Construction of Derivative Works

Firms are presented with two primary creative challenges in the production of derivative works. These challenges can be largely conceived of as choices

TABLE 5.1.   The Charactersitics of Renewals and Reinventions

Type of Change	Reason	Usual Goal	Common Mistake
Renewal (Incremental Change)	Upkeep	Revise, maintain, and improve products	Adding new elements that eliminate or interfere with the core elements of the original property
Reinvention (Radical Change)	Crisis	Save a firm or product	Throwing the good out with the bad; radical reinvention without keeping what works
	Stagnation	Resuscitate a stagnant intellectual property	Change for change's sake; altering a property without understanding the audience
	Absence	Evoke nostalgia for a once-popular work	Bringing back only surface elements; not understanding what is core about the original property

about elements of similarity and elements of difference between the new product and the original. With regards to similarity, it is vital that the new product be identifiably derived from the old. That is, the new product must be similar in a way(s) that can be easily recognized as a new version of the old creative work. Difference is simply the corollary of similarity. The new product must be different enough from the old to be considered a new, useful, interesting version. Psychologist Dean Keith Simonton's research on classical music demonstrates a similar point on a large scale, using a data set of over 15,000 classical music compositions. He shows that compositions considered to be creative in a given time period tend to be different enough from accepted musical norms of the time to be considered novel, but similar enough to these norms to still be popular.[9] The norms of a musical genre are much more "broad" than the norms surrounding a single piece of intellectual property, but the message is still the same; audiences expect for creative works to be simultaneously recognizable *and* novel.

The problem creative firms face is that there is always a degree of ambiguity surrounding the question of precisely what combinations of old and new elements will be considered creative. Creativity is generally thought to be the production of solutions that are novel, non-obvious, and valuable.[10] But none of these three concepts lend themselves to clearly defined objective measures. It is difficult to measure newness because all ideas are rooted in older ideas to some degree.[11] Indeed, absolute newness would be impossible in the case of derivative works since they are always based directly on an older work. It is similarly difficult to measure whether something is not obvious. Whether something is obvious or not is a matter of perception, not fact. Helen Fielding's 1996 novel *Bridget Jones's Diary* might be a clever use of Jane Austen's *Pride and Prejudice* for one person and a tired retread of an old theme for another.

Measuring value is no easier. With primarily utilitarian products such as computer servers or industrial adhesives, there are readily available objective standards for measuring the value of a new version. 3M's new version of Scotch-Weld epoxy adhesive works better than previous versions by any technical measure and is therefore valuable.[12] But many creative works have substantial design components that depend more on taste and fashion than on utility. It would be very difficult say to that Natalie Cole's remake of her father Nat King Cole's classic song *Unforgettable* is valuable in any objective sense. It would be just as absurd to say that the new cut of this year's Brooks Brothers blue blazer was more valuable than last year's model. A measure based on sales or critical acclaim could be used, but people would (appropriately) argue about the validity of the measure.

The novelty, non-obviousness, and value of a derivative work are impossible to accurately define before the fact. This is because the audience for a derivative work will ultimately determine whether it meets their criteria. This audience-contingent nature of creativity is something scholars refer to as "social construction."[13] For firms, the social construction of creativity means that it isn't enough to just "be creative" or "think outside the box" when renewing or reinventing old products. Designers attempting to make a new, creative version of an old product must also attempt to predict what the audience will construe as a new, interesting version of the old. "What we call creativity," writes psychologist Milhaly Csikzentmihaly, "is a phenomenon that is constructed through an intersection between producers and audience."[14] In the case of derivative works, the original intellectual property is situated at this intersection. Thus, producers must seek to understand the complex network of audience attachments to the property in order to produce creative derivative works based on the property.

Case Studies

In this section, I present four case studies of renewal and/or reinvention of well-known intellectual properties. The cases were selected in order to present a relatively diverse sample of industries, product types, and issues encountered by firms. Each case focuses on a specific audience-related problem inherent to the production of derivative works (see Table 5.2 for a summary of these case studies).

Socially Uninformed Change: The Case of New Coke

The first thing that must be considered regarding renewal or reinvention is whether change is needed at all. The pressure to change existing creative works can be intense in some areas, but it isn't always a good idea. This is

TABLE 5.2. Summary of Case Studies

Firm	Industry	Product	Primary Issue Encountered
Coca-Cola	Beverage	New Coke	Getting information about *consumer attachment* to the original product
Apple	Consumer electronics	iPod	Maintaining *continuity* from iteration to iteration of the product
BMW	Automobile	Mini	Understanding what the original version *meant* to consumers
Warner Bros.	Comics/Film	*Batman Begins*	Selecting from *multiple histories* of the original intellectual property

particularly true when the work being changed has a loyal following. Change in these cases must be undertaken cautiously because audiences tend to develop strong attachments with successful works. The audience may have a history with the work that will cause them to resist change when it is not obviously needed. In this case, changing the original work may be the worst thing a firm can do.

This was most certainly the case when the Coca-Cola Company somewhat infamously attempted to reinvent the original Coca-Cola soft drink formula in 1985. It is understandable why executives thought changing the formula was appropriate. Coca-Cola's market share had eroded from 60 percent just after World War II to less than 24 percent in 1983. Pepsi-Cola was steadily gaining ground on Coke in both market share and brand loyalty (as measured by the willingness to accept substitute soft drinks). And, to further bolster the argument for change, the previous effort at creating a variation on the original Coke, Diet Coke, had been a runaway success.[15]

The reinvented Coca-Cola, a sweeter variant dubbed New Coke, was released with the slogan "The Best Just Got Better" in April of 1985. New Coke initially sold as well as the original version (which was immediately put out of production), with most Coke drinkers making the switch without complaint. The sociocultural response, however, was unexpectedly (for the Coca-Cola Corporation) passionate and vocal. An organization of old Coke fans, named the Old Coca-Cola Drinkers of America, was formed to lobby Coca-Cola in hopes of bringing back the old formula. Their efforts included tens of thousands of letters, a class action lawsuit against Coca-Cola, and efforts to procure original Coca-Cola from overseas sources. The media quickly caught wind of the backlash and Coke's "mistake" entered the popular culture, appearing in late-night talk-show monologues, editorial cartoons, and even rival Pepsi's advertising. In July of 1985, Coca-Cola responded by reintroducing the original formula as Coca-Cola Classic, a move that eventually led Coca-Cola to regain market share from Pepsi.[16]

There are several competing explanations regarding exactly what went wrong with New Coke, ranging from conspiracy theories to thoughtful ruminations on the relationship between products and consumers. Some consumers suspect that Coca-Cola planned the reintroduction all along, hoping to capitalize on a flood of attention and publicity. There is, however, almost no evidence for this theory.[17] The Coca-Cola Corporation proffers a populist version, arguing that the introduction of New Coke ignited an underestimated passion for Coke in the American public. "There is a twist to this story which will please every humanist and will probably keep Harvard professors puzzled for years," said Donald Keough, president and chief operating officer, at a press conference the day of Coca-Cola Classic's release, "The simple fact is that all the time and money and skill poured into consumer research on the new Coca-Cola could not measure or reveal the deep and abiding emotional attachment to original Coca-Cola felt by so many people."[18]

Business historians and marketing scholars prefer to think that Coca-Cola did not understand, despite ample evidence, the power of a vocal minority of emotionally attached consumers.[19] In focus groups conducted by Coca-Cola before New Coke's release, 10–12 percent of the subjects were angered by the idea of introducing a substitute for Coke.[20] More interestingly, they were shown to exert indirect peer pressure on the other subjects to respond unfavorably to the proposed change. This response (anger and peer pressure) is presumed to have played out on a national scale once New Coke was introduced.[21]

What is interesting here (for the purposes of this chapter) is not which version of the New Coke story is accurate—both parties (Coca-Cola and academic writers) make a persuasive argument. Rather, what is interesting is the "social thread" that runs through both accounts. In both cases, the Coca-Cola Corporation underestimated the power and influence of social dynamics (as compared to product qualities and features) surrounding the original Coca-Cola product. They failed to fully comprehend both the scope and nature of attachment to the original formula and the alienation that some customers would experience as a result of introducing a reinvented product and removing the original from the market.[22] Alienation is a concept derived, in part, from the sociology of modern societies.[23] Alienation here means the separation or estrangement of people from the *things* (e.g., objects, brands, ideas) they were formerly attached to. Alienation has powerful emotional repercussions, leaving people feeling isolated, bitter, and angry, to varying degrees. Whether the American public in general or a vocal minority experienced this alienation, the introduction of New Coke brought it to the fore.

The introduction of New Coke makes clear the stakes of producing derivative works. The audience of a work (consumers in this case) may have substantial attachment to the original work. Reinvented derivative works that do not preserve or improve this attachment can cause substantial alienation on the part of the attached audience.

Adhering to Continuity—The Case of Apple's iPod

Of course, change is not always bad and many times is necessary. Soft drinks are products without any clear utilitarian advantage over each other. It cannot be said, for instance, that the original Coca-Cola formula is technologically superior to New Coke. But many products have substantial technological elements and must be revised in order to keep pace with the rest of the market. Keeping the product the same for long periods is simply not an option. This does not mean, however, that the social context ceases to be a factor. It remains important and must be considered in concert with technical changes to product features.

In the case of renewal, substantial elements of the old work are often still perceived to be desirable. Thus, any changes made should not abandon those elements. A powerful example of this is Apple Computer's near-clockwork renewal of the iPod digital music player. At least every six months since its initial release, Apple has come out with a new version of the basic iPod model (the larger, hard drive-based device simply named iPod). These new versions have added small changes to the same core product—better screens, longer-lasting batteries, slightly smaller form factors, and video functionality. But, crucially, each new iteration of the core iPod line is still easily recognizable as an iPod.[24] Both obvious and subtle aspects of the shape, finish, materials, and interface are largely the same across the entire history of the product. The iPod iterations can be said to exhibit *continuity* with regard to certain features and qualities. This continuity is echoed in Apple's online advertising: "Witness the evolution of the revolution. First it played songs. Then photos. Then podcasts. Now iPod plays video, changing the way you experience your music and more."[25]

The various iterations of the basic iPod line are examples of renewal, but the complete iPod line also contains examples of reinvention. Reinventions of the original iPod have appeared periodically in the form of dramatically smaller versions (the Shuffle, Mini, and Nano). Though each is recognizable as an iPod because of basic design similarities, the difference between the new version and the old basic design is significant enough to be understood as a reinvention. The Shuffle maintained the white gloss and rounded edges of the original iPod. And the Mini and Nano shrunk the basic form factor of the original to a more pocketable size at the expense of storage capacity. These products were reinventions of the old iPod but still maintained enough similarity to be recognizable members of the iPod family.

But how did Apple maintain continuity through both renewal and reinvention of the iPod? How did they decide what was core, central, and enduring about the iPod line? Though much has been written on the design of the first generation of iPod, Apple is notoriously secret about its ongoing design processes. It is clear, however, that Apple has a considerable advantage over its competitors in identifying customer attachments simply by virtue of the substantial amount of public debate that revolves around the question of what, precisely, is so innovative about the iPod. "You can say that the iPod is innovative," said reporter Rob Walker in *The New York Times*, "but it's harder to nail down whether the key is what's inside it, the external appearance or even the way these work together."[26] Many consumers love the scroll wheel that controls volume and menu navigation. Others admire the sleek, almost seamless body of the device.[27]

Some clues as to the elements of continuity may be found in Apple's first efforts at an iPod-like phone. Apple lent its name and software interface to a music-playing cellular phone from Motorola called the ROKR. The phone exhibited none of the design factors (aside from the software) most associated with the iPod. It lacked the minimalist button layout, the solid build quality, and the sleek, rounded shape of the iPod line. Aesthetic continuity was not adhered to by the designers of the ROKR, and the phone ended up being somewhat jarringly different from the iPod. Not surprisingly, the phone was panned by critics and consumers alike, inspiring not just lackluster sales but also more general criticism of Apple and Motorola. Fortunately for Apple, Motorola received most of the criticism, with many critics not believing that Apple under Steve Jobs could make such a design blunder.[28]

Continuity of design is an absolutely vital aspect of both the renewal and the reinvention of intellectual property. But it is very easy to lose core, central, and enduring aspects of the original design if existing audience attachments are not attended to. Apple successfully achieves this with the iPod through careful, periodic iteration that rarely seems to infringe on the audience's relationship with the product. The lesson here is not necessarily to copy Apple. Indeed, it isn't entirely clear how they identify the elements to keep continuous. Rather, the lesson lies in being cognizant of the potential dangers of abrubt, discontinuous extensions of intellectual property (e.g., the ROKR) and the sheer power of continuity for maintaining audience attachment.

Mining Nostalgia—The Reinvention of the Mini

Designers of the recently re-released Mini automobile grappled mightily with the problem of understanding the social context of their work. While the designers of the iPod only have to contend with a fairly continuous product history dating back to late 2001, designers of the Mini were faced with a comparatively rocky, but just as public, history dating all the way back to the late 1950s. After its invention by Sir Alec Issigonis in 1957 as a response to VW's Beetle, the Mini went through numerous design changes, two "retirements," multiple periods of popularity and stagnation, and, ultimately, a sale to BMW in the mid-1990s. Trying to get a fix on exactly what was core, central, and enduring about the Mini design was, understandably, no easy task.

The central difficulty with reinventing a creative work like the Mini is that during its lifetime, the Mini has "meant" many things to different audiences.[29] Despite only incrementally changing from its debut until production completely ceased in 2000, the vehicle had acquired multiple cultural meanings. In his book on the Mini as a design icon, historian L.J.K. Setright isolates several aspects of the car's identity over the years in his chapter headings: "Upstart" (the Mini as an innovative piece of design and engineering—with its small size, front-wheel drive, and transverse engine), "Gamine" (the car became a fashion statement in the 1960s, due in part to BMC loaning Minis to various celebrities), "Workhorse" (as a family car, and with various models used as taxicabs), "Racer" (the model produced by the John Cooper Garages—the Mini Cooper—had three victories in the Monte Carlo Rally [race] in the 1960s), "Film Idol" (prominent in many British films), and "Freak" (highlighting various bizarre customizations by enthusiasts over the years).[30] The multifaceted nature of the Mini is further emphasized by archivist Anders Clausager, who noted that in the U.K.,[31] "[the Mini's] functionality and ubiquity has made it the automotive equivalent of the Dr. Martens boot. Classless and ageless, it is a car for the dustman as well as the Duchess."[32]

Given the difficulty of discerning exactly what the Mini "meant," BMW chose to emphasize the design features that cut across the product's history. The compact size (at least relative to other vehicles) was preserved. The fuel economy was kept high, despite an updated high-performance engine. And the easy customizability (including the option of a British flag painted on the roof by the factory) was implemented at the factory level. Marketing in the U.K. played down innovative design elements like the new rigid chassis (for better cornering), the vastly improved suspension, and new safety devices.[33] In short, BMW emphasized what was iconic in order to invoke a sense of nostalgia in the audience, and made design (and thus creative) decisions that preserved aesthetic continuity with the past. When people look at the new Mini, they are meant to see the old in the new design.

Cultural historian David Platt explores this evocation of nostalgia through design in his analysis of a British magazine ad for the Mini. In the ad is a small boy in an old-fashioned British schoolboy uniform peering into the window of a current model Mini parked in a barn. On the wall above the car are ads for British 1960s-era Spark Plug Service and car Battery companies (old British companies). The child is carrying a toy version of a Mini and behind him are framed black and white photographs of old Minis in car rallies. Platt argues that the advertisement is an example of "hyperreality," a simulation of the past that attempts to be more "real" than the original. Consistent with psychology research regarding remembrance of past emotions, the ad attempts to elicit a sort of positive "retrospective bias" regarding feelings and memory about old versions of the Mini.[34] The garage full of Mini memorabilia with the young boy peering into the car is, in Platt's opinion, a way for BMW to both evoke nostalgia and communicate to customers that BMW understands how important the history of the Mini is.[35]

Evoking nostalgia is not, however, simply a matter of advertising or marketing. It involves creative decisions about the elements from the old work that must remain in the derivative work. Just as in the case of the iPod, this requires an understanding of what elements of the design must remain in order to not alienate the audience. One can imagine the reaction if the new Mini had not been identifiably tied to the old using the iconic design elements. Not only would the Mini experience poor sales, but BMW would possibly have been critiqued for their betrayal of Mini owners.

Drawing from Multiple Histories: Batman Begins

When DC Comics considered what to do with the Batman film franchise following the critical and commercial failure of 1997's *Batman and Robin*, further alienation of their loyal fan base was of paramount concern. DC, a subsidiary of Warner Brothers, knew that the increasingly "campy" film portrayals of Batman (since Tim Burton's 1989 film started the series) were not adequately capturing what was core, central, and enduring about the character of Batman.[36] Furthermore, there wasn't any one iconic version of Batman to which they could turn for inspiration.

While the Mini had multiple meanings associated with one relatively continuous past, Batman's creative history consists of many disparate versions of the Batman character. Batman began life in 1939 as a vigilante in the style of "film noir." Then, from 1941 to 1970, Batman appears as a law-abiding, fairly standard superhero in the mold of Superman and Wonder Woman, painted in bright colors and entirely heroic in demeanor. This period also saw the famous, and much ridiculed, television show starring Adam West, which ran from 1966 to 1968. The 1970s returned Batman to his original incarnation as a dark, brooding loner, and narratives of this era resembled detective stories rather than science fiction. This transformation was capped by author and artist Frank Miller's 1986 story *The Dark Knight Returns*, which portrayed a bitter, jaded, and retired Batman in a dystopian future. Miller wrote in a realistic tone that focused on Batman's inner life, significantly fleshing out what eventually came to dominate Batman's present incarnations; more recent changes have tended to build on Miller's foundation.[37]

The central point here is that finding a single continuous history from which to draw is impossible in the case of Batman. This problem extends beyond comics. Consider the similar challenge facing the creators of James Bond films. Five different actors have played Bond, all in decidedly different ways. However, none of them necessarily lays claim to being *the* "iconic" Bond, and much argument about the subject persists among fans. In an article about the difficulty of selecting a new Bond, Avi Arad of Marvel Studios (one of DC's competitors) opined that, at least for Marvel, securing big-name actors isn't necessary when a company is in possession of a strong brand name.[38] Securing big-name actors may not be necessary, but ensuring that the film preserves (or establishes) what is considered core, central, and enduring about a property certainly is. In the eyes of the audience, the circumstance of multiple histories does not excuse the creators from this responsibility.

What, then, constitutes the core of a creative work that has multiple histories? For Warner and DC, answering this question involved several years of development, many scripts, and countless conversations with fans, creators, and potential writers and directors.[39] The Batman film franchise produced no films from 1997 to 2005 as DC probed both the potential audience for a new Batman film and the creators who were most attached to the property. As eventual director Christopher Nolan puts it, the creators of the film needed to find "[the] elements [that] have stuck through [Batman's] history. Those were then the key elements that we felt helped to pin down the character and the mythology that we had to stick to."[40] Far from adhering to any sort of clearly established continuity, the new film picks and chooses existing elements from Batman's history based on knowledge drawn from those with strong relationships to the original work.

Nolan and screenwriter David Goyer quickly homed in on Miller as a primary source for these mythic elements. Miller had reinvented Batman at a time (1986) when the editors felt that the character's complicated histories were becoming too overwhelming. Miller's response was to change not the history of the character but the tone of the comic, as described above. Using Miller's Batman as the core inspiration for the 2005 cinematic version was an admitted attempt on the part of the editors not just to stick with core elements of the character but "to fuse and clarify certain elements of the mythology that have always been around."[41] "I felt I had the responsibility to make the most sincere effort to make a great version of the character as I understood him from studying the history of the comics," said Nolan.[42] Consequently, the new film draws from both Miller's *Batman Year One* and *Dark Knight Returns* for many aesthetic, thematic, and plot-based elements. Sprinkled in were ideas and characters drawn from other stories, such as writer Jeph Loeb's *The Long Halloween* and *Dark Victory*; these borrowed elements, while adding to the depth of the narrative, remained compatible with the identifiable Miller aesthetic.

This is not to say that the end result, *Batman Begins*, was without novel elements. Selecting the areas of similarity defined the space where novelty and innovation could occur. Referring to the addition of the character of Rachel, Goyer said, "She is an invention of ours. We wanted a female lead who would be integral to the mystery/crime aspects of the story, but there didn't seem to be an appropriate character in the existing canon." Certain aspects of the old also had to be adjusted for the film medium. It was important to Nolan not to be "aping the form of the comic book itself, so all the elements of design, photography, and the selection of storyline are based upon the same sort of terms of logic, realism, and attention to detail that would apply to any thriller or action film."[43]

Batman Begins was an immense commercial and critical success.[44] Nolan attributes the success of his film, in part, to his (and screenwriter David Goyer's) ability to "come up with the cinematic equivalent of the key elements of the comic book mythology." *The New York Times* agreed, noting that "what makes this Batman so enjoyable is how Mr. Nolan balances the story's dark elements with its light, and arranges the familiar genre elements in new, unforeseen ways."[45] This was also the reaction of fans, who took to both the borrowed elements in the film and the novel ones.[46] Thus DC managed to preserve, and possibly even improve, the relationship between Batman's audience and the character of Batman by taking this relationship seriously. Goyer and Nolan analyzed the social context of the Batman property. They used this information to pick and choose a set of core, central, and enduring elements from among multiple histories of the property. And they transformed these elements into a successful derivative work.

IMPLICATIONS FOR CREATIVITY

The audience-centered perspective and the cases of New Coke, the iPod, the Mini automobile, and *Batman Begins* are presented in this chapter to make the following argument—choosing areas of similarity and difference for renewed or reinvented works is difficult, particularly because the audience's reception of the new work is contingent on the audience's relationship to the original work. New Coke failed as a direct result of this relationship. New iterations of the iPod have to adhere to an established continuity of design regardless of what innovation occurs at a technological level. The new Mini had to evoke nostalgia for the old, despite having its utilitarian features upgraded and improved. And *Batman Begins* needed to borrow from the appropriate histories of Batman in order to be received well by those already familiar with Batman.

Audiences have complicated relationships to creative works. And new versions of creative works often succeed by preserving or improving the relationship between the audience, the creators, and the product itself. Though this challenge is related to design, it is ultimately a social concern. George Lucas's release of *The Phantom Menace*, for instance, was much criticized for not adhering to the elements that made the original Star Wars trilogy so loved. Many fans expressed anger and a sense of betrayal. Avoiding these sorts of mistakes requires an understanding of how the audience for a product (consumers, fans, creators) relate to it. How do they identify with the product? What do they believe can be changed? What cannot? Where are they willing to accept risk taking with regard to new features and details? In short, and yet again, what do they find core, central, or enduring about an old product? These are tough questions to answer, but are crucial to the success of a derivative work.

Finally, I want to address the general implication of this argument for our understanding of creativity. First, the argument suggests that whether a creative work is considered to be an incremental or radical innovation depends significantly on context. Firms may think they are making incremental changes to a product when, in fact, customers interpret the change as radical (and therefore potentially threatening). For instance, some readers may have argued with my assessment of the Shuffle, Mini, and Nano as reinventions of the iPod. After all, compared to the reformulation of Coca-Cola into New Coke, these new models of iPod seem to be relatively minor retoolings. This problem of scale and relative difference is precisely what makes definitions of either reinvention or renewal so difficult. It is also what makes creativity and innovation potentially dangerous when not tempered by an understanding of the social context of change.

Second, and most important, the argument suggests that "supply-side" perspectives on creativity and innovation that emphasize producer agency need to be balanced by audience-focused perspectives. I believe, however, that much of both the popular press and business scholarship is guilty of overemphasizing the role of firms and fields (the producers) while simultane-ously ignoring markets (the audience). I don't want to make the same mistake by overemphasizing the role of the audience in the creative process. Ingenuity, genius, inspiration, and intuition still play a vital role in the creativity and innovation. Hopefully this chapter has demonstrated, however, that it is impossible to understand creative processes without considering the audien-ce's role in the process.

NOTES

1. Claude Levi-Strauss, *The Savage Mind* (Oxford, U.K.: Oxford University Press, 1962).

2. Andy Hargadon and Robert Sutton, "Technology Brokering in a Product Devel-opment Firm," *Administrative Science Quarterly* 42 (1997).

3. S. Albert and D. Whetten, "Organizational Identity," in *Research in Organiza-tional Behavior*, ed. B. M. Staw (Greenwich, CT: JAI Press, 1985).

4. Cyclingnews, *Trek Rolls out New Weapons for Discovery Tour Campaign* [Web page] (Cyclingnews, June 16, 2005 [cited November 2, 2005]); available from http://www.cyclingnews.com/tech.php?id=tech/2005/features/discovery_tour_bikes.

5. Eric von Hippel, *The Sources of Innovation* (New York: Oxford University Press, 1988).

6. Robert William Kubey, *Creating Television: Conversations with the People Behind 50 Years of American TV* (Mahwah, NJ: Lawrence Erlbaum Associates, 2004).

7. Gary Levin, *Retooled "Practice" Ready to Return* [Web article] (*USA Today*, 2003 [cited October 4 2005]); available from http://www.usatoday.com/life/television/news/2003-07-15-practice_x.htm.

8. Warren Brown, "Detroit Yells a Rowdy Howdy" [Web page] (*Washington Post*, 7/31/2005 2005 [cited November 13, 2005]); available from http://www.washingtonpost.com/wp-dyn/content/article/2005/07/29/AR2005072901646.html, DaimlerChrysler Corpo-ration, *Chrysler Group, Brands & Products, 2006 Dodge Charger* (2005 [cited November 20, 2005]); available from http://www.daimlerchrysler.com/dccom/0,0-5-470118-1-480957-1-0-0-0-0-0-36-479389-0-0-0-0-0-0-0,00.html http://www.daimlerchrysler.com/dccom/0,0-5-470118-1-480350-1-0-0-0-0-0-36-479389-0-0-0-0-0-0-0,00.html http://www.daimlerchrysler.com/dccom/0,0-5-470118-1-480960-1-0-0-0-0-0-36-479389-0-0-0-0-0-0-0,00.html, Roland Jones, *"Dukes" Flick Jump-Starts Charger's Popularity* [Web article] (MSNBC, 8/15/2005 2005 [cited November 4, 2005]); available from http://msnbc.msn.com/id/8813484/.

9. D. K. Simonton, "Thematic Fame, Melodic Originality, and Musical Zeitgeist: A Biographical and Transhistorical Content Analysis," *Journal of Personality and Social Psy-chology* 38 (1980): 972–983.

10. T. M. Amabile, "A Model of Creativity and Innovation in Organizations," in *Research in Organizational Behavior*, ed. B. M. Staw and L. L. Cummings (Greenwich, CT: JAI Press, 1998).

11. T. B. Ward, "What's Old About New Ideas?" in *The Creative Cognition Approach*, ed. S. M. Smith, T. B. Ward, and R. A. Finke (Cambridge, MA: MIT Press, 1995).

12. 3M Corporation, *3M Scotch-Weld Epoxy Adhesive 2214 Hi-Temperature New Formula* [Web catalog] (3M Corporation, 2005 [cited October 12, 2005]); available from http://products3.3m.com/catalog/us/en001/manufacturing_industry/engineered_adhesives /node_GS9ZRNKGJ7be/root_GST1T4S9TCgv/vroot_WHG0MWH6QPge/gvel_GVTSZT9B QQgl/theme_us_adhesivetape_3_0/command_AbcPageHandler/output_html.

13. Peter L. Berger and Thomas Luckmann, *The Social Construction of Reality: A Treatise in the Sociology of Knowledge* (New York: Anchor Books, 1966).

14. Csikzentmihaly advocates a systems perspective on creativity that, among other things, does not artificially separate the audience's perceptions from the decisions made by producers of creative works. See Milhaly Csikzentmihaly, "Implication of a Systems Perspective for the Study of Creativity," in *Handbook of Creativity*, ed. Robert J. Sternberg (Cambridge, U.K.: Cambridge University Press, 1999).

15. Mark Pendergrast, *For God, Country, and Coca-Cola: The Definitive History of the Great American Soft Drink and the Company That Makes It* (New York: Basic Books, 2000).

16. Coca-Cola, *Cokelore* [Web page] (The Coca-Cola Company, 2005 [cited August 1, 2005]); available from http://www2.coca-cola.com/heritage/cokelore_newcoke.html.

17. Matt Haig, *Brand Failures: The Truth About the 100 Biggest Branding Mistakes of All Time* (London: Kogan Page, 2003).

18. Ibid.

19. L. L. Garber, E. M. Hyatt, and R. G. Starr, "Measuring Consumer Response to Food Products," *Food Quality and Preference* 14, no. 1 (2003); Pendergrast, *For God, Country, and Coca-Cola: The Definitive History of the Great American Soft Drink and the Company That Makes It*.

20. Robert M. Schindler, "The Real Lesson of New Coke: The Value of Focus Groups for Predicting the Effects of Social Influence," *Marketing Research* 4 (1992).

21. Ibid.

22. Contrast Coca-Cola's strategy with that of Adidas, who has kept the much-loved Copa Mundial soccer shoe largely unchanged and still available since 1979. This is despite substantial and persistent technological innovation being applied to other soccer shoes in its line. See Adidas Corporation, *Adidas—About Us* (2005 [cited October 3, 2005]); available from http://www.adidas.com/us/shared/aboutadidas.asp?strCountry= us&strBrand=performance&lpos=Header&lid=About&parameter='About%20Adidas'; http:// www.press.adidas.com/en/desktopdefault.aspx/tabid-4/79_read-1487/; http://www.press.adi- das.com/en/desktopdefault.aspx/tabid-28/41_read-1209/, Adidas Corporation, *Adidas Orginals Brings Diversity of Authentic Concepts* (2005 [cited October 4, 2005]); available from http://www.press.adidas.com/en/desktopdefault.aspx/tabid-70/96_read-329/.

23. Karl Marx, *The Communist Manifesto* (New York: Signet, 1998); James S. Coleman, *Foundations of Social Theory* (Cambridge, MA: Harvard University Press, 1990).

24. Leander Kahney, *Cult of iPod* (New York: No Starch Press, 2005).

25. Apple Computer, *Apple—iPod* (2005 [cited December 10th 2005]); available from http://www.apple.com/ipod/ipod.html.

26. Rob Walker, "The Guts of a New Machine" [Web archive of newspaper article] (*The New York Times*, 11/20/2003 2003 [cited December 9, 2005]); available from

http://select.nytimes.com/search/restricted/article?res=F30816F93A5F0C738FDDA80994 DB404482.

27. Ibid.

28. Frank Rose, *Battle for the Soul of the Mp3 Phone* [Web page] (Wired, November 2005 [cited November 21, 2005]); available from http://www.wired.com/wired/ archive/13.11/phone.html, Nick Santilli, *Did Apple Sabotage the Rokr?* (the AppleBlog, 2005 [cited December, 2005]); available from http://www.theappleblog.com/2005/11/ 09/did-apple-sabotage-the-rokr/.

29. David Platt, *Meaning and the Mini: Nostalgia, Hyperreality and Changing Meaning* (Stanford, CA: Stanford University Press, 2004).

30. L. J. K. Setright, *Mini: The Design Icon of a Generation* (London: Virgin, 1999).

31. In the U.S., the Mini enjoyed a period of popularity in the 1960s, but was taken off the market in 1967 because it did not meet new fuel emissions standards. BMC deemed it too expensive to fix the problem and the only Minis used in the States after this period were modified by collectors.

32. Anders Ditler Clausager, *Essential Mini Cooper: The Cars and Their Story 1961– 71 and 1990 to Date* (Bideford, U.K.: Bayview, 1997).

33. BMW, *The Mini Story* [Web advertising] (2005 [cited July 23, 2005]); available from http://www.mini.com/com/en/mini_story/index.jsp.

34. Linda J. Levine et al., "Remembering Past Emotions: The Role of Current Appraisals," *Cognition and Emotion* 15, no. 4 (2001).

35. Platt, "Meaning and the Mini: Nostalgia, Hyperreality and Changing Meaning."

36. Sean Axmaker, *Christopher Nolan's Realistic Superhero* (GreenCine, 2005 [cited November 10, 2005]); available from http://www.greencine.com/article?action=view& articleID=247.

37. Ruth Morrison, *Batman Masterpieces: Portraits of the Dark Knight and His World* (New York: Watson-Guptill Publications, 2002).

38. Bob Tourtellotte and Mike Collett-White, *007 Secret Safe So Far as James Bond Casting Looms* [Web article] (Ezilon Infobase, 12/5/2005 2005 [cited December 6, 2005]); available from http://www.ezilon.com/information/article_11293.shtml.

39. Manohla Dargis, "Dark Was the Young Knight Battling His Inner Demons" (*The New York Times*, 2005 [cited December 8, 2005]); available from http://www.nytimes. com/2005/06/15/movies/15batm.html?ex=1134622800&en=ebc42153c15e78e9& ei=5070.

40. Claudia Kalindjian and Editors of DC Comics, *Batman Begins, the Official Movie Guide* (Time Inc. Home Entertainment, 2005).

41. Axmaker, *Christopher Nolan's Realistic Superhero* ([cited]), Dargis, *Dark Was the Young Knight Battling His Inner Demons* ([cited]), Kalindjian and Editors of DC Comics, *Batman Begins, the Official Movie Guide*.

42. Axmaker, *Christopher Nolan's Realistic Superhero* (cited).

43. Kalindjian and Editors of DC Comics, *Batman Begins, the Official Movie Guide*.

44. Scott Holleran, *Wink Kid: An Interview with Christopher Nolan* (Box Office Mojo, 2005 [cited October 27, 2005]); available from http://www.boxofficemojo.com/features/ ?id=1921&p=.htm.

45. Dargis, *Dark Was the Young Knight Battling His Inner Demons* (cited).

46. Comics2Film, *Review: Batman Begins* [Web review] (Comics2Film, 2005 [cited November 15, 2005]); available from http://www.comics2film.com/StoryFrame.php? f_id=13754&f_sec=6, Holleran, *Wink Kid: An Interview with Christopher Nolan* (cited).

REFERENCES

Adidas Corporation. 2005. Adidas - About Us. http://www.adidas.com/us/shared/abou tadidas.asp?strCountry=us&strBrand=performance&lpos=Header&lid=About&para meter='About%20Adidas'; http://www.press.adidas.com/en/desktopdefault.aspx/tabid-4/79_read-1487/; http://www.press.adidas.com/en/desktopdefault.aspx/tabid-28/41_read-1209/ (accessed October 3, 2005).

———. 2005. Adidas Originals Brings Diversity of Authentic Concepts. http:// www.press.adidas.com/en/desktopdefault.aspx/tabid-70/96_read-329/. (accessed October 4, 2005).

Albert, S., and D. Whetten. "Organizational Identity." In *Research in Organizational Behavior*, ed. B. M. Staw, 263–295. Greenwich, CT: JAI Press, 1985.

Amabile, T. M. "A Model of Creativity and Innovation in Organizations." In *Research in Organizational Behavior*, ed. B. M. Staw and L. L. Cummings, 123–67. Greenwich, CT: JAI Press, 1998.

Apple Computer. 2005. Apple—iPod. http://www.apple.com/ipod/ipod.html (accessed December 10, 2005).

Axmaker, Sean. 2005. "Christopher Nolan's Realistic Superhero." http://www.greencine. com/article?action=view&articleID=247 (accessed November 10, 2005).

Berger, Peter L. and Thomas Luckmann. *The Social Construction of Reality: A Treatise in the Sociology of Knowledge*. New York: Anchor Books, 1966.

BMW. 2005. The Mini Story. http://www.mini.com/com/en/mini_story/index.jsp (accessed July 23, 2005).

Brown, Warren. 2005. "Detroit Yells a Rowdy Howdy." In *On Wheels*, ed. Warren Brown. http://www.washingtonpost.com/wp-dyn/content/article/2005/07/29/ AR2005072901646.html (accessed November 13th, 2005).

Clausager, Anders Ditler. *Essential Mini Cooper: The Cars and Their Story 1961–71 and 1990 to Date*. Bideford, U.K.: Bayview, 1997.

Coca-Cola. 2005. Cokelore. http://www2.coca-cola.com/heritage/cokelore_newcoke. html (accessed August 1, 2005).

Coleman, James S. *Foundations of Social Theory*. Cambridge, MA: Harvard University Press, 1990.

Comics2Film. 2005. Review: Batman Begins. http://www.comics2film.com/StoryFrame. php?f_id=13754&f_sec=6 (accessed November 15th, 2005).

Csikzentmihaly, Milhaly. "Implication of a Systems Perspective for the Study of Creativity." In *Handbook of Creativity*, ed. Robert J. Sternberg, 313–335. Cambridge, U.K.: Cambridge University Press, 1999.

Cyclingnews. 2005. Trek Rolls out New Weapons for Discovery Tour Campaign. http://www.cyclingnews.com/tech.php?id=tech/2005/features/discovery_tour_bikes (accessed November 2, 2005).

DaimlerChrysler Corporation. 2005. Chrysler Group, Brands & Products, 2006 Dodge Charger. http://www.daimlerchrysler.com/dccom/0,0-5-470118-1-480957-1-0-0-

0-0-0-36-479389-0-0-0-0-0-0-0,00.html   http://www.daimlerchrysler.com/dccom/
0,0-5-470118-1-480350-1-0-0-0-0-0-36-479389-0-0-0-0-0-0-0,00.html   http://
www.daimlerchrysler.com/dccom/0,0-5-470118-1-480960-1-0-0-0-0-0-36-479389-
0-0-0-0-0-0-0,00.html (accessed November 20, 2005).

Dargis, Manohla. 2005. Dark Was the Young Knight Battling His Inner Demons.
http://www.nytimes.com/2005/06/15/movies/15batm.html?ex=1134622800&en=
ebc42153c15e78e9&ei=5070 (accessed December 8, 2005).

Garber, L. L., E. M. Hyatt, and R. G. Starr. "Measuring Consumer Response to Food
Products." *Food Quality and Preference* 14, no. 1 (2003): 3–15.

Haig, Matt. *Brand Failures: The Truth about the 100 Biggest Branding Mistakes of All Time*.
London: Kogan Page, 2003.

Hargadon, Andy and Robert Sutton. "Technology Brokering in a Product Development
Firm." *Administrative Science Quarterly* 42 (1997): 716–749.

Holleran, Scott. 2005. Wink Kid: An Interview with Christopher Nolan.   http://
www.boxofficemojo.com/features/?id=1921&p=.htm (accessed October 27, 2005).

Jones, Roland. 2005. *"Dukes" Flick Jump-Starts Charger's Popularity.*   http://msnbc.
msn.com/id/8813484/ (accessed November 4, 2005).

Kahney, Leander. *Cult of iPod*. New York: No Starch Press, 2005.

Kalindjian, Claudia and Editors of DC Comics. *Batman Begins, the Official Movie Guide*:
Time Inc. Home Entertainment, 2005.

Kubey, Robert William. *Creating Television: Conversations with the People Behind 50 Years
of American TV*. Mahwah, NJ: Lawrence Erlbaum Associates, 2004.

Levi-Strauss, Claude. *The Savage Mind*. Oxford, U.K.: Oxford University Press, 1962.

Levin, Gary. 2003. Retooled "Practice" Ready to Return.   http://www.usatoday.com/life/
television/news/2003-07-15-practice_x.htm (accessed October 4, 2005).

Levine, Linda J., Vincent Prohaska, Stewart L. Burgess, John A. Rice, and Tracy M.
Laulhere. "Remembering Past Emotions: The Role of Current Appraisals." *Cognition and Emotion* 15, no. 4 (2001): 393–417.

Marx, Karl. *The Communist Manifesto*. New York: Signet, 1998.

Morrison, Ruth. *Batman Masterpieces: Portraits of the Dark Knight and His World*. New
York: Watson-Guptill Publications, 2002.

Pendergrast, Mark. *For God, Country, and Coca-Cola: The Definitive History of the Great
American Soft Drink and the Company That Makes It*. New York: Basic Books, 2000.

Platt, David. *Meaning and the Mini: Nostalgia, Hyperreality and Changing Meaning*. Stanford, CA: Stanford University Press, 2004.

Rose, Frank. 2005. Battle for the Soul of the Mp3 Phone.   http://www.wired.com/
wired/archive/13.11/phone.html (accessed November 21, 2005).

Santilli, Nick. 2005. Did Apple Sabotage the Rokr?   http://www.theappleblog.com/
2005/11/09/did-apple-sabotage-the-rokr/ (accessed December 2, 2005).

Schindler, Robert M. "The Real Lesson of New Coke: The Value of Focus Groups for
Predicting the Effects of Social Influence." *Marketing Research* 4 (1992): 22–27.

Setright, L. J. K. *Mini: The Design Icon of a Generation*. London: Virgin, 1999.

Simonton, D. K. 1980. "Thematic Fame, Melodic Originality, and Musical Zeitgeist: A
Biographical and Transhistorical Content Analysis." *Journal of Personality and Social
Psychology* 38: 972–983.

3M Corporation. 2005. 3M Scotch-Weld Epoxy Adhesive 2214 Hi-Temperature New
Formula.   http://products3.3m.com/catalog/us/en001/manufacturing_industry/engine

ered_adhesives/node_GS9ZRNKGJ7be/root_GST1T4S9TCgv/vroot_WHG0MWH6QPge/
gvel_GVTSZT9BQQgl/theme_us_adhesivetape_3_0/command_AbcPageHandler/output_
html (accessed October 12, 2005).

Tourtellotte, Bob and Mike Collett-White. 2005. 007 Secret Safe So Far as James Bond
Casting Looms. http://www.ezilon.com/information/article_11293.shtml (accessed
December 6, 2005).

von Hippel, Eric. *The Sources of Innovation*. New York: Oxford University Press, 1988.

Walker, Rob. 2003. The Guts of a New Machine. http://select.nytimes.com/search/
restricted/article?res=F30816F93A5F0C738FDDA80994DB404482   (accessed
December 9, 2005).

Ward, T. B. "What's Old About New Ideas?" In *The Creative Cognition Approach*, ed.
S. M. Smith, T. B. Ward and R. A. Finke, 157–178. Cambridge, MA: MIT Press,
1995.

6

Organizational Design for Corporate Creativity in the Indian Setting

PRADIP N. KHANDWALLA and KANDARP H. MEHTA

E arly but still influential organization scholars argued that organizations have considerable difficulty innovating. Managers tend to have limited problem-solving, information-processing, and choosing capabilities (bounded rationality), and this bounded rationality predisposes the organization to rely on precedents, rules of thumb, familiar solutions, and standard operating procedures rather than on innovation (Cyert & March, 1963; March & Simon, 1958). When the organization is large, it tends to get bureaucratic, that is, it favors extensive functional and role specialization and hierarchy of authority (Pugh, Hickson, Hinings, & Turner, 1969), and this further impairs the organization's capacity to innovate with respect to those innovations that require intensive interdepartmental coordination (Burns & Stalker, 1961). Because of the aforementioned reasons, organizations tend to get inertial, with limited capacity to respond effectively to environmental jolts. As a consequence, populations of organizations that are suddenly confronted with major environmental discontinuity will tend to show heightened mortality rate (Hannan & Freeman, 1984).

On the other side of the spectrum, a number of scholars believe that corporate organizations need to be highly innovative to be able to survive in today's times (Drucker, 1985; Kimberly, 1981; Quinn & Rivoli, 1991). Even executives in Third World countries, long insulated from global competition through protectionism, have begun to appreciate the need for innovation. Reportedly, in a recent survey conducted in India by the Boston Consulting

Group and the Confederation of Indian Industries, 82 percent of the executives polled believe that generating growth through innovation has become essential for success in their industry (*Economic Times*, 2005). Obviously, therefore, if organizational inertia is pervasive and innovation is essential, then both organizational scholars and practitioners need to understand better the sort of organizational design(s) that can counter inertia and deliver innovativeness. This chapter sets out a model of organizational design for corporate creativity and presents evidence in support of it.

WHAT IS CORPORATE CREATIVITY?

Corporate creativity or innovativeness is the ability of a corporate organization to conceive and sustain a continuing stream of reasonably successful (for the organization) innovations and new initiatives. Creativity is generally considered as the ability to come up with novel (in the context) but appropriate solutions to problems, while innovation consists of those processes that transform a creative idea into a *usable* unique product or process or activity (Khandwalla, 2003). Corporate creativity not only includes but goes well beyond technical inventions powered by R&D and patents. It includes small innovations and improvements in operations (kaizen), innovations in the decision-making process and the style of management, in business growth, competitive, and survival strategies, in organizational structure, in organizational practices and culture, in various management systems such as control, coordination, human resource management, marketing, information and communications, R&D and design, financing, operations, management of projects and innovations, etc. Several examples given below illustrate the power and ambit of corporate creativity.

Examples of Corporate Creativity

Five cases are presented below. Three cases are of European airlines reeling from powerful new competition in the early 1980s that was unleashed by the deregulation of the western airlines industry. Two are of Indian companies struggling to come to terms with the competitive forces unleashed by India's liberalization and globalization that began in earnest in 1991.

Aer Lingus

The Irish national airline found itself in troubled waters. Following the deregulation of the airline industry in the early 1980s in the West, it lost over 11 million Irish pounds on a turnover of 500 million Irish pounds in 1981–82, and lost money also in 1982–83. To turn around in the intensely competitive environment, it leveraged its computerization skills for designing a turnkey reservation system for a West Asian airline; it leveraged its skills in overhauling aircraft engines by setting up a plant to offer overhauling services to other airlines at the relatively cheaper Irish rates; and it leveraged its personnel management competencies to equip and operate a hospital in Iraq and nursing homes in Britain (Arbose, 1986; Kennedy, 1988). Aer Lingus earned 20 million Irish pounds in 1984–85. Aer Lingus offers an interesting example of innovations in growth strategy.

British Airways

Ill-reputed in the 1970s as the airline of last choice, the government-owned British Airways sought to change the work culture innovatively in the early 1980s to overcome its weaknesses and to compete effectively (Leahey, 1990). The entire frontline staff, some 40,000 persons, was put through a two-day-long program called Putting People First, which emphasized good interpersonal relations. This move was effective in that employees became much more sensitive to the importance of good relations both among themselves and with customers. Several cross-functional teams were formed to accelerate various aspects of the change process, such as a team for designing management information systems (MIS) support for the change effort, another to refurbish livery, etc. Surveys were conducted and the results were fed back to the staff to stimulate changes and innovations. The staff members in the human resources management area were trained to perform agent change roles and assist managers in bringing about changes and innovation. A novel system was devised to provide emotional support to those who were stressed by providing high-quality service in a very demanding environment. Another system provided peer group support to people who had undergone the Managing People First program. As a customer relations management initiative, multilingual troubleshooters were stationed at Heathrow Airport to welcome and assist non-English-speaking passengers arriving for the first time in the U.K. Later, a worldwide program was launched on leadership to strengthen customer relations. British Airways won the best airline of the year award several times in the 1980s, and turned around from a loss of £545 million on revenues of £2,060 million in 1982 to a profit of £216 million on revenues of £2,510 million in 1984. British Airways offers a good example of innovations in the human resource management and customer relations management areas.

Scandinavian Airlines

SAS lost 63 million Swedish Kroners in 1980, with a comparable loss in 1981. Jan Carlzon, the new CEO, stepped up communications with the staff. He gave pep talks at staff parties, in aircraft hangars, and in other unlikely places. He traveled around the world to meet practically every one of the 16,000 employees, and sought their views on what to do to revive the airline.

The staff rose to the occasion, and suggested some 150 projects that would cost about 40 million Swedish Kroners. A little red book of about fifty pages titled *Let's Get in There and Fight* incorporated the turnaround strategy and was distributed to the entire staff. The booklet was written to charm the reader and included many cartoons. The message was efficiency and service quality. Some 150 study groups were set up with wide staff participation to reinvent the company. Some 10,000 frontline staff were put through a customer service training program, and 2,500 middle-level managers were sent to a three-week course in new management and business philosophies. To make the orientation more business oriented, the sales office was moved to the business area. Several new profit centers were set up, and the whole structure was revamped for greater decentralization with accountability. Even flight routes were turned into profit centers. Some 1,300 jobs were eliminated, but mostly on the basis of attrition. The fleet was refurbished, and a computerized reservation system was installed. Business class passengers were specially targeted, and the airline was promoted as the "businessmen's airline." SAS Destination Service provided door-to-door service to passengers, along with hotel reservations in the destination city. SAS began to earn between 70 and $80 million Swedish Kroners a year. In 1983, *Fortune* called it the best airline of the year, and in 1984 it was selected as the "Airline of the Year" by an international magazine. SAS offers an interesting account of innovations in human resource management, communications, leadership and style of management, customer services and relations, operations, marketing, and organizational structure (Carlson & Nelson, 1988; Lefebure, Jorgensen, & Staniforth, 1988).

Ramon & Demm

The company was was set up in India in 1964 to produce gears. It thrived initially in India's protectionist economy, but began to falter badly when liberalization picked up steam (Sareen, 1996; Gupta, 1998). The company was taken over by the Eicher Group in 1992. The new CEO initiated a flurry of innovations and initiatives that were new for the company, which turned the company around by 1995. He met all the stakeholders, including the representatives of unions, suppliers, and distributors, to better understand their problems. Market surveys revealed severe erosion of brand value. The CEO wrote a letter to the employees inviting cooperation and holding out a vision of the company regaining its lost glory. Safety was improved, and employees began to get their salaries on a regular basis. The staff was given extensive training on quality and teamwork. A turnaround promotion scheme was launched to provide incentives to the staff, and the incentives were pegged as sales value added (value of sales minus material costs) to promote sales productivity and customer service. A voluntary retirement scheme was launched that reduced manpower from 850 to 700 without "hire and fire" methods.

Just-in-time and proper materials handling techniques were introduced. A strenuous effort to reduce machine breakdown and power consumption led to reductions of machine breakdown by 80 percent and power consumption by 30 percent. A large sum was spent on plant reconditioning. Improvements in production panning led to a doubling of turnover per unit of inventory. Vendors were rationalized from thirty to ten high-quality, loyal vendors. Productivity nearly doubled.

Export of high margin gears was pushed, and unprofitable products were replaced by profitable products, while some of the existing products were repositioned as niche products. Aggressive promotion was aimed not at garage owners but at garage mechanics. Unsuitable distributors were replaced. Sales rose from Rs. 200 million in 1993–94 to Rs. 500 million in 1995–96, and profitability increased from a loss of Rs. 50 million in 1993–94 to a profit of Rs. 50 million in 1995–96. This case illustrates the power of initiatives and innovations in the areas of operations, sales and marketing, value chain, productivity, and communications that bore dramatic fruit.

Asoka Spintex

This Indian company (Gupta, 1999), a producer of fabrics and part of the Lalbhai Group, suffered grievously after the late 1980s from competition from the small-scale power loom weavers, freer imports of filament fiber, and an ill-timed expansion into polyester fiber and modernization. There were also sharp rises in input costs that added to the company's woes. A young MBA scion of the business group was appointed as CEO. The management was able to get suppliers to resume sales to the company on credit after they were assured that they would be paid on time. It also negotiated an agreement with the power supplier not to disconnect power supply on account of accumulated debts. Hints were conveyed to the workers that the company was likely to close down, so that they could become more amenable to rationalization of surplus manpower. The union's cooperation was secured for downsizing. Other stakeholders, such as the tax authorities and the financial institutions, were also co-opted into the turnaround. Friendlier communications and interactions, and an open-door policy for the staff, were initiated. At the same time, "troublemakers" and nonperformers were eliminated and discipline was restored. The entire white collar staff was required to wear a uniform to foster the "we" feeling. Workers' suggestions were sought to improve quality and productivity. Incentives in terms of promotions and pay packets were initiated. Quality control was tightened, and work on getting an ISO certification was begun. A TQM consultant was brought in, and quality circles were introduced in all departments. A three-shift system was introduced. A human resource management executive was appointed for the first time, and the recruitment of talented and qualified employees was emphasized. Also emphasized were multiple skills, job rotation, training, and upgrading of skills. The company benchmarked its management systems on the most successful company in the business group. Planning and interdepartmental coordination were improved, and annual goals and targets began to be set and disseminated to the staff. Massive downsizing, rare in India, was initiated, and about 80 percent of the workforce was removed, mainly in the highly unprofitable weaving and fabric processing units. The company concentrated only on the profitable spinning operations. Modernization of spinning facilities enabled the company to export 25 percent of its yarn, so that exports increased from Rs. 50 million in 1995–96 to Rs. 250 million in 1996–97. More responsiveness of dealers was initiated. All these initiatives, some innovative in the context of the company and the industry, resulted in profits. After losing money for eight years, the company earned Rs. 53 million on sales of Rs. 608 million in 1996, and continued to remain profitable the next year despite a recession. The management's initiatives in stakeholder management, operations management, strategic divestment, downsizing, and so forth, many of them innovative in the Indian context of the time, bore rich fruit.

WHY CORPORATE CREATIVITY?

In this chapter we argue that organizations are not fated to be inertial, rigid, and vulnerable in a volatile environment, and that it is possible to design them in such a way that they produce a sustained stream of successful technological, operations-related, and managerial innovations (corporate creativity) that can raise their viability even in a turbulent, highly competitive environment, and indeed can help them flourish in such an environment. This possibility becomes highly significant in the context of globalization.

Globalization has created immense competitive pressures on corporations, as well as global opportunities. The emergence of the knowledge economy, intense global competition, creation of new trade blocks, greater integration of global markets, and the fast pace of technological, economic, and social change have positioned creativity and innovation as key elements for sustained competitive advantage. Creativity and innovation help organizations produce the new products, processes, and systems required for adapting to, and profiting from, changing markets, technologies, and modes of competition. The focus of this chapter is not the effective management of R&D or particular innovations, but the organization's *innovativeness* and the organizational design that can facilitate a sustained stream of successful product, process, and management-related innovations.

Innovation is equally important for both developed as well as developing countries. Organizations in developed countries are facing a sudden threat to survival from companies in emerging market economies like China and India. Industries are dispersing quickly all over the world. Many "smokestack" industries are migrating to the developing countries from their countries of origin. The U.S. and European firms have been taking a beating even in relatively high-tech industries like memory-chip, office-automation, consumer-electronics, and auto-parts industries. Asian challengers have dethroned many Western giants in their respective industries. Xerox has lost its dominance to Sharp and Sony, Panasonic and Toshiba have edged out Canon, and Motorola has outpaced Zenith and RCA. The Western pioneers of auto industry have had a tough time coping up with the likes of Toyota, Honda, and Nissan.

Corporations in emerging economies like South Korea, China, and India that have invested heavily in education, especially technical and managerial education, seem to have gained considerably in terms of competitiveness. Emerging countries possess a cost advantage not only in terms of unskilled labor cost; some of them are also able to provide high-quality intellectual capital at a lower cost than developed economies can. The U.K. government has estimated that China's wage costs are 5 percent of the wage costs in the U.K. (Innovation Report, 2003). South Korea's labor costs are just 50 percent of the wage costs in the U.K., while the proportion of graduates in the working population is identical (Innovation Report, 2003). China, with a steel output equal to the combined production of the U.S., Japan, and Russia—the next three largest producers—has emerged as the manufacturing hub for many industries, while India has emerged as a programming and R&D hub for multinationals. Since developing countries are quick to adapt to new technologies, organizations from developed countries are under sustained pressure to retain the position of technological leadership. In order to gain a competitive edge over their counterparts in the developing world, these corporations need to be *quick* at developing new technologies and technologically superior products, and marketing them globally, to garner the first mover advantage. This requires a high order of creativity and innovation.

Developing countries also require creativity and innovation. Many of them are far behind the developed countries in manufacturing technology and productivity, customer service, product quality and so forth. India, for instance, ranked forty-ninth on product-process sophistication in 2002–03, compared to ranks of fourth and sixth for Japan and the U.S., respectively; fifty-ninth on customer orientation versus third and first for Japan and the U.S., forty-sixth on extent of staff training versus sixth and third for Japan and the U.S., and forty-sixth on capacity for innovation versus fourth and sixth for Japan and the U.S. (Cornelius, 2003). These huge gaps cannot be bridged rapidly without a high order of creativity and innovation.

Globalization and liberalization have enabled developing countries to import Western technology and build up a cost advantage on the basis of much lower labor costs. However, corporations in developing countries need to adapt imported technology to local needs and conditions, which requires ingenuity. Globalization has also opened up doors of thus-far protected markets of these countries to multinational corporations, and the resultant fierce competition in the premium quality high-margin segments needs to be met with creativity and innovation by the domestic players. Finally, firms in emerging economies have to be innovative to create new markets and to break into lucrative foreign markets. Though some emerging countries, especially India, have emerged as R&D hubs for companies like Motorola, Microsoft, and HP, organizations in these countries need to capitalize upon advantages in their home bases to penetrate foreign markets and remain viable in them. All these challenges cannot be met without designing corporate organizations to yield high levels of creativity and successful innovations.

Creativity and innovation can benefit organizations in emerging economies in different ways. Improving production or operations-related routines through innovation may provide them with a cost advantage over competitors. Innovative organizational redesigning can increase managerial productivity. The production- or operations-related strategy could be reinvented to increase production flexibility, reduce lead times, improve working conditions, and reduce staff costs. Similarly product strategy can be reinvented to improve product quality, replace obsolete products, and extend the product range, and marketing strategy can be reinvented to open new domestic or foreign markets or protect existing market shares. Research on designing organization for creativity and innovation indicates how these benefits can be garnered.

CORPORATE CREATIVITY AND ORGANIZATIONAL DESIGN: SOME STUDIES

Research indicates that innovative firms grow faster and tend to be more profitable than non-innovative firms (Geroski & Machin,1993; Khandwalla, 1985; Kleinknecht, Oostendorp, & Pradhan, 1997). A crucial question, therefore, is how an organization can be designed in such a way that it can maximize innovativeness and innovational success. Some scholars have argued that there is yet no consensus on what factors influence innovational success (Downs and Mohr, 1976; Wolfe, 1994). Wolfe (1994) has concluded: "the most consistent theme found in the organizational innovation literature is that its research results have been inconsistent." An attempt, therefore, to evolve a consensus on the organizational design needed to promote successful innovativeness is an urgent necessity. Based on a number of previous studies briefly outlined below, we have made an attempt to evolve such a design and validate it with the help of data on sixty-five Indian corporate organizations (Khandwalla & Mehta, 2004).

An early but influential British study tried to find out why in the post-World War II era some new companies in the electronics industry could innovate quite successfully while some older companies in the same industry that had been highly successful during the war failed to be innovative after the war was over (Burns & Stalker, 1961). Based on a study of twenty companies, the researchers concluded that the style of management was the decisive factor for determining the innovative capability of an organization. In the older companies the management tended to be "mechanistic"—that is, hierarchy and fairly rigid functional jurisdictions were more important, and lateral communications were discouraged. Departmental loyalties were fierce due to absence of interdepartmental mobility, and interdepartmental disputes were usually pushed upwards to top management for resolution. Hence, innovations requiring interdepartmental cooperation either were not implemented or were implemented with delays. The style that was suitable to innovativeness was the one the researchers labeled "organic," in which there was not only extensive decentralization and much freer flow of lateral and vertical communication, but the management stressed getting results over following the laid-down rules and procedures, encouraged improvisation, let decisions emerge through the interaction of all the stakeholders in the decision, and gave experts on the subject greater say in the making of a decision than the person formally designated as in charge.

Steiner argued that to be innovative the organization should be ambidextrous, that is, be effective both at generating creative ideas and at implementing selected ideas effectively (Steiner, 1965). The organization needs to have a free-wheeling, "boundaryless" brainstorming culture to generate creative ideas, as in a creative ad agency or an R&D lab. For effective implementation, a professionalist culture is needed, with strong systems of planning, control, coordination, evaluation of proposals, rewards and incentives for superior performance, performance review for course correction, cross-functional teams for better coordination, and so forth. It is frequently difficult for organizations to change gears between the phases of "invention" (creative ideation) and "innovation" (effective implementation of a creative idea), and some organizations try to separate the two wings entirely—one portion to ideate creatively, another to innovate successfully (Kimberly, 1981).

A third influential idea concerning organizational design for innovativeness is that the organizational design for breakthrough innovations may differ from the design for numerous incremental innovations throughout the organization—what the Japanese call kaizen (Gluck, 1985; McMillan, 1984). Breakthrough innovations need "skunk works"—small, dedicated teams of bright, creative individuals fanatically pursuing breakthrough innovations despite modest resources, epitomized by Steve Jobs' Apple Computers. The organization is small, or broken up into relatively small teams. Each team is headed by an innovation champion. There is usually considerable disrespect for systems, procedures, budgetary discipline, and the like. The organization perpetually operates in a fire-fighting mode, and tinkering, improvisation, and trying out odd approaches is part of the organizational culture. Opposed to this "gung-ho" management culture is the cozy "clan" culture of the kaizen, with consensual, participative decision making, lifetime learning, a culture of continuous improvements, paternalism, job security, collaborative rather than adversarial relations with internal and external stakeholders, bonuses to everyone (though tied to corporate performance), etc. In its heyday in Japan, this management culture yielded excellent results: from 1967 to 1987, Japan's manufacturing productivity grew two to three times faster than that of the

U.S. and other leading Western nations (Quinn & Rivoli, 1991). The Japanese corporations appeared to convert R&D-based ideas into successful products faster than their U.S. counterparts, although they did not match the Americans in breakthrough inventions.

Khandwalla's (1985) study of policy frameworks used by a sample of seventy-five Indian companies yielded one that he labeled "pioneering—innovative." This consists of a group of policies that favor pioneering of novel, technologically sophisticated, high-quality products in an emerging market economy, emphasis on innovation and experimentation in all the operations of the organization, entrepreneurial risk taking, operating flexibility, and hiring of creative youngsters with considerable operating responsibility and autonomy. On average, the group of companies using this policy cluster grew 50 percent faster than the group of companies that were traditionally managed, and also averaged better profitability.

In another study of ninety Indian corporate organizations, Khandwalla identified three top management styles that had the largest correlations with the organization's rated innovativeness (Khandwalla, 1995, chapter 7). These adhered to the entrepreneurial style of pursuing big but risky growth opportunities, the organic style that emphasizes improvisation and operating flexibility discussed earlier, and the participative decision-making style. In addition, while these three styles had the largest number of significant correlations with organizational mechanisms for *generating* innovative ideas, the styles with the largest number of significant correlations with organizational aids for *implementing* innovations and changes were the bureaucratic and altruistic styles of management that stressed accountability, the following of rules and regulations, and business ethics. The styles with the largest number of significant correlations with organizational mechanisms for *stabilizing* the changes were the altruistic, the bureaucratic, and the participative styles (Khandwalla, 1995, chapter 4). Thus, for the organization to be successfully innovative, it may not be enough to have an entrepreneurial and organic style of management; it may also be necessary for the management to emphasize widespread participation in implementing innovative initiatives, accountability for performance, and also norms, values, and ethics to generate the trust and commitment of the stakeholders in the bona fides of the management and its innovative initiatives.

Jacobs' study (1998) of four pairs of Indian organizations indicates that organizational design for innovativeness is a strategic choice of the management. Each pair shared the same industry or activity or parent organization, and yet one in the pair displayed relatively high innovativeness (corporate creativity) while the other one displayed a distinctly lower innovativeness. A striking difference was within a pair of advertising organizations, both based in Ahmedabad. Mudra Communications was set up in 1980 by the Reliance business group; Bidhan Advertising, started a decade earlier, was a proprietorship. Mudra was highly entrepreneurial; Bidhan found a niche early in its life and stuck to it tenaciously. By 1988, Mudra already had a diversified portfolio of activities—nurturing of small clients that Mudra tried to help grow fast, an example being Pioma Industries, the producer of Rasna line of drinks (which enjoyed fantastic growth and brand creation during the 1980s); market research and advertising support functions; production of videos; a distribution house; and fashion and textile design. In another decade, Mudra added many more activities, such as value-adding information for clients; outdoor media work; public relations assignments; product designing; promotions, exhibitions, road shows, and event management; creation of Web sites for clients; graphics; sponsored television programs; creation of corporate brands, etc. All these diversifications catapulted Mudra into one of the four largest communications companies in India.

In contrast, Bidhan stuck primarily to producing more or less conventional advertising copy for less than a score of loyal clients; twenty years after its founding, it had notched up barely 2 percent of Mudra's revenues. Mudra won innumerable awards for communications excellence and creativity; Bidhan simply never entered that race. Organizationally, Mudra was highly divisionalized, had a flat structure, and was regionally decentralized; Bidhan was run as a tight ship, with the proprietor insisting on overseeing every account personally. Mudra aggressively hired creative, dynamic youngsters, many from India's premier management schools, and gave them autonomy in pursuing challenging assignments; Bidhan had no such policy. Mudra entered into collaboration with a major American media company; Bidhan never pursued this route. Mudra blended professional management into its entrepreneurship. For example, it carefully studied the long-term prospects of targeted industries and developed high-quality communications products based on market research for presentation to actual or potential sophisticated clients looking for quality and custom-tailored communications services. It targeted not industry leaders, but the relatively underserved segment of smaller but dynamically managed companies hungry for growth. Mudra also fully computerized its operations, and hired a doctorate holder to head the IT function. Mudra's CEO traveled incessantly, practicing "management by moving around" (Peters & Waterman, 1982); he liked to play the roles of a mentor, coach, and motivator. Bidhan's CEO primarily played the role of a controller. Mudra developed an internal work climate favoring creativity and innovation. A survey showed that its score on this dimension was thirty-five, versus sixteen for Bidhan. Mudra also displayed an altruistic and visionary streak—it set up a pioneering institute of communications to train communications professionals, not just for itself, but also for the entire industry. Bidhan stayed away from any such entrepreneurship, strategizing, professional management, or altruism.

An American study on 141 pairs of projects conducted by Teresa Amabile and associates also provides interesting insights (Amabile, Conti, Coon, Lazenby, & Herron, 1995). In each pair, one project was judged to be high on creativity while the other was judged to be low on creativity. The "creative" projects significantly outscored the "uncreative" projects on six aspects of workplace practices: reportedly, greater challenge was provided in work, greater encouragement to creativity, greater work group support to individuals, greater sense of autonomy as well as of ownership, and greater encouragement provided by superiors to subordinates. In another study, it was found that when people jointly identified work-related problems, there was not only a greater feeling of participation, but the solutions individuals found to problems tended to be more creative (Plunkett, 1990).

In their review of forty-three studies of factors behind success and failure of innovative projects, Van der Panne, Van Beers, and Kleinknecht (2003) identified some common factors affecting innovative success of organizations. According to them, firm-related factors that are relevant for innovational success are: (1) an innovation-fostering culture, (2) the firm's previous experience with innovative projects, (3) the characteristics of the R&D team (like the team's configuration and the presence of a product champion), (4) a pro-innovation strategy, and (5) a flexible organizational structure. They also identified complementarity of various functions of the organization with the project, management style, and top management support for the innovation project as factors that determine success or failure of an innovation project in an organization.

Ford (1996) emphasized the role of domains in fostering organizational creativity. Domains of the organization include its markets, the outsider professional institutions that educate and train the staff members of the organization, government agencies, labor associations, relevant industry leaders, and other stakeholders. Meeting disparate and exacting demands requires acquisition of a wide range of skill sets and information, and controlled, well-directed creativity. Thus, the critical influencers of the design of the creative organization are the domains it chooses to operate in, the system that management develops to interpret these domains, the system developed to acquire the needed knowledge and skills for creative action, and the system that selects which creative actions will be taken and which will be excluded.

Service and Boockholdt (1998) surveyed the literature on organizational innovations and identified eight broad factors that affect innovativeness. The sort of environment the organization operates in and the way the organization responds to it, strategically and otherwise, is one factor. The kind of management the organization has—management style—and the quality of management is another factor. The structure of the organization and the control system is the third factor. The organization's human resource management system is the fourth factor. The existence of key innovation promoters and change agents and the roles they play form the fifth factor. The organization's culture and work climate is the sixth factor. The nature of the innovations—management-related versus technical, incremental versus breakthrough—is the seventh factor. The eighth factor is the organization's marketing and customer response system.

This brief review of the empirical work having a bearing on the organization's innovativeness suggests that innovativeness is fostered by a number of factors. Chief among these are the style of top management, the organization's culture and practices, its strategic posture and policies, especially vis-à-vis risk taking, and its organizational structure and management systems, especially human resource management. Important for innovational success is how individual innovations are conceived, planned, implemented, and reviewed for course correction.

Obviously, having to attend to so many factors can make the job of designing an innovative organization quite difficult, especially if there is lack of clarity on how these factors are to be utilized. More specific guidelines are needed on how to proceed. We have attempted to include these factors into a prescriptive model of organizational design for sustained and successful innovativeness.

APPROACHES TO DESIGNING THE ORGANIZATION FOR CORPORATE CREATIVITY

Three approaches are especially useful for designing organizations for sustained and successful innovativeness.

1. The contingency theory approach eschews all universally best designs and argues that for the organization to be able to survive, its structure and functioning must be adapted to such features of its operating context as the environment it operates in, the nature of its industry or domain, its size, its technology, etc. (Donaldson, 2001).

2. The strategic choice approach argues that in any context, organizations can adopt a variety of designs depending upon the strategic choices they make (Child, 1972; Hrebiniak & Joyce, 1985). The key stakeholders of the organization choose elements of organizational design, such as the organization's values and vision, competitive and growth strategies, structure, management style, key management functions, the decision-making and other processes, and the capabilities of its human resources. Some corporations, especially the "prospector" types (Miles & Snow, 1978), may choose such visions, values, strategies, structures, and practices that foster innovativeness, while others may choose visions and other elements that either do not foster innovativeness or may even impede it.

3. The synergy, or "good fit," approach argues that for superior performance, the various elements of organizational design indicated above must be properly aligned, that is, must support each other rather than work at cross purposes (Lawrence & Lorsch, 1969; Khandwalla, 1973; Miller & Friesen, 1984).

Drawing on both the literature summarized earlier and the tenets of these three approaches, the following model of organizational design for corporate creativity is proposed for the corporations of emerging economies like India's that are undergoing liberalization and globalization.

ORGANIZATIONAL DESIGN FOR CORPORATE CREATIVITY

When a business environment becomes significantly more competitive, turbulent, and exacting, as during the liberalization and globalization of a once protectionist economy, organizations need to reconfigure their organization design. This is the contingency theory expectation. However, some organizations may choose to change their design in innovativeness-congruent directions, while others may not choose to change in this fashion, or may choose to change, but to a much lesser extent. This is because the "prospector" types of management would tend to see more opportunities than threats through change and innovation, while managements with more conservative mindsets may prefer a wait-and-watch attitude, or see more threats than opportunities from change and innovation (Miles & Snow, 1978). Thus, what response the organization makes to an environmental jolt or discontinuity is a strategic choice.

Organizations that do adopt an innovation-friendly design can display substantially higher corporate creativity, that is, they can be copiously and successfully innovative, provided they align their choices of vision, values, strategy, structure, and other elements appropriately. This is the synergy, or "good fit," approach. However, this is not easy, and may require a good deal of experimentation. Thus, innovating successfully requires a good deal of learning. But once a facilitative organizational design is identified and the process of innovating successfully is mastered, the management would feel encouraged to try out many more innovations and changes required to operate in a turbulent, competitive, and demanding environment. Organizations that are copiously and successfully innovative may have a strong competitive advantage, as evidenced by an above-average performance on a variety of effectiveness indicators. This is because there is a time lag between a successful innovation in an organization and its diffusion among its rivals, so that the more numerous the successful innovations, the larger overall, and possibly longer would be the performance advantage of the innovating organization. Figure 6.1 summarizes the above model.

Implications of the Model

There are several implications of the model. First, if globalization represents a major discontinuity, as in the case of China after 1979, and India and Russia after 1991, many organizations will seek to adopt a corporate creativity-friendly organizational design. However, in a given economy, globalization may not proceed with equal rapidity for all industries and sectors. In India, for instance, there still are a few industries reserved for the public sector because of their defense-related or strategic significance, and customs tariffs, though much lower than in 1991, still differ from industry to industry. Thus, in any given economy, the tendency for adopting a corporate creativity-friendly organizational design will be stronger the more an industry is

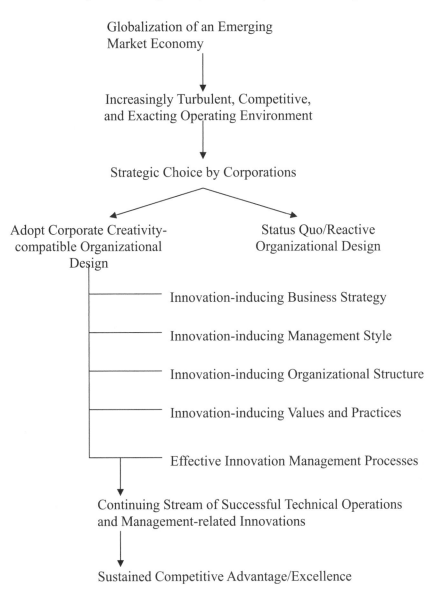

Globalization of an Emerging
Market Economy

Increasingly Turbulent, Competitive,
and Exacting Operating Environment

Strategic Choice by Corporations

Adopt Corporate Creativity-
compatible Organizational
Design

Status Quo/Reactive
Organizational Design

Innovation-inducing Business Strategy

Innovation-inducing Management Style

Innovation-inducing Organizational Structure

Innovation-inducing Values and Practices

Effective Innovation Management Processes

Continuing Stream of Successful Technical Operations
and Management-related Innovations

Sustained Competitive Advantage/Excellence

FIGURE 6.1.   Organizational Design for Corporate Creativity

globalized (that is, the more it is subjected to global competition). Second, in a globalized environment that was previously statist or protectionist, corporations will tend to vary in how corporate creativity friendly their organizational designs are. There is as yet no generally accepted model to emulate; the conservatism of the management's mindset varies from organization to organization; and the extent of change may also depend upon how creativity friendly the organization was earlier—if it was already substantially creativity friendly, it will tend to change more modestly than those organizations that did not previously have a creativity-friendly design and now want to make good the deficit. In other words, the strategic choice of the management and the inherited organizational design will influence how creativity friendly the new design is. Third, those organizations that do manage to adopt a creativity-friendly design in a globalized economy/industry will tend to do better than those that do not do so or that make only partial changes toward that design.

STUDY

The model of corporate creativity was broadly validated in a study of sixty-five Indian organizations (public as well as private) from different industry sectors (Khandwalla & Mehta, 2004). In the study, conducted during the period from late 1999 to early 2003, data were secured from a fairly wide spectrum of corporate organizations. Since the study was published in an Indian journal, for the convenience of non-Indian readers, the Appendix provides the sample characteristics, operational definitions of the variables, their basic statistics, regression results, etc. The data were secured through a questionnaire completed anonymously by an average of five top and senior-level executives of each company.

In the questionnaire, the data were gathered through ratings by participants on a number of six-point scales, anchored by a statement at each extreme. All the responses from each organization were averaged, and converted into percentage scores for the organization as shown in the Appendix. The following variables were measured (see Appendix for operational definitions and other details):

1. Environmental Pressure
2. Innovation-supportive Strategic Management
3. Innovation-supportive Management Style
4. Innovation-supportive Organizational Structure
5. Innovation-supportive Practices
6. Effective Management of Innovation
7. Corporate Innovational Success (Corporate Creativity)
8. Competitive Excellence.

For each of the above variables, the organization's scores were computed for the "present" situation and the situation three years earlier, and thereafter the extent of change scores were computed by subtracting the score for three years prior to the "present" score (see Appendix for details). When we work with first differences of "past" scores, as we have in this study, it is easier to see how and to what extent the corporate sector in a country has been changing, and also the causal connections between various dimensions of this change. The reliabilities (Cronbach's Alpha) of these first difference variables were quite reasonable for a pioneering study. They ranged from .76 to .94. The basic statistics (means, standard deviations, reliabilities of the variables, and the inter-correlations of the change variables) are shown in the Appendix.

Major Findings of the Study

The results of the study reported earlier (Khandwalla & Mehta, 2004) were interesting:

- For the three-year period for which data were secured, environmental pressure intensified by about 20 percent, though there was considerable variation in the sample on the reported change in environmental pressure.
- Interestingly, the increase in organizational design variables (creativity-friendly strategy, top management style, organizational structure, innovation-supportive practices, and management of innovations) lagged behind the magnitude of increase in environmental pressure, though only by a few percentage points. The maximum change was in strategic management, and the minimum change was in management of innovation. All the variables varied fairly widely across the sample.
- There was significant improvement in innovational success over the three-year period, but the improvement in competitive excellence lagged far behind, suggesting that it was getting tough to improve performance in the increasingly high-pressure environment.
- The correlations of change in environmental pressure with the organizational design change variables were quite small, suggesting that movement toward a corporate creativity-friendly organizational design is not inevitable in a more turbulent and demanding environment. This is seemingly contrary to the tenets of contingency theory (Donaldson, 2001).
- There was much stronger evidence favoring organizational design as a strategic choice (Hrebiniak & Joyce, 1985). Two clusters each were identified in the scores of the organizational change variables for the condition of relatively large perceived increase and for the condition of relatively small perceived increase in environmental pressure. In each condition, one cluster indicated a relatively large movement toward a corporate creativity-friendly organizational design, and the other of a much smaller, merely incremental movement. Thus, in the large increase in environmental pressure condition, some organizations chose to move decisively toward a corporate creativity-friendly design, while others did not; and in the relatively low increase in environmental pressure condition, too, despite the low necessity, some opted to change toward a corporate creativity-friendly design while others did not.
- The model seemed to be robust. In regressions, the organizational change variables accounted for 75 percent of the variance in improved innovational success, while the organizational change variables plus improved innovational success explained nearly 50 percent of the variance in improved perceived corporate performance.

- Improvement in innovational success was strongly correlated with improved corporate performance, thus underscoring the importance of innovativeness for sustained competitive advantage.
- The strongest predictors of improved innovational success were better management of innovations, closely followed by more innovation-supportive practices, management style, and strategic management.

Study's Extensions

As extensions of the above study, two new issues are examined in this chapter. The first issue is which organizations change the most toward a corporate creativity-friendly organizational design—the ones that are already relatively close to it, or the ones whose designs are quite far from it. The conjecture is that those already relatively close to the needed organizational design—the organizational pace setters—will not change much, but the ones that are far off—the organizational laggards—will tend to change the most. The second conjecture is that the larger the change, the greater will be the improvement in innovational success and competitive excellence.

Responses of Initial Pace Setters versus Laggards

To test the first conjecture, the "past" organizational design variables were subjected to cluster analysis, and a three-cluster solution was selected, each cluster representing an organizational design type (see Figure 6.2). Cluster 1 (nineteen observations) was highest on all the organizational design variables, while Cluster 3 (ten observations) was the lowest on all variables but one. Cluster 2 (thirty-six observations) was second on all but one of the variables and in that variable, too, it was only marginally behind the second-ranked cluster on this variable. Thus, it seems appropriate to consider the Cluster 1 organizations as having a relatively highly creativity-friendly organizational design (the pace setters), the Cluster 2 organizations as having a moderate creativity-friendly design (the cautious followers), and the Cluster 3 organizations as having the least creativity-friendly design (the laggards) at the inception of the three-year period.

A similar cluster analysis was done on the "present" organizational design variables to extract three types of organizational design (see Figure 6.3). Here again, the Cluster 1 (twenty-two observations) organizations can be considered highly creativity friendly (pace setters), the Cluster 2 (eleven observations) organizations as moderately creativity friendly (cautious followers), and the Cluster 3 (thirty-two observations) organizations as the least creativity friendly (laggards). A comparison of Figures 6.2 and 6.3 shows that all three types moved up in their scores during the three-year period. Indeed, the scores of the relatively highly creativity-friendly "past" design were not much higher than the scores of the "present" least creativity-friendly design.

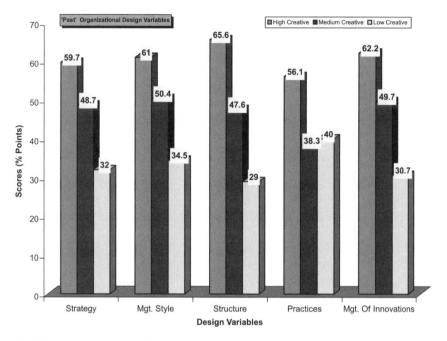

FIGURE 6.2. Past Organizational Design
Note: The numbers represent percentage scores of the cluster.

The question is: did the pace setters, cautious followers, and laggards in Period 1 also remain pace setters, cautious followers, and laggards respectively in Period 2 (three years after Period 1), or was there change in their relative statuses? For an answer, the number of organizations that maintained their status from each "past" type to each "present" type was computed (see Table 6.1).

The bulk of the "past" pace setters remained "present" pace setters and the vast bulk of the laggards remained laggards three years later. The bulk of the cautious followers regressed to being laggards. Even among Period 1 pace setters, as many as 42 percent regressed. On the other hand, 20 percent of the Period 1 laggards improved their classification, as did 25 percent of the cautious followers. The data suggest considerable inertia in adapting to an increasingly turbulent and demanding environment, with half the sample classified as laggards in Period 2.

But this may not be the whole truth. The laggards of Period 2 had substantially higher scores on the organizational variables than the laggards of Period 1, and though many of the latter did not change enough to move to the next higher class, they may have changed quite a bit in relation to their scores in Period 1. To examine this matter more closely, organizational *change* variables ("present" score minus "past" score) were subjected to cluster analysis and a three-cluster solution was extracted (see Table 6.2). Cluster 1 was highest by

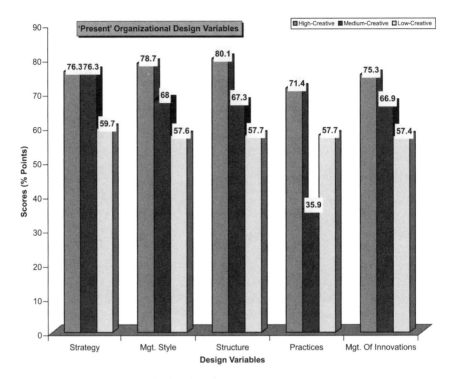

FIGURE 6.3. Present Organizational Design
Note: The numbers represent average percentage scores for the cluster.

far on four out of five organizational change variables, and therefore was labeled the high change type. Cluster 2 group was medium on all but one organizational change variable and therefore was called medium change type. The third cluster was the lowest on all organizational change variables, and therefore was called the low change type.

TABLE 6.1. Transition Table Past to Present Types

		Sample Size	Present Type					
			Pace Setters		Cautious Followers		Laggards	
Past Type	Pace Setters	(N=19)	11	58%	4	21%	4	21%
	Cautious Followers	(N=36)	9	25%	6	17%	21	58%
	Laggards	(N=10)	1	10%	1	10%	8	80%
	Sample Size		(N=21)		(N=11)		(N=33)	

TABLE 6.2.   Types of Change Magnitudes in Organizational Design Variables

	Strategy Change	Management Style Change	Structure Change	Practices and Culture Change	Management of Innovations Change
Cluster 1 (N=19)	13.7	27.6	32.8	24.2	27.8
Cluster 2 (N=34)	16.4	13.2	12.8	14.4	12.3
Cluster 3 (N=12)	4.8	2.3	3.7	1.6	0.3

Note: The numbers represent percentage points.

Next, a calculation was made of how many pace setters, cautious followers, and laggards in Period 1 were Types I, II, and III in terms of the extent of change. Table 6.3 shows the computations.

Table 6.3 shows that initial pace setters exhibited predominantly moderate or low change. The initial cautious followers tended, however, to exhibit moderate to high change. The surprise was with respect to the initial laggards. Unlike the picture of inertia presented in Table 6.3, these tended to exhibit the largest change of all three types. Thus, the initial laggards were not inertial at all. Most of them took what for them were *relatively* big steps toward a creativity-friendly design; but their initial base was so low that even these steps were not enough to catapult them into higher categories in the subsequent period. Perhaps these organizations were willing to change, but their management's competence or conceptual base was not strong enough for them to change far enough.

To sum up, the data suggest a nearly paradoxical blend of organizational inertia and proactivity in the face of a major environmental change favoring creativity and innovation-friendly organizational design. Inappropriately designed organizations (the initial laggards) tend to show the maximum relative (to their base) forward movement but not enough in an absolute sense to escape their organizational design type.

TABLE 6.3.   Magnitude of Change in Design Variables of Initial Pace Setters, Cautious Followers, and Laggards

Initial Design Type	Large Change Type		Medium Change Type		Low Change Type		Total
Pace Setters	1	5%	10	53%	8	42%	19
Cautious Followers	11	31%	21	58%	4	11%	36
Laggards	7	70%	3	30%	0	0%	10

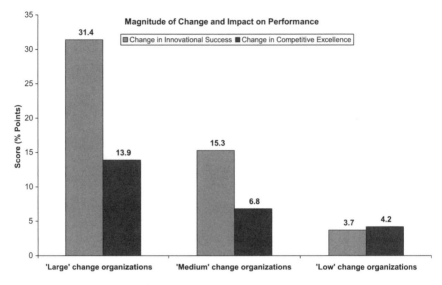

FIGURE 6.4. Change–Magnitude and Impact
Note: The numbers are in percentage points.

ORGANIZATIONAL DESIGN CHANGE AND PERFORMANCE CHANGE

The question is: if organizations change toward a contextually appropriate organizational design, do they improve their performance? This is the implicit assumption of what has been called configurational contingency organization theory (Doty, Glick, & Huber, 1993). The central tenet of contingency organization theory is that to remain viable, organizations tend to adopt contextually appropriate organizational designs. An extension of the reasoning is that those organizations that in fact do adopt these designs will tend to perform better than those that do not adapt well to their operating context.

To test the preceding supposition, the extent of improvement on two indices of performance (perceived innovational success and competitive excellence) was computed for each magnitude of change type. Figure 6.4 shows the results.

Clearly, there is a strong positive relationship between how *much* change in creativity-friendly organizational design the organization initiates (relative to its base) and improvement in its innovational success and competitive excellence. Interestingly, the major performance improvements in terms of both criteria seem to arise not in going from low change to medium change, but from going from medium change to large change relative to the organization's starting position.

DISCUSSION AND SUGGESTIONS FOR PRACTITIONERS

The analysis shown above has a clear message. A creativity-friendly organizational design is a strategic choice that pays off. However, creativity is not a one-off event in a corporate setting. For an organization to be durably and strikingly innovative, a synergistic blend of various organizational design elements is essential. The study presents fairly strong evidence that redesigning organizations for sustained and copious technical, operations-related, and management-related creativity and innovation (corporate creativity) can provide a powerful performance edge to organizations in a globalizing economy. In the face of higher environmental pressure, an organization needs to respond through an aligned and *relatively large* change in its strategy, management style, structure, practices, and the way it manages innovations.

This realignment of the organization in the emerging market economies is quite difficult. The biggest hurdles are ingrained conservative mindsets and a gerontocratic corporate power structure. The energy, the ideas, and the fire in the belly for change and innovation are often at levels far below the top management, and the challenge is to provide innovation space to these potential change agents, innovators, and intrapreneurs. Hope lies in the young scions of the promoter family that are often educated in institutions of excellence, and should they come to power, as in the case of Asoka Spintex (described earlier), the transition could be fast but not necessarily painless. Even if this does not happen, enlightened top management could do a lot. Here are some tips for the practitioners based on research on pioneering and innovative Indian entrepreneurs (Manimala, 1999) and the authors' consultancy experiences:

- Conduct a diagnosis of the design of your organization. How conducive are the present business strategy, top management style, organizational structure, management processes and culture, and the management of innovations to corporate creativity? A diagnostic instrument is available (Khandwalla, 2003, Appendix II) that can provide fairly detailed information on where your organization stands against a benchmark of some highly innovative and successful corporations. Most effective are diagnostic efforts that involve the participation of the organization's stakeholders *and* are done with reasonably high expertise so that the findings are credible.
- Identify the items where the gaps are the largest. Form a cross-functional team to tackle each major gap area, with a mandate to find effective and innovative ways of closing the gap. The teams may initially need some training in creative problem solving in an organizational context.
- After reviewing participatively the recommendations of the cross-functional teams, identify consensually the most productive action points for quick implementation. This can build momentum for innovation and change.
- Ensure widespread brainstorming for novel but effective solutions. Ensure also that after a large number of options are generated, a participative process is employed to short-list the most promising ideas and that a consensus is then sought on the way forward.
- Create an organizational mechanism to seek continuously and widely, both within the organization and outside, new growth areas. Encourage the taking up of high potential initiatives even if they are risky, but then ensure that a thorough effort is made to mitigate the risks.

- Develop innovative ideas in house rather than merely borrowing solutions from outside. If outside ideas or systems need to be adopted, make sure that they are appropriately modified to suit the situation of the organization.
- Break up the organization into numerous profit and responsibility centers. Identify potential change agents, innovators, and intrapreneurs, give them the requisite training in strategic and cross-functional management, team building and teamwork, leadership and so forth, and put them in charge of these profit and responsibility centers. An outstanding example of how this was done is the German IT major Siemens Nixdorf (Kennedy, 1998). This does not mean that the senior and top-level managers should be removed. But their roles need to be redefined, and they need to be trained to migrate from hands-on, operational management roles to the roles of policy makers, mentors, designers of management systems, global hunters for best practices and opportunities, and example setters.

The scales in the Appendix that make up the variables used in the organization design for corporate creativity can provide further cues on what else to do.

Governments and industry associations can play supplementary roles in disseminating a better understanding of what is needed to be done to create innovative organizations. Not only at the organizational level, but also at the industry level and even the national level, major awards and similar reward mechanisms could be created for the most innovative corporations and managers. Institutions could be set up to train agents of change and innovation. Creativity training and training in the effective management of innovations could be imparted more widely not only in these specialized institutions but also in schools and colleges.

Corporate creativity is part of a wider movement of human creative striving that has transformed how we live. This movement has yielded many great "goods" but also some fearsome "bads" Enron and WorldCom were fearsomely innovative in the way they committed fraud. Such misuse of creativity needs to be avoided. Corporate management needs to understand corporate creativity better, use it effectively, and align it with ethical and socially responsive striving.

REFERENCES

Amabile, T. M., Conti, R., Coon, H., Lazenby, J., & Herron, M. (1995). Assessing the work environment for creativity. *Academy of Management Journal, 39*(5), 1154–1184.

Arbose, J. (1986). The unlikely diversifications helping to keep Aer Lingus afloat. *International Mangement, 41*(5), 57–63.

Burns, T., & Stalker, G. M. (1961). *The management of innovation*. London: Tavistock.

Carlson, J., & Nelson, R. (1988). Scandinavian Airlines (SAS). In Nelson, R. and Clutterback, D. (eds), *Turnaround: How twenty well-known companies came back from the brink*. London: Mercury Books of W. H. Allen, 115–124.

Child, J. (1972). Organizational structure, environment and performance: The role of strategic choice. *Sociology, 6*, 1–22.

Cornelius, P. (ed.). (2003). Global competitiveness report 2002–3 of World Economic Forum. New York, Oxford University Press.

Cyert, R., & March, J. (1963). *A behavioral theory of the firm*. Englewood Cliffs, NJ: Prentice-Hall.

Donaldson, L. (2001). *The Contingency theory of organizations*. Thousand Oaks, CA: Sage.

Doty, D., Glick, W., & Huber G. (1993). Fit, equifinality, and organizational effectiveness: A test of two configurational theories." *Academy of Management Journal, 36*, 1196–1250.

Drucker, P. (1985). *Innovation and entrepreneurship*. London: Heinemann.

DTI (Department of Trade & Industry, Gov. of U.K.) (2003). Innovation report—Competing in the global economy. *Innovation Challenge, December 2003,* Overview, 4. www.dti.gov.uk.

Ford, C. (1996). Striking inspirational sparks and fanning creative flames: A multi-domain model of creative action taking. In Ford, C. and Gioia, D. (eds.), *Creative action in organizations: Ivory tower visions and real world ones*. Thousand Oaks, CA: Sage Publications. 330–354.

Geroski, P., & Machin, S. (1993). The profitability of innovating firms. *RAND Journal of Economics, 24* (2), 198–211.

Gluck, F. (1985). Big bang management. In Kuhn, R. L. (ed.), *Frontiers in creative and innovative management*. Cambridge, MA: Ballinger.

Gupta, P. (1999). Asoka Spintex. *Vikalpa, Vol.24* (4), 43–60.

Gupta, S. (1998). Little cheer. *Business Standard's The Smart Investor, 15* (June), 4.

Hannan, M., & Freeman, J. (1984). Structural inertia and organizational change. *American Sociological Review, 49,* 149–164.

Hrebiniak, L., & Joyce, W. (1985). Organizational adaptation: Strategic choice and environmental determinism. *Administrative Science Quarterly, 30,* 336–349.

Jacob, N. (1998). *Creativity in organizations*. New Delhi: A. H. Wheeler.

Kennedy C. (1998). The roadmap to success: How Gerhard Schulmeyer changed the culture at Siemens and Nixdorf. *Long Range Planning, 31* (2), 262–271.

Kennedy, D. (1988). Aer Lingus. In Nelson, R., & Clutterback, D. (eds.), *Turnaround: How twenty well-known companies came back from the brink*. London: Mercury Books of W. H. Allen.

Khandwalla, P. N. (1973). Viable and effective organizational designs of firms. *Academy of Management Journal, 16,* 481–495.

Khandwalla, P. N. (1985). Pioneering innovative management: An Indian excellence. *Organization Studies, 6* (2), 161–183.

Khandwalla, P. N. (1995). *Management styles*. New Delhi: Tata McGraw-Hill.

Khandwalla, P. N. (2003). *Corporate creativity: The winning edge*. New Delhi: Tata McGraw-Hill.

Khandwalla, P., & Mehta, K. (2004). Design for corporate creativity. *Vikalpa—A Journal of Decision Makers, 1,* 13–28.

Kimberly, J. R. (1981). Managerial innovation. In Nystrom, P. C., & Starbuck, W. H. (eds.), *Handbook of organizational design, vol. 1,* New York: Oxford University Press.

Kleinknecht, A., Oostendorp, R., & Pradhan, M. (1997). Patterns and economic effects of flexibility in labour relations in the Netherlands. An exploration of the OSA demand and supply panels (in Dutch). *The Hague: Scientific Council for Government Policy* (WRR, V99), Sdu Publishers (ISBN: 90 399 1383 8).

Lawrence, P., & Lorsch, J. (1967). *Organization and environment.* Boston: Graduate School of Business Administration, Harvard University.

Leahey, J. (1990). *Changing the culture at British Airways: Harvard Business School case 9-491-009.* Boston: President and Fellows of Harvard College.

Lefebure, R. B., Jorgensen, J., & Staniforth, D. (1988). Scandinavian Airline System (SAS) in 1988, INSEAD-CEDEP case. Fontainbleu, France: INSEAD.

Manimala, M. (1999). *Entrepreneurial policies and strategies: The innovator's choice.* New Delhi: Sage.

March, J., & Simon, H. (1958). *Organizations.* New York: John Wiley.

McMillan, C. (1984). *The Japanese industrial system.* Berlin: Walter de Gruyter.

Miles, R. E., & Snow, C. (1978). Organization strategy, structure, and process. New York: McGraw-Hill.

Miller, D., & Friesen, P. (1984). *Organizations: A quantum view.* Englewood Cliffs, NJ: Prentice-Hall.

Peters, T. J., & Waterman, R. H. (1982). *In search of excellence: Lessons from America's best-run companies.* New York: Harper & Row.

Plunkett, D. (1990). The creative organization: an empirical investigation of the importance of participation in decision-making. *Journal of Creative Behavior, 24* (2), 140–148.

Pugh D., Hickson, D., Hinings, C., & Turner, C. (1969). The context of organization structures. *Administrative Science Quarterly, 14*, 91–114.

Quinn, D. P., & Rivoli, P. (1991). The effects of American and Japanese style employment and compensation practices on innovation. *Organization Science, 2* (4), 323–341.

Sareen, S. (1996). Synchromeshed revival. *The Economic Times*, 24–30 May, 3.

Service, R. W., & Boockholdt, J.L.(1998). Factors leading to innovation: A study of manager's perspectives. *Creativity Research Journal, 11* (4), 245–307.

Steiner, G. (1965). Introduction. In Steiner, G. (ed.), *The creative organization.* Chicago: University of Chicago Press. 1–24.

The Economic Times. Innovation is only way forward, December 14, 2005, Ahmedabad edition, 9.

Van der Panne, G., Van Beers, C., & Kleinknecht, A. (2003). Success and failure of innovations: A literature review. *International Journal of Innovation Management, 7*, (3) 309–338.

Wolfe, R. A. (1994). Organisational innovation: Review, critique and suggested research directions. *Journal of Management Studies, 31* (3), 405–431.

APPENDIX

Sample Characteristics
Sample: 65 Indian Corporations

Particulars	Number	Percentage (%)
Size (Rs. = Indian Rupees)		
Large (Sales/Revenue exceeding Rs. 5000 Mn Indian Rupees)	19	29%
Medium (Sales/Revenue between Rs. 1000 Mn and. 5000 Mn.)	25	38%
Small (Sales/Revenue below Rs. 100 Mn.)	20	31%
Unknown	1	2%
Nature of Activity		
Manufacturing (e.g., textiles, steel, aluminum, chemicals, automobile, auto ancillary, cement, fibers, pulp, paper, etc.)	48	74%
Service (e.g., banks, telecommunication, financial services, Internet-enabled services, network solutions, etc.)	17	26%
Ownership		
Government	7	11%
Private—Indian	49	75%
Private——MNC	9	14%
Listing on Stock Exchanges		
Listed	27	42%
Non-listed	38	58%

Operational Definitions of Variables

1. *Environmental Pressure* was measured on four aggregated scales. The first scale measured how **turbulent the product market environment** of the corporate was, in terms of having to cope with unexpected changes in the organization's output markets. The second scale measured the **turbulence in the organization's input markets,** involving having to cope with unexpected changes in the prices and availability of key inputs like power/fuel, components, raw materials, equipment, human resources, funds, etc. The third scale measured the **sophistication of the organization's clients/customers,** and how demanding they were in terms of quality, price, delivery, etc. The fourth scale measured **the vulnerability of the organization to competitive pressures** or other hostile acts of outside forces. High aggregated scores for

the four scales reflected high environmental pressure on the organization, while low aggregated scores represented low environmental pressure.

2. *Innovation-supportive Strategic Management*: Scores on six scales were aggregated to measure innovation-supportive strategic management. The higher the score, the more innovation-conducive the organization's strategic management was. The first scale measured **the management's desire to position the organization as a unique one** in its industry in the way it operated. The second scale measured the **management's commitment to diversify the organization's products/activities** and enter new markets. The third scale measured the **management's commitments to offer customized products/services**. The fourth scale measured the **management's preference for pioneering new or novel products/services,** that is, for the organization being the first in the market to offer new products/services. The fifth scale measured **the management's priority to product differentiation and superior quality offerings**. The sixth scale measured the **management's preference for sophisticated, "high-tech" technologies,** products, or services.

3. *Innovation-supportive Management Style*: Aggregated scores on eight scales measured the extent of innovation-supportive management style. The first scale measured the **management's preference for calculated risk taking and entrepreneurship**. The second scale measured the **management's emphasis on getting results through operating flexibility,** operating autonomy for managers but with accountability for results, and interactive evolving of decisions. The third measured the **management's rewarding of successful innovation,** creativity, resourcefulness, experimentation, and improvisation. The fourth scale measured the **aggressiveness with which the management scanned the national and international environment for opportunities** even if these did not relate directly to the organization's areas of current priorities. The fifth scale measured the **interactivity of the top managers with customers, suppliers, and competitors** for securing or testing out ideas, suggestions, and possible joint ventures. The sixth scale measured the **management's preference for commissioning periodically professional market surveys,** SWOT-diagnostic studies, reorganization studies, morale surveys, customer satisfaction surveys, etc. to identify new opportunities and areas of innovation and improvement. The seventh scale measured the top management's **emphasis on business ethics and corporate social responsibility**. The eighth scale measured the top management's **commitment to participative and consultative decision making**.

4. *Innovation-supportive Organizational Structure*: Aggregated scores of four scales measured the extent of innovation-supportive organizational structure. The first scale measured the **extent of administrative flexibility,** as evidenced by changes of roles, creation of new sections and disbanding of old sections, and interdepartmental transfers of people. The second scale measured the **flatness of the managerial hierarchy**. The third scale measured the **extent of decentralization of operating decisions** from the top to lower levels in the organization. The fourth scale measured the **extent to which the organization resembled a matrix structure,** with specialist staff belonging to functional departments also assigned to project teams, divisions, etc., that is, having dual responsibility.

5. *Innovation-supportive Practices and Culture*: Scores on eight scales were aggregated to secure the score on this variable. The first scale was **the extent of usage of multidisciplinary project teams** and took forces for probing problem areas and for developing fresh but workable options and opportunities. The second scale measured **the emphasis at work on professional norms** and peer group pressure. The third measured the **extent to which the management disseminated to the rank-and-file the challenges** faced by the organization and invited suggestions for meeting these challenges. The fourth scale measured **the management's encouragement to the employees to form quality circles** and the like. The fifth scale measured the **involvement of the staff during target-setting exercises** and the eliciting of their views and ideas. The sixth scale measured **the encouragement by the management to the employees to resolve their personal differences** with each other directly rather than by the intervention of their bosses. The seventh scale measured **the emphasis on learning and skills** enhancement through planned human resource development. The eighth scale measured the **management's priority to recruiting bright, innovative young professionals** and to giving them challenging assignments.

6. *Effective Management of Innovation*: Ratings on thirteen scales were aggregated to secure the score for this variable. The scales ranged over **practices** to generate fresh ideas, planning of innovations, rewards for creativity, implementation of innovations and review mechanisms, etc. The extent of usage of group brainstorming for generating fresh ideas on key issues was measured on the first scale. The second scale measured the **management's encouragement** to managers and technical staff to participate in seminars and conferences and to visit leading organizations to pick up ideas for innovation. The third scale measured the **use of benchmarking** for generating potential innovations. The fourth scale measured the organization's **commitment to R&D**. The fifth scale measured the **organization's reliance on technical collaboration** ventures to procure and develop innovative products and processes. The sixth scale measured **the latitude to bending or bypassing rules** that obstruct desirable innovations and changes. The seventh scale measured the **extent of careful planning**, phasing, and reviewing of innovations. The eighth scale measured **the usage of an effective system for rewarding creative ideas** of employees. The ninth scale measured **the usage of post-implementation reviews** of innovations for making suitable modifications. The tenth scale measured **the usage of special cross-functional teams** for implementing innovations. The eleventh scale measured **the top management's involvement in monitoring** the progress of innovations. The twelfth scale measured **the management's commitment to intrapreneurship** (internal entrepreneurship). The last scale measured the extent to which the management forced **the pace of innovations**, such as through stretch targets for sales from new products, percentage increase in productivity, percentage decrease in costs, and the securing of patents or innovation awards.

7. *Corporate Innovational Success (Corporate Creativity)*: Scores on five scales were aggregated to derive the score for this variable. The first measured how excellent the **organization's image** was of being **an innovative organization**.

The second scale measured the extent to which **current revenues** were **derived from product innovations** during the past three years. The third scale measured the record of the **organization for successfully implementing a stream of technological process innovations** during the previous three years. The fourth measured the organization's record for **successfully implementing operations related innovations** (such as BPR, TQM, QC, etc.) during the previous three years. And the fifth measured the organization's record of **successfully implementing innovations in strategy, structure, management systems and practices, etc.**

8. *Competitive Excellence*: Ratings on twelve scales were aggregated to derive the score for this variable. Each scale measured **the relative performance of the organization** vis-à-vis the best performers in the organization's relevant sector, industry, or line of business in India. The twelve performance indicators were: level of profitability, growth rate of sales, morale of employees, financial strength of the organization, public image and good will, adaptability (ability to diversify successfully, quickly change strategies, seize opportunities, etc.), stability in the level of performance from one year to another, operating efficiency, innovativeness, impact on industry/sector (through impact making new products, technologies, activities, etc.), corporate social responsibility, and business ethics.

All the scales used were six-point scales, with 1 representing very low or nil value of the dimension measured and 6 measuring very high or maximum value. For interpreting convenience, each rating was converted into a percentage score, with 1=0, 2=20%, 3=40%, 4=60%, 5=80% and 6=100%. All the converted ratings from the organization were averaged to secure the organization's percentage score for the scale.

For each scale used in the above eight variables, two ratings (and therefore two percentage scores) were obtained from each respondent: the first, of the current situation; and the second, of the situation three years earlier. Subtracting the "past" score from the "present" score yielded the direction and magnitude of change. By averaging the organization's scores of the changes for the scales constituting a variable, it was possible to derive the change score for the variable for the organization. Since the ratings were converted into percentages, the change scores were in percentage points. As an example, if five respondents rated an organization on all the scales utilized in this study, and after conversion into percentages, the "present" scores for the four scales constituting environmental pressure (averaged across the five respondents) were, respectively 80%, 75%, 68%, and 62%, and similarly calculated "past" scores (in percentage points) were 58%, 62%, 65%, and 57%, the "change" scores, in percentage points would be 22, 13, 3, and 5, and the score for the variable for the organization would be 43/4 or 10.75.

Basic Statistics of the Sample
Sample: 65 Indian Corporations

Change Variables	Average (in % points)	Std. dev.	Reliability (Cronbach's Alpha)	Product Moment Correlations with						
				CSM	CMS	COS	CMP	CMI	CIS	CCE
1 Change in Environmental Pressure (CEP)	20.1	12.7	0.78	0.03	0.03	−0.10	0.01	0.05	−0.03	−0.20
2 Change in Innovation-supportive Strategic Management (CSM)	18.8	13.2	0.76		0.79**	0.31*	0.65**	0.64**	0.73**	0.35**
3 Change in Innovation-supportive Top Management Style (CMS)	15.4	11.5	0.80			0.40**	0.77**	0.75**	0.79**	0.40**
4 Change in Innovation-supportive Organizational Structure (COS)	14.9	15.0	0.80				0.36**	0.28**	0.38**	0.40**
5 Change in Innovation-supportive Management Practices and Culture (CMP)	17.0	12.6	0.87					0.76**	0.79**	0.35**
6 Change in Effective Management of Innovation (CMI)	14.6	12.2	.90						0.80**	0.40**
7 Change in Corporate Innovational Success (CIS)	17.9	12.9	.90							0.63**
8 Change in Corporate Competitive Excellence (CCE)	8.4	10.2	.94							

* Statistically significant at 95% confidence level (two-tailed)
** Statistically significant at 99% confidence level (two-tailed)

Regression Results
Sample: 65 Indian Corporations

Dependent Variable	Independent Variables	Multiple Correlation Coefficient	Total Variance Explained*	Statistically Significant Predictors**
Change in Corporate Innovational Success	Change in Environmental Pressure and five organizational change variables	0.88	0.75 (F=33.1)	1. Change in Management of Innovation 2. Change in Management Practices 3. Change in Strategic Management
Change in Corporate Competitive Excellence	Change in Environmental Pressure, five organizational change variables, and Change in Corporate Innovational Success	0.74	0.49 (F=9.7)	1. Change in Corporate Innovational Success 2. Change in Management Practices 3. Change in Organizational Structure

* Adjusted R^2
** At the 95% confidence level (two-tailed)

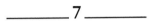

7

Managing Global Innovation Projects

MAXIMILIAN VON ZEDTWITZ and OLIVER GASSMANN

MORE GLOBAL R&D LEADS TO MORE GLOBAL INNOVATION PROJECTS

The Rise of International R&D

Until the mid-1980s, international R&D was a marginal phenomenon. However, decentralization of power, control to divisions, and the desire to be more market oriented subsequently led to a "jungle growth" of dispersed R&D activities. In addition, corporate R&D established research laboratories dedicated to tapping into local knowledge pools. By the late 1990s, the internationalization of R&D had reached more than 50 percent in small countries such as the Netherlands and Switzerland, 30 percent in all of Western Europe, and about 10 percent in the United States (see e.g., Dunning, 1994; Patel, 1995; Roberts, 1995; von Zedtwitz & Gassmann, 2002). Within less than a decade, many companies found themselves overseeing distributed R&D networks with complicated management and control structures (e.g., De Meyer, 1993; Chiesa, 1996; Gassmann & von Zedtwitz, 1999).

Challenges for R&D Project Management

Most traditional R&D project management approaches were designed for collocated teams or ignore physical distances between team members. Commonplace techniques such as brainstorming or rapid prototyping assume that project team members (including project leader, project experts, lead customers, etc.) are able to meet face-to-face in the same room, not only in order to

147

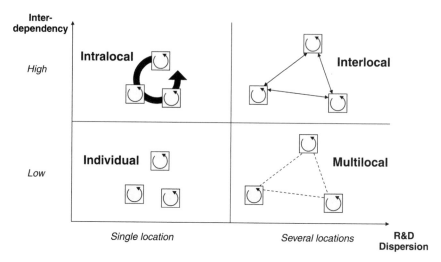

FIGURE 7.1. Classification of International R&D Projects

exchange ideas but also to exchange sketches and notes, demonstrate the practicality and feasibility of suggested designs, and build rough drafts and plans of product features to be detailed out later. Much of the early-stage creative work favors collocation (see e.g., Tushman, 1979; von Hippel, 1988; Gassmann & von Zedtwitz, 2003b); the development of distributed collaborative work environments and tools (e.g., virtual reality, rich media conferencing, etc.) has so far advanced only slowly (e.g., O'Hara-Devereaux & Johansen, 1994; Boutellier, Gassman, Macho, & Roux, 1998).

A key challenge is to integrate new R&D units so that they become productive partners in the company's global R&D network. Integration is necessary as R&D work tends to be interdependent, i.e., changes in one place of the system architecture are likely to impact changes elsewhere in the architecture. Only in later-stage R&D, with the system architecture fully defined and modules and components delineated, can interdependency be removed from the system level (see e.g. Gassmann & von Zedtwitz, 2003b; Sosa, Eppinger, & Rowles, 2004).

In a classification of international R&D projects (see Figure 7.1) differentiating the dispersion of R&D units (one versus many) and the degree of interdependency of R&D work within projects (weak versus strong), the challenge of global innovation is particularly strong within interlocal R&D projects. Here, interunit R&D collaboration is necessary. These projects are notorious for being difficult to manage, costly to execute, never on time, and ineffective toward their goals. Regarding global innovation projects, R&D managers are thus divided into two groups: one believing in the additional potentials offered by multiculturalism and multiple perspectives, and one rejecting the idea based on extra costs and inefficiencies incurred.

International R&D Management

With increasingly numerous R&D projects de-facto becoming international projects, a better understanding is necessary of when global innovation projects are feasible and how they should be organized. There is no single optimal solution for all projects and companies: the decision to use a global innovation team is often a necessity and not a choice; being "virtual" is in most cases not a strategy but an operational reality. For purposes of clarity, this chapter is structured in three parts:

1. A review of ten central characteristics of innovation projects and how they influence project globalization.
2. The description of four typical team structures used in executing of global innovation projects: 1) self-organizing decentralized teams; 2) teams with a system integrator; 3) teams with a core coordination team; and 4) centralized venture teams.
3. The presentation of four principal determinants for global project organization: 1) the type of innovation pursued; 2) the systemic nature of the project; 3) the modes of knowledge conversion; and 4) the degree of resource bundling.

REVIEW OF PROJECT MANAGEMENT LITERATURE

Despite substantial research in project management, R&D managers acknowledge the inadequacy of traditional project management training for managing transnational innovation processes. In the literature, few authors present descriptions of transnational R&D project organizations, and even fewer authors provide a guiding framework for project execution. In our analysis, we have considered ten characteristics describing project management and organization: power of the project manager, funding mechanism, project goals, ownership, system interdependencies and knowledge, project coherence, cross-functional integration, communication tools, organizational structure and processes, globalization, and externalization of R&D. Table 7.1 lists some important literature outlining and elaborating on these factors, partly with reference to virtual or international project forms. Empirical research indicated that virtual projects differed substantially in these ten factors (Gassmann & von Zedtwitz, 2003a).

The first such characteristic is the role and *power of the project manager*. Burgelman (1984) describes the problems internal group and venture leaders are faced with, recommending additional support roles by corporate and middle-level managers. In a study on the locus of power between project and functional

TABLE 7.1.   Overview of relevant literature on factors affecting the management of global innovation projects (based on Gassmann and von Zedtwitz, 2003a)

Project Determinants	References
Power of the project manager	Burgelman (1984); Katz and Allen (1985); Thamhain and Wilemon (1987); Roussel, Saad, and Erickson (1991); Wheelwright and Clark (1992)
Funding mechanism	Ellis (1988); Crawford (1992); Szakonyi (1994a, b); Madauss (1994); EIRMA (1994, 1995)
Project goals	Roussel, Saad, and Erickson (1991); Dimanescu and Dwenger (1996)
Project owner	Rubenstein et al. (1976); Katzenbach and Smith (1993a); Leavitt and Lipman-Blumen (1995)
System interdependencies and knowledge	Nadler and Tushman (1987); Henderson and Clark (1990); Madauss (1994); Nonaka and Takeuchi (1995); Carmel (1999)
Project coherence	van de Ven (1986); Thamhain and Wilemon (1987); Roussel, Saad, and Erickson (1991)
Cross-functional integration	Burgelman (1983); Imai, Nonaka, and Takeuchi (1985); Nadler and Tushman (1987); Wheelwright and Clark (1992); Szakonyi (1994a, b); Carmel (1999)
Communication tools	Allen (1977); Tushman (1979); Albers and Eggers (1991); Howells (1995); Dimanescu and Dwenger (1996); Jensen and Meckling (1996)
Organizational structures and processes	Bartlett and Ghoshal (1990); de Meyer (1991); Cooper and Kleinschmidt (1991); O'Hara-Devereaux and Johansen (1994); O'Connor (1994); Madauss (1994); Ancona and Caldwell (1997); Gassmann and von Zedtwitz (1998, 1999)
Globalization and externalization of R&D	Rubenstein (1989); de Meyer and Mizushima (1989); von Boehmer, Brockhoff, and Pearson (1992); Ridderstråle (1992); Beckmann and Fischer (1994); Howells (1995); Medcof (1997); Gassmann and von Zedtwitz (1998); Naman, Dahlin, and Krohn (1998); *Research Policy* 28(special issue), Nos. 2–3 (1999); Reger (1999); von Zedtwitz and Gassmann (2002)

managers, Katz and Allen (1985) argue for considerable power in the hands of project managers in order to improve organizational support and coordination authority. Four team structures—between functional and heavyweight—were finally typified by Wheelwright and Clark (1992). Closely related to the degree of leadership authority in teams is the *significance of the project* and its success to the corporation (e.g. Burgelman, 1984; Thamhain & Wilemon, 1987; Roussel, Saad, & Erickson, 1991).

While much has been written about *funding* of R&D in general, the allocation criteria for funding specific R&D projects are still intensively debated (e.g., Madauss, 1994, EIRMA, 1994, 1995; Ellis, 1988). Different exposure and assessment to risk asks for different funding models. Based on comparative analysis of 300 companies, Szakonyi (1994a, b) points at the poor relations of R&D with finance and accounting departments. Specific information about funding sources and costs of projects are sometimes disclosed in case studies and other accounts of R&D project management. Large-volume projects are categorized and reviewed differently from regular projects, and their project management is often given more autonomy and authority. Although *costs* are typically better tracked and accounted for in projects than in functional environments, hidden costs occur particularly in accelerated product development (Crawford, 1992).

Clear *project aims* seem to be a necessary condition for project success (e.g., Roussel, Saad, & Erickson, 1991: 151; Dimanescu & Dwenger, 1996: 82). The project must reach a reasonable balance between a great idea and what is technically feasible. On the one hand, the *project owner* as the main protagonist and champion of the product idea exerts significant influence over technology and market targets (see e.g., Rubenstein, Chakrabarti, O'Keefe, Souder, & Young, 1976). Project ownership and commitment creates direction, momentum, and a common purpose (Katzenbach & Smith, 1993a; Leavitt & Lipman-Blumen, 1995). On the other hand, technical uncertainties (Madauss, 1994), organizational inertia and structures (Henderson & Clark, 1990), reciprocal interdependencies (Nadler & Tushman, 1987) as well as difficulties in knowledge mode conversions (Nonaka & Takeuchi, 1995) make the definition of *system interfaces* a less than trivial task.

Besides content-specific integration, appropriate planning, reporting, control and information systems help to manage the R&D process (e.g., Roussel, Saad, & Erickson, 1991). But special efforts in establishing team culture or aligning individual project objectives are needed to achieve *project coherence* (van de Ven, 1986; Thamhain & Wilemon, 1987). R&D groups that create their own dynamic orderliness have been referred to as "self-organizing teams" (Burgelman, 1983; Imai, Nonaka, & Takeuchi, 1985). Self-organizing teams as well as project teams composed of members of diverse functional specializations are capable of cross fertilization. In the above-mentioned study, Szakonyi (1994a, b) observes that the commitment toward establishing *cross-functional integration* is present but in general is weakly supported. Liaison officers, cross-unit groups, project integrators, or matrix organization could achieve such structural linking (Nadler & Tushman, 1987).

During integrated problem solving, communication between members of the team is particularly intensive (Wheelwright & Clark, 1992). *Communication tools* and communication facilitators have long been recognized to improve R&D

quality and effectiveness. Based on Allen's (1977) seminal work, R&D managers lay out R&D facilities to enhance and facilitate communication. Tushman (1979) observes, however, that communication patterns differ with function (research, development, and technical service) and operational needs both within and outside the firm (operational, professional). As Dimanescu and Dwenger (1996) argue, it is important to maximize the opportunity for interaction and information exchange and not the actual information flow.

With the trend toward empowerment and decentralization (see e.g., Albers & Eggers, 1991; Jensen & Meckling, 1996; Gassmann & von Zedtwitz, 1999), communication tools have become a vital ingredient for effective *coordination*. Conventional R&D coordination tools (e.g., Cooper & Kleinschmidt, 1991; Madauss, 1994; O'Connor, 1994) are being complemented by new organizational structures (de Meyer, 1991; Gassmann & von Zedtwitz, 1998), modern communication instruments (O'Hara-Devereaux & Johansen, 1994), and boundary-crossing individuals (Bartlett & Ghoshal, 1990; de Meyer, 1991; Ancona & Caldwell, 1997).

Although impressive advances have been made in these areas, we have difficulties finding specific literature concerning global R&D project management. Most research in this field either pertains to organizational issues in R&D but disregards the *project* dimension (e.g., the gatekeeper concept), or it fails to differentiate between centralized and globally *dispersed* projects (e.g., the development funnel). There are, however, a number of exceptions.

Authors of global R&D management have at least implicitly pointed at increased impediments of communication and coordination in international R&D (e.g., Rubenstein, 1989; de Meyer & Mizushima, 1989; von Boehmer, Brockhoff, & Pearson, 1992; Beckmann & Fischer, 1994; Boutellier, Gassman, Macho, & Roux, 1998). De Meyer & Mizushima (1989) introduced "the half-life effect of electronic communication," pointing out that e-mail is at best complementary to face-to-face contact. O'Hara-Devereaux and Johansen (1994) described groupware and its usefulness in sharing know-how worldwide. The use of ICT in R&D has been studied by Howells (1995); in particular, he summarizes some preconditions for cross-border R&D teamwork. With ICT a familiar tool for many engineers and scientists, its utilization for R&D management was just a matter of time. The adoption of global project coordination mechanisms has been somewhat slower, with software development being at the forefront of decentralized R&D management (e.g., Carmel, 1999). Nevertheless, we see dedicated global R&D management structures emerging (Gassmann & von Zedtwitz, 1998; Naman, Dahlin, & Krohn, 1998; Reger, 1999).

We describe the ten principal project characteristics in a model of four principal project organizations (see Figure 7.2) presented originally by Gassmann (1997) and Gassmann and von Zedtwitz (2003a):

1. Decentralized self-coordination,
2. System integration coordinator,

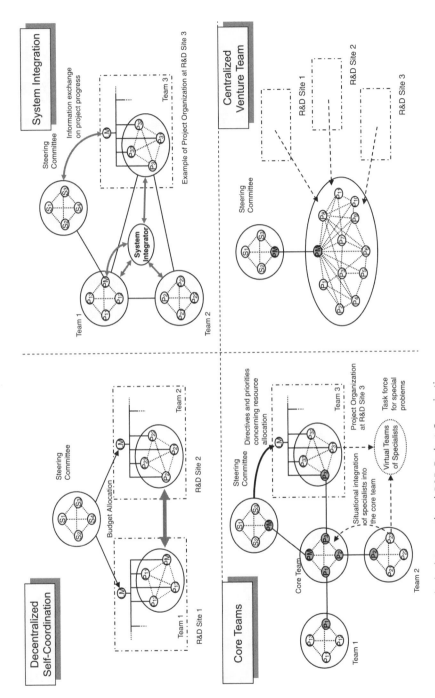

FIGURE 7.2. Four Principal International R&D Project Organizations

3. Core team as system architect, and
4. Centralized venture team.

These concepts are presented in the order of increasing central authority of the project coordinator, along with case studies to illustrate global innovation projects in industry. Particular emphasis is placed on interface management, both technical and interpersonal, as well as project management and project organization.

DECENTRALIZED SELF-COORDINATING INNOVATION PROJECTS

In the absence of a strong project manager, no single authority enforces a rigid time schedule or a defined list of objectives. A mutually shared ambition guides cooperation. Project objectives are not vital to the company's business and hence receive only casual management attention. As in many highly dispersed teams, communication and coordination are primarily based on modern information and communication technologies such as the Internet, shared databases, groupware, telephone, and fax. As there are no dedicated project budgets, travel is kept to a minimum or is coincidental. A strong corporate or professional microculture sometimes compensates for the lack of team or project spirit otherwise found in traditional project teams. Intrinsic motivation is important and must keep in check, potentially diverging individual interests. Coordination is relatively weak, and company-wide soft management practices and company culture provide operational guidelines for project members.

Self-organized teams often originate from R&D bootlegging. They may also be set up by a superior manager who later yields project control to the group (e.g., collaborative basic research projects). Once initiated, only some administrative support is necessary. Decentralized self-coordinated projects are common in research, where they help scientists stay in touch with their peers around the world and draw on their ideas for the benefit of related internal R&D projects. In these very early stages of R&D, system integration is often not an issue as it is still unclear what systems, technologies, and products will be affected. In development, decentralized self-coordinating teams emerge only if standards for interfaces between locally developed modules are already available and clearly defined, as for instance in IBM's established VSE and MVS systems. Such standards may give rise to relatively autonomous product development with low system specificity, resulting in modules that can be produced and distributed independently. This is the case in dominant design industries in which the overall product architecture is shared by all major parties and the focus of innovation is on process improvement, as in the elevator industry.

Decentralized self-coordination is poorly suited for problems with highly integrated solutions. Should critical project situations arise and priorities need to be set, overall project goals may be sacrificed at the expense of local interests (e.g., resources, local over global design, local autonomy). "Mirror organizations" in participating R&D sites help to identify required specialists in more complex settings. Such a symmetrical organization of teams greatly supports direct communication between corresponding specialists at the operative project level without expanding administrative project chores.

Decentralized self-coordination is well suited for organizations with independent business units that have a high self-interest in the development of the product component they manufacture. The overall project is supervised by a steering committee that approves and assigns the project budget. Regional line managers assume control over local module development. Such independent and multilateral coordination of teams succeeds best in incremental or highly modular innovation. As technical interfaces are well defined, potentially diverging project objectives for component development have only a limited impact on the entire project.

Decentralized self-organizing teams may be created if the emergence of a more powerful centralized project organization is prevented by market forces (e.g., autonomous web developers) or company-internal principles (e.g., interdivisional competition). However, if a decentralized self-organized project rises in significance and managerial problems are expected, an individual will be vested with formal coordination authority to ensure more efficient system integration.

Mini-Case: Decentralized Self-coordinating Teams—Hewlett-Packard's Technology Transfer Project

The Technology Transfer Project at Hewlett-Packard (HP) was started by an HP scientist trying to improve transfer of technologies to HP business units with a project management tool-base. On his own initiative, he raised the interests of colleagues, the support of his management, and the financial commitment of the WBIRL grant committee. He also identified supporters in HP Labs research centers in the U.S., England, and Italy; these participants in turn recruited new members.

The workload was highly distributed, and most of the communication took place by e-mail or videoconference. The early attempts to "get going on the work" failed because the distributed team members had not yet established common goals and objectives, so a few day-long face-to-face workshops helped overcome emerging frustrations.

Greatly aided by other HP scientists, the team developed a technology transfer toolbox that included external industry benchmarks. As it selected some preexisting process reference documentation templates, the toolbox was adopted quickly within the HP R&D community.

Mini-Case A2: Decentralized Self-coordinating Teams—Hitachi's European Virtual Research Laboratory

Hitachi's European Virtual Research Laboratory had a more formal foundation than HP's technology transfer project. Because Hitachi had no significant manufacturing operations in Europe at that time, Hitachi aimed to pursue fundamental research in close connection with local universities and research institutes, and had established research centers at the universities of Cambridge (microelectronics), Dublin (information science), Munich, and Milan with more than eighty researchers by 1997. The administrative headquarters were at the European R&D headquarters in Maidenhead, U.K.

In 1997, Hitachi created a virtual research laboratory called "Hitachi European Telecommunications Lab." The goal was to pursue research in telecommunications systems and the development of network system software. Research was designated to four of the most suitable locations: Cambridge (U.K.), Dublin (Ireland), Sophia-Antipolis (France), and Dallas (U.S.). Each location had a designated technical competence but could dynamically reallocate and group collaboration projects as needed. Overall research administration remained in Maidenhead. Access to standardization consortia was also important. For instance, Sophia-Antipolis is known for expertise in mobile computing and communications, as well as competence in European framework programs such as EURECOM, ESPRIT, and ETCI.

Research was distributed among ten scientists in those five places. Individual scientists were given a lead by "holonic management," which yields a maximum of power and freedom to the individual while making sure that the research understands and pursues the overall goals of the research laboratory and how his work affects his own research and that of his colleagues. Although each scientist is a fully integrated researcher in his local community, he relies on the work of his virtual colleagues and shares his results with them.

SYSTEM INTEGRATOR AS R&D COORDINATOR

A system integrator helps with overcoming some of the coordination problems. A system integrator harmonizes interfaces between modules, defines work packages, and coordinates decentralized R&D activities. The system integrator's interface management includes four aspects:

1. A system integrator harmonizes physical, logical, and process interfaces between modules and supervises overall system integration (*technical interface management*).
2. The system integrator is also responsible for ensuring that the work packages in a project are completed on time (*temporal interface management*).
3. The system integrator tracks and controls the contribution of all participating profit centers (*administrative interface management*).
4. Moreover, the system integrator must build a common project understanding between different functional and regional units in the project team (*social interface management*).

The system integrator has a central role in an otherwise highly decentralized project. Several system integrators or a dedicated project integration office may supervise particular complex or collaborative decentralized projects, facilitating the coordination and coherence between dispersed product management teams and the project aims. These teams act highly independently, and as long as they fulfill previously agreed-upon specifications, the system integrator should not interfere. Often, this project organization is used to tap locally available expertise for product upgrades or refinement work.

As participating teams are often from very different technological or cultural backgrounds, the system integrator is responsible for managing knowledge transformation and translation processes, bridging different contexts of language, business versus technical aspects, and culture. In order to overcome functional differences, a system integrator must opt for system thinking in favor of local technological optimization. Although project coordination is aided considerably by modern ICT, an initial workshop with principal team members and subsequent regular face-to-face contacts are crucial for system integration. A geographically central location of the integrator's office is important in order to reduce otherwise significant travel burden, and to facilitate meetings between teams and integrator.

The principal threat to projects supervised by a system integrator is teams with diverging interests and conflicts of interest. Since the system integrator has no formal decision authority over project teams, he must rely on intensive communication, strong personal commitment, and frequent travel to build an informal network and at least a rudimentary form of team spirit. If conflicts still cannot be handled this way, he will summon team leaders to meet face-to-face in order to settle the dispute or solve the problem. Much patience, sensitivity, and experience are required to align the individual objectives of each partner team, making sure that they agree on a shared understanding of what is to be achieved and how each partner prefers to contribute to this goal. Mutually demonstrated appreciation of each other's work (e.g., in top-management reviews) is very helpful for continuous motivation in an extremely complex international environment.

Mini-Case: System Integrator as an R&D Coordinator—VSE Development at IBM

The development of IBM's Virtual Storage Extended (VSE) system software was distributed over eleven R&D units. For reasons of compatibility, 90 percent of the old code was reused for the new release. Project management and system responsibility resided with IBM's R&D unit in Böblingen, Germany. Four integrators coordinated the development and revision of twenty VSE components. Their responsibilities included the collection and technical evaluation of new project ideas, technical system design, project supervision and coordination, project documentation, and VSE product planning. Ideas for completely new functions (leading to radical innovation) were also reviewed and considered for potential development in Böblingen, or assigned to a better-suited IBM R&D unit.

There was a substantial potential for goal conflict since each development team was part of an independent profit center. Direct instructions from one team to another team were not possible. Although this empowerment promoted self-coordination, team autonomy was limited by IBM-internal integration. The low-authority system integrator had to rely on the readiness of all R&D teams to cooperate, often using soft forms of persuasion. When no agreement could be reached, Böblingen considered internal development or outsourcing, which often resulted in complex profit distribution schemes and intellectual property conflicts.

After many years of VSE development experience, project planning became a highly standardized process with clearly defined project goals, interfaces, and abundant boundary conditions. The project office tended to restrict developmental freedom in project teams. Once the VSE development reached a predefined checkpoint, the specifications were frozen. Component design was almost entirely entrusted to local R&D units, but the project office continued to supervise and coordinate the development process (including system design, implementation, code scaffolding, module integration, and customer testing).

Mini-Case: Decentralized Research in European Community Projects

Research in European Community projects is extremely decentralized. REWARD, a one-year project aimed at designing and implementing reengineering methods in R&D, was formed of teams from five large companies, three smaller companies, and three research and consulting service providers, including a total of twenty-five researchers from eight countries. One of the firms assumed coordination responsibilities to organize and administer start-up workshops, regular face-to-face meetings, and online communication. Its central location (in Germany) was important for frequent personal contact between contributing partners and the coordinator himself.

The project was split down according to work tasks. Three problems occurred. First, handover of preliminary and final work package results was often complicated by incompatible computer and information systems. Second, after a team had concluded its part of the work, the entire project was given a lesser priority, thus hindering the efficient project continuation for the rest of the teams. Third, the project coordination office (system integrator) responsible for coordination and control was given only weak influence and decision power, thus lacking the strong authority needed to keep decentralized activities on track.

Although all project partners were European, the Europe-internal cultural differences had been underestimated. Furthermore, decentralized project work involving several partners required a different mindset from the efficiency-oriented work routines used in single-location projects. The project office was thus eventually strengthened to control efficient use of file transfer exchange and e-mail, and to call more frequently for face-to-face meetings between key team members. REWARD was eventually completed on budget and ahead of schedule, and its team received recognition for improved project management in European projects.

THE CORE TEAM AS A SYSTEM ARCHITECT

Collocating all project members and equipment may be very costly and sometimes impossible. Companies whose R&D teams work closely together control their product development processes better (Takeuchi & Nonaka, 1986). Studies on communication and team performance suggest a physical collocation of R&D in one place (e.g., Allen, 1977; Katz & Allen, 1985; Takeuchi & Nonaka, 1986; Katzenbach & Smith, 1993b). But the advantages of intralocation are in fundamental contrast to the many multisite necessities in R&D projects (Lullies, Bolinger, & Weltz, 1993).

In the core team approach, key decision makers meet regularly in one location to direct decentralized R&D work. This approach is characterized by a higher intensity of interlocal communication and a more integrated problem solution than the two previously described project organizations. The core team usually consists of the leaders of the most important subteams and perhaps of internal business customers. To be functional, the core team rarely exceeds ten to fifteen people.

The core team develops the system architecture of a new product and maintains coherence of the system during the entire project duration. It assumes the role of a system architect and integrator but also has the authority to enforce its directives. The core team is thus in a better position to resolve deadlocks between functional and local units and to translate between differing cognitive contexts ("cognitive bridging," Ridderstråle, 1992: 14). The core team also maintains a good link to the supervising project steering committee to guarantee direct information flow between project teams and the product champions. In strategic projects, the steering committee has direct influence on line managers concerning the prioritization of projects and resource allocation, in order to resolve responsibility conflicts occurring in a complex matrix organization.

Core teams can address problems on an integrative level, and find solutions outside predefined concepts. Problem solving in core teams differs substantially from independent local search paths of self-coordinating teams or the mediation by system integrators. The core team organization is best for highly innovative product development, and when intralocal project execution is impossible due to limited resources.

A defining feature is the temporary inclusion of technical experts from local R&D teams. The core team thus varies in size and composition as necessary, although a maximum size should not be exceeded for efficient decision making. Tele- or videoconferences may suffice to bring together the input from other specialists, but if the problem is particularly complex and involves several modules, specialist teams are created and supervised by the core team.

Mini-Case: Intelligent Machine Development at Rockwell Automation

In January 1996, based on a set of customer requirements, Rockwell Automation initiated an ambitious eighteen-month program to develop an intelligent motor product, integrating existing experience as well as novel, yet-to-be-developed technologies.

The core team consisted of three senior managers in marketing, R&D, and engineering. New team members were included in the project team as needed, often from another Rockwell division. A one-page product brochure communicated a clear, common, and concise objective. The project's internal visibility, strong customer drive, and a keen sense of urgency ensured team coherence, although only one person was employed full time on the project.

Formal project management was established, including project reporting and tracking, weekly one-page updates, and a central data repository. Software revisions and document control were administered by the core team. Still, a key success factor was the considerable amount of informal communication: it was customary for team participants to contact anyone on the project as needed, despite the fact that the teams were located in faraway places in the U.S. and Europe. Issues and results from semiformal communication were copied to the appropriate core team leader responsible for the area of activity.

Team members were chosen based on their professional expertise as well as their previous record to work in distant collaborative teams. Individual team members from remote locations spent time at other project locations performing joint R&D tasks. As project management was done from a distance, trust and transparency of leadership were critical. The R&D representative on the core team spent a quarter of his time traveling and coordinating R&D activities with local team engineers, contractors, and customers. Competent and empowered team leaders in each location helped align local activities with the overall project objective. Despite the adversities of geographical separation, the project turned out to be very successful: The overall development time was shortened from the projected eighteen months to twelve months while staying within the predefined budget. A testimony of the success of this project is multiple industry and patent awards for eventual product.

Mini-Case: Xerox's Translation and Authoring System

The two Xerox research centers in Palo Alto, California, and Grenoble, France, had strong expertise in linguistic technologies. Based on promising results of a feasibility project conducted in Grenoble, a team was put in place to develop a product and service offering for a translation and authoring software called XTRAS, develop a business case and business plan, and find early customers. A small core team consisted of research managers, internal business customers, internal business development consultants, and external consultants. The project itself was organized in a straightforward manner: a project leader, a business team, and a technical team. Seven Xerox organizations participated in the project distributed across four sites in the United States and Europe.

The majority of the core management team participated on a part time basis only. The main management challenges were identified as:

- Managing an internationally distributed team;
- Coordinating and collaborating with potentially competing teams (the business to be created could be seen as competing with current product and service offerings, as well as internal translation services); and
- Validating the product/service concept and business models.

Management coordination made heavy use of collaborative tools such as videoconferencing, significantly reducing the requirement, frequency, and cost of face-to-face meetings. The technical team was collocated in Grenoble, with the project leader.

The project was a success because of the tight coordination between the technical and business teams, with multiple collaborations at various levels of decision authority. However, while at the working level a large number of collaborations existed between the various teams, the business teams' management was not engaged early enough through their respective participants in the project, contrary to the assumptions made by the core project management team, which resulted in slow decision making and nearly delayed the business launch. The XTRAS core team, recognizing this shortfall, organized a crash program to get the appropriate management levels involved.

The distributed aspect of the project, both geographically and organizationally, offered the most significant management challenges. However, the richness brought by the various views of the different cultures and organizations was a key to its success.

CENTRALIZED VENTURE TEAM

Distance between R&D employees significantly decreases the likelihood of communication (Allen, 1977), and coordination and information exchange become more difficult in international R&D settings. Physical collocation of scientists, engineers, and project managers thus tend to make the execution of R&D projects more efficient. Due to high costs of relocating dispersed R&D personnel and resources in one location, the centralized venture team is used only for strategic innovation projects.

The geographically centralized venture team is responsible for planning and execution of an R&D project, including idea generation, product system definition, technology and product development, testing, and often even the product's market introduction. A heavyweight project manager exercises unrestricted command over the resources assigned to the project. To effectively implement his decisions, he is fully empowered to pursue new and original solutions without repeatedly asking for approval. Full technical and business responsibility is likely to lead to radical new product and process concepts. Due to its strategic importance, project funding is often provided from corporate sources.

Through physical proximity and intensive project-internal communication, the centralized venture team is able to pursue integrated solutions. Collocation, face-to-face communication, and good informal linkages between team members are key factors for effective short-term development. Simultaneous engineering (rugby team approach) is possible if cross-functional collocation overcomes compartmental thinking.

Centralized venture teams have been labeled "High-impact projects" at ABB, "Top projects" at Bosch, and "Golden badge projects" at Sharp. They are strategic in nature, and their budgets may be very large. However, staying within budget limits is less of a priority than achieving technical goals and time-to-market. Frequently, such projects are crucial for developing attractive business opportunities or for closing gaps to fast-moving competitors. Dispatched to the central project location, project members are exempted from line duties in other R&D locations. Specialists are often intensely engaged in such activities, and their removal from their parent location imposes great opportunity costs for venture teams. Direct costs are less important compared to the opportunity costs of collocating the team. The development of a strong project culture complicates the reintegration of the project members into their previous line functions.

Although the venture team is centralized in one place, this location is not necessarily the corporate R&D center. The venture team's separation and independent organization from its original R&D department can be critical. Removed from the company's line organization, a venture team allows the unrestricted cooperation of specialists from several functional areas.

Despite the strong centralization, these venture teams are increasingly international, with cross-border cooperation necessary with lead customers, specialized suppliers, and external research partners.

Centralized venture teams are the most costly approach to global innovation teams and result in difficult overcapacity situations at the termination of the project. But centralizing R&D teams may be the only way to accomplish challenging objectives under strong time pressure. Especially when information can easily be converted to code and team members know each other already from previous projects, a substantial amount of cost-intensive centralization can be reduced to kick-off and review meetings. Yet modern information and communication technologies cannot replace face-to-face contacts for extended periods of time without reducing trust among its team members (De Meyer, 1991).

Mini-Case: ABB's Think-Tank for the Gas Turbine Development GT24/26

ABB's GT24/26 gas turbine development represented a breakthrough innovation project with more than 100 patents filed. Realizing that they were lagging behind, ABB launched a major effort to catch up with competitors. Although technical foundations had to be developed as well, it was paramount to hit the optimal market entry time window.

An R&D project team of several hundred researchers, engineers, and manufacturing specialists from twenty nations was concentrated in a single open-space office in a two-story building in Gebensdorf, Switzerland. Much of the R&D and engineering work was done simultaneously. ABB engaged in turbine development before the necessary materials research was completed, and the design of production tools was started before the product development phase was concluded. This created serious coordination challenges. For instance, the rotor development team and its manufacturing personnel were relocated from Mannheim to Baden in order to ensure the necessary intensity of collaboration.

Despite all efforts to centralize, a substantial piece of the work had to be provided from remote suppliers. As secrecy was critical to maintain an edge over competition, everyone involved in the project was sworn into confidence. This—along with the extreme stretch goals in time and quality—created a common project spirit and innovation culture.

Almost needless to say, the GT24/26 project had a top priority in ABB's Power Generation unit. The project leader reported directly to the head of development and the general manager. Most of the project members were fully assigned to the project and reported only to the heavyweight project manager; he had exclusive power of the use of their time and other resources. The project manager was responsible for all activities of research, development, and manufacturing, including the completion of the first two gas turbines and their installation at the customer sites.

The main success factors of the GT24/26 development were the centralization of the project team in one location, the coordinated parallelization of activities and cross-functional cooperation, strong top-management commitment, and the integration of potential and lead customers. ABB's top management fully supported the project, yielding considerably authority and decision power to the GT24/26 project manager. Cross-functional teams, lead users, researchers, and development engineers collaborated during the entire project. The GT24/26 generation was a technological breakthrough and turned ABB into a serious competitor in the field of high-end turbines within a short timeframe. Compared to previous projects, time-to-market could be reduced by 60 percent and the number of modules by nearly 50 percent.

Mini-Case D-2: Daimler-Benz's Centralized "Projekthaus" Necar

Daimler-Benz's fuel-car development had its origins in its Dornier subsidiary's work on fuel cells for space-related applications. After feasibility studies done in the research & technology (R&T) department showed promising results for automotive applications (No-Emission Car 1, i.e., Necar-1 in 1994), a concept car was jointly developed between R&T and Mercedes-Benz Advanced Development (Necar-2, 1996). Project management and a large part of the project responsibility were assumed by development. Nebus, suitable for operation as a normal city bus, followed in 1997. Necar-3 (a fuel cell-based A-class vehicle) went into production in 1999.

R&D on the fuel cell with forty-two engineers was concentrated in a "Project-House Fuel Cell" about thirty kilometers away from the company's headquarters in Stuttgart, but close enough to Mercedes-Benz development. An additional 200 engineers of R&D partners were located in the Project-House for efficient collaboration. Being a key future technology and possibly a successor to traditional engine technology, it received close attention from almost twenty different boards and several steering committees.

Additional attention was given to infrastructure development, fuel methanol logistics, and the development of fuel cell service requirements. This had to be done in partnership with other companies. Already in 1992, a strategic collaboration was formed with the Canadian Ballard Power Systems, a global leader in fuel cell technologies and a spin-off from General Electric's former fuel cell research. By 1997, a joint venture was founded to develop the entire fuel cell system, and another joint venture was created for distributing the fuel cell-powered engines. In December 1997, Ford joined Daimler-Benz and Ballard to secure a greater market access for fuel cell cars. Necar-5 was delivered in 2000 and set new distance and speed records. The technology has since been introduced in SUVs, minivans, and buses, and is being mass tested in other car types.

DETERMINANTS OF TRANSNATIONAL R&D ORGANIZATION

The most evident differences between the described project organizations are the power of the project manager and the geographic distribution of the greater part of the team. However, these differences do not explain *why* a particular organization of global innovation project execution was chosen—they only highlight *how* an organization prefers to address more fundamental determinants and constraints of transnational R&D work. A total of four determinants were identified as central in choosing a specific organizational form of global R&D organization (see Figure 7.3):

1. Type of innovation: incremental versus radical;
2. Nature of the project: systemic versus autonomous;
3. Knowledge mode: explicit versus tacit; and
4. Degree of resource bundling: redundant versus complementary.

Type of Innovation: Incremental versus Radical

The novelty of an innovation is determined by the number, extent, and predictability of deviations from the experience and know-how base of a

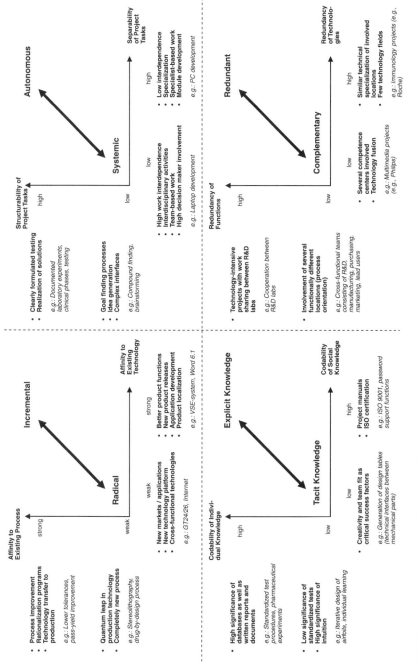

FIGURE 7.3. Determinants for Choosing R&D Organizational Forms

company. Incremental innovation is characterized by a great affinity of the R&D effort to existing technology and processes, higher continuity, routinization, and more gradual improvement. Examples for strong process affinity are R&D efforts to reduce tolerance levels or improve pass-yield quotas; products with a high affinity to existing technologies are, for example, software application updates such as Word 6.1 or platform-based car derivatives.

Radical innovation is often the result of a breakthrough project in a new technology or process, involving completely new markets, new technological designs, or the integration of formerly unrelated technologies for novel applications. Since technology and process affinity is weak, project dynamics and uncertainties concerning attainability and execution are high. Examples of radical innovation are drug-by-design processes in the pharmaceutical industry, ABB's GT24/26, and Daimler's Smart Car.

Incremental innovation is better suited for decentralized execution, as the required technologies are known and system interfaces are defined. R&D is more likely to target module-internal innovation, leaving the overall product system intact. While incremental innovation is often a sine qua non condition for maintaining or expanding an existing line of business, its R&D projects usually do not enjoy the same internal visibility or attract the same attention from top management.

Nature of the Project: Systemic versus Autonomous

The systemic nature of the innovation project depends on the interdependence and configuration of individual project work tasks. Highly structured projects with separable work tasks are examples of autonomous innovation projects. Structure implies a defined input-output process as well as cause-and-effect knowledge about individual tasks. Work is split up into work packages with well-defined interfaces, and can be carried out without much interaction with other work packages. Highly modularized product systems such as the personal computer (memory chips, monitors, disk drives, integrated circuits, etc.) lend themselves to great decentralization of innovation. The rigorous testing and research process established in many academic and industrial R&D laboratories is a good example for highly structured innovation.

Highly interdependent work tasks indicate a systemic nature of innovation, and is often found in the early phases of R&D projects, when technical and procedural concepts have not yet been defined. In product development, wide tolerances between functional parts also reduce separability.

Thompson's (1967) four types of interdependence (pooled, sequential, reciprocal, and team-oriented) also apply global innovation projects: pooled interdependence is based on restricted access to shared resources. Sequential interdependence links the output of a work package with the input of another work task. Reciprocal interdependence implies mutual coordination of temporal and logic dependencies, as in technical specifications of highly integrated products. In team-oriented interdependence, high module-internal interdependencies require a strong coordination and mutual integration of work package goals within every team. These constraints are present, for example, in laptop development, where tightly packed modules require close physical and functional alignment, which makes a clear separation of module development impossible. Also, highly creative processes (e.g., brainstorming) function better when structural rigidities are removed.

If no previous relevant experience is available according to which project should be structured, innovation tends to be systemic. With increasing knowledge and experience, work tasks and interdependencies are delineated. In complex R&D projects, however, many technical design interfaces are initially unknown and emerge only in the course of the project (see also Sosa, Eppinger, & Rowles, 2004). Systemic innovation is better approached with cross-disciplinary teams not only because their input may be more diverse but also because they are believed to adapt faster to unexpected change. In autonomous innovation, system integration occurs at a lower level and is typically not time critical. Coordination and communication are asynchronous and are determined beforehand by technical and managerial constraints. High interdependence and systemic projects are poorly suited for interlocal execution, whereas autonomous work packages and highly structured projects may be decentralized to remote but higher qualified R&D units.

Knowledge Mode: Explicit versus Tacit

In innovation, the pooling and transfer of knowledge among team members is extremely important, particularly in international projects that aim at exploiting specific location advantages. If knowledge is to be exchanged across large distances, the distinction between tacit and explicit knowledge becomes even more important (see Nonaka & Takeuchi, 1995; Polanyi, 1966). Explicit knowledge is easily articulated and documented, but tacit knowledge is difficult to communicate. We can extend on this terminology by introducing individual knowledge and social knowledge. Social knowledge is knowledge shared among a group of individuals, its interpretation being subjective to the composition of this group. There is a high degree of redundant knowledge that provides identity to this group. Individual knowledge is specific to every human being; it is present and producible without other people having to be around.

In innovation projects, individuals as well as teams engage in knowledge creation and knowledge transfer. Learning occurs both at the individual level and at the team level. The codifiability of knowledge defines learning modes and knowledge exchange patterns. Examples of highly codifiable individual knowledge are fact-based accounts or context-unspecific results. Codified social knowledge is found in laws and written norms and standards, as for instance in R&D project manuals, ISO certifications, or password-recovery functions. Difficult-to-codify individual knowledge includes many individual "how-to" skills at the border to what we may call art or intuition; it may also be more trivial knowledge that an individual is unaware of and assigns little relevance to be articulated. Hard-to-codify social knowledge is at the core of group dynamics and the success of creating the "right" team.

Tacit knowledge includes both individual knowledge and social knowledge. Examples are decisions based on intuition and "coordination without words." The transformation of knowledge (socialization, externalization, internalization, combination) from one mode to another is not trivial and is crucial for effective learning and know-how transfer. In the start-up phase of an R&D project, mutual agreements and procedures must be established (socialization). This tacit knowledge is eventually externalized (i.e., codified and transformed into standards and specifications). The processing of explicit knowledge into more explicit knowledge (combination) is increasingly supported by modern information technologies, particularly multimedia-based means of context-rich communication.

These transformations are highly affected by the cultural and behavioral background of the project members. Project coherence may be based on shared cultural or social knowledge, or mutually shared social knowledge can be established in order to reduce difficulties resulting from cultural differences. Interlocal project execution presupposes that tacit knowledge can be externalized and communicated over distance. It is the project manager's responsibility to facilitate the transformation of individual know-how to knowledge available to the entire team.

Resource Bundling: Redundant versus Complementary

In international R&D projects, resources such as capital, equipment, and people are pooled over a number of locations. Within a project, the deployment and bundling of these resources can be either redundant (i.e., there are overlaps in competencies and skills) or complementary (there are no such overlaps).

There can be bundling of resources in both functional and technological capacities. Strong functional redundancy is present in projects with team members performing similar functions. Project-internal communication then tends to be less problematic since all members use the same terminology and share the same referential framework. Functional redundancy is low if different functions are involved, such as R&D, suppliers, and lead users. As their contexts are not strongly related, communication tends to be more complicated and requires more face-to-face contact and externalization. Strong functional redundancy occurs when subteams are deployed in parallel to prepare competing solutions to the same problem; cross-functional teams are typically characterized by low functional dependency.

Technological redundancy is high if only few or highly related technological areas are involved: all participating R&D teams share similar technological competencies. Researchers of the same scientific discipline also share the same cognitive base and terminology, which, as with functional redundancy, helps low-context ICT or telephone communication by making reference to well-understood frameworks. Examples of strong technological redundancy are projects in clinical drug development, where a specific drug candidate is being tested in similar circumstances across a multitude of hospitals. Low technological redundancy is given if many different technologies are to be combined and only a few experts are available. This is the case in cutting-edge R&D where the number of experts is limited, such as in intelligent machine design or laser research.

Redundancy is often associated with the duplication of R&D efforts and the waste of available resources. However, redundancy in resources and competencies (usually tied to people or teams) provides a buffer against the unforeseeable loss of key people or the elimination of technical alternatives. Epistemological redundancy thus improves the knowledge creation process in R&D projects. Redundant and overlapping knowledge improves the parallelization of R&D work and cross-functional collaboration. Interlocal projects are more difficult to carry out if there is little or no functional and technological redundancy.

CONCLUSION

Although from a technical and scientific point of view the optimal form of innovation is almost always a decentralized one (due to the global distribution of know-how, experts, and infrastructure), coordination and collaboration requirements (due to managerial inefficiencies and human communication limitations and preferences) require greater centralization. Truly decentralized global innovation projects are possible only under certain conditions, specifically if the innovation is more incremental, the project work is autonomous, the knowledge involved is available in explicit form, and the resources are mostly redundant. Global innovation projects must be centralized if the innovation is radical, the project is systemic, knowledge is present mostly in tacit form, and resources are complementary.

Projects may adapt their organizational form if the project environment and requirements change. For instance, project work is centralized because the strategic importance of the work is recognized and time and costs become issues to the rapid success of the project. Or, project work is decentralized because the overall work load was successfully broken down into work packages that are assigned to remote/specialized R&D units. This happens typically during the development stages, following the exploratory stages when technological uncertainty is low and clear interfaces have been developed.

It is important to notice that firms learn how to organize and execute global innovation projects with time and experience. Advances in information and communication technologies, improvements in collaborative project management software applications, and personal ease in handling sophisticated communication technology add to the popularization of global innovation. The four determinants outlined in this chapter should indicate what form of project organization is necessary, which in turn should indicate a preference for the various project management configurations mentioned in the beginning of this chapter. Not every project is equally suited for decentralized global execution. It is important to recognize that the decision of project organization still has to be made case-by-case.

REFERENCES

Albers, S., & Eggers, S. (1991). Organisatorische Gestaltungen von Produktinnovations-Prozessen. Führt der Wechsel des Organisationsgrades zu Innovationserfolg? *Zeitschrift für Betriebswirtschaftliche Forschung, 43,* 1, 44–64.

Allen, T. J. (1977). *Managing the flow of technology—Technology transfer and the dissemination of technological information within the R&D organization.* London: Cambridge University Press.

Ancona, D., & Caldwell, D. (1997). Making teamwork work: Boundary management in product development teams. In Tushman, M., & Anderson, P. (eds.), *Managing strategic innovation and change.* New York: Oxford University Press, 433–442.

Bartlett, C. A., & Ghoshal, S. (1990). Managing innovation in transnational corporation. In Bartlett, C. A., Doz, Y., & Hedlund, G. (eds), *Managing the global firm.* New York: Routledge, 215–255.

Beckmann, C., & Fischer, J. (1994). Einflußfaktoren auf die Internationalisierung von Forschung und Entwicklung in der Chemischen und Pharmazeutischen Industrie. *Zeitschrift für Betriebswirtschaftliche Forschung, 46,* (7/8), 630–657.

Boutellier, R., Gassmann, O., Macho, H., & Roux, M. (1998). Management of dispersed R&D teams. *R&D Management, 28* (1), 13–25.

Burgelman, R. (1983). A model of internal corporate venturing in the diversified major firm. *Administrative Science Quarterly, 28,* 223–244.

Burgelman, R. (1984). Managing the internal corporate venturing process. *Sloan Management Review, Winter,* 33–48.

Carmel, E. (1999). *Global software teams—Collaborating across borders and time zones.* Upper Saddle River, NJ: Prentice Hall.

Chiesa, V. (1996). Managing the internationalization of R&D activities. *IEEE Transactions on Engineering Management, 43* (1), 7–23.

Cooper, R. G., & Kleinschmidt, E. J. (1991). New product processes at leading industrial firms. *Industrial Marketing Management 20,* 137–147.

Crawford, C. (1992). The hidden costs of accelerated product development. *Journal of Product Innovation Management, 9,* 188–199.

De Meyer, A. (1991). Tech talk: How managers are stimulating global R&D communication. *Sloan Management Review, 32* (3), 49–58.

De Meyer, A. (1993). Management of an international network of industrial R&D laboratories. *R&D Management, 23* (2), 109–120.

De Meyer, A., & Mizushima, A. (1989). Global R&D management. *R&D Management 19* (2), 135–146.

Dimanescu, D., & Dwenger, K. (1996). *World-class new product development.* New York: Amacom.

Dunning, J. (1994). Multinational enterprises and the globalization of innovatory capacity. *Research Policy, 23*, 67–88.

EIRMA (1994). *Funding and financing industrial R&D*. Paris: EIRMA Conference papers XLIII.

EIRMA (1995). *Funding R&D for industrial innovation*. Paris.

Ellis, L. W. (1988). Managing financial resources. *Research Technology Management 31*, (4), 21–38.

Gassmann, O. (1997). *Internationales F&E-Management—Potentiale und Gestaltungskonzepte transnationaler F&E-Projekte*. Oldenbourg: München, Wien.

Gassmann, O., & von Zedtwitz, M. (1998). Organization of industrial R&D on a global scale. *R&D Management, 28* (3), 147–161.

Gassmann, O., & von Zedtwitz, M. (1999). New concepts and trends in international R&D organization. *Research Policy, 28,* 231–250.

Gassmann, O., & von Zedtwitz, M. (2003a). Trends and determinants of managing virtual R&D teams. *R&D Management, 33* (3), 243–262.

Gassmann, O., & von Zedtwitz, M. (2003b). Innovation processes in transnational corporations. In Shavinina, L. (ed.), *The international handbook on innovation*. Oxford: Pergamon, 702–714.

Henderson, R. M., & Clark, K. B. (1990). Architectural innovation: The reconfiguration of existing product technologies and the failure of established firms. *Administrative Science Quarterly, 35,* 9–30.

Howells, J. (1995). Going global: The use of ICT networks in research and development. *Research Policy, 24,* 169–184.

Imai, K., Nonaka, I., & Takeuchi, H. (1985). Managing the new product development process: How Japanese companies learn and unlearn. In Clark, K., Hayes, R., & Lorenz, C. (eds), *The uneasy alliance*. Cambridge, MA: Harvard University Press.

Jensen, M. C., & Meckling, W. H. (1996). Specific and general knowledge, and organizational structure. In Myers, P. S. (ed.), *Knowledge management and organizational design*. Newton, MA: Butterworth-Heineman, 17–38.

Katz, R., & Allen, T. (1985). Project performance and the locus of influence in the R&D matrix. *Academy of Management Journal, 28* (1), 67–87.

Katzenbach, J., & Smith, D. K. (1993a). The discipline of teams. *Harvard Business Review, 71,* 111–120.

Katzenbach, J., & Smith, D. K. (1993b). *The wisdom of teams*. Boston: Harvard Business School Press.

Leavitt, H., & Lipman-Blumen, J. (1995). Hot groups. *Harvard Business Review, 73,* 109–116.

Lullies, V., Bolinger, H., & Weltz, F. (1993). *Wissenslogistik: Über den betrieblichen Umgang mit Wissen bei Entwicklungsvorhaben*. Frankfurt, New York.

Madauss, B. J. (1994). *Handbuch projektmanagement*, 5. Aufl., Stuttgart: Schaeffer-Poeschel.

Nadler, D., & Tushman, M. (1987). *Strategic organization design*. Glenview, IL: Scott Foresman and Company.

Naman, J., Dahlin, K., & Krohn, M. (1998). *Managing international R&D for global platforms and local adaptations*. Carnegie-Bosch Institute working paper No. 98-1.

Nonaka, I., & Takeuchi, H. (1995). *The knowledge-creating company: How Japanese companies create the dynamics of innovation*. New York: Oxford University Press.

O'Connor, P. (1994). Implementing a stage-gate process: A multi-company perspective. *Journal of Product Innovation Management, 11,* 183–200.

O'Hara-Devereaux, M., & Johansen, R. (1994). *Globalwork: Bridging distance, culture, and time.* San Francisco: Jossey-Bass.

Patel, P. (1995). Localised production of technology in global markets. *Cambridge Journal of Economy, 19,* 141–153.

Polanyi, M. (1966). *The Tacit dimension.* London: Peter Smith.

Reger, G. (1999). How R&D is coordinated in Japanese and European multinationals. *R&D Management, 29* (1), 71–88.

Ridderstråle, J. (1992). *Developing product development: Holographic design for successful creation in the MNC.* Competitive Paper for EIBA Annual Meeting. Reading.

Roberts, E. B. (1995). Benchmarking the strategic management of technology I. *Research Technology Management 38* (1), 44–56.

Roussel, P. A., Saad, K. N., & Erickson, T. J. (1991). *Third generation R&D: Managing the link to corporate strategy.* Boston: Harvard Business School Press.

Rubenstein, A., Chakrabarti, A., O'Keefe, R., Souder, W., & Young, H. (1976). Factors influencing innovation success at the project level. *Research Management, 19, 3.*

Rubenstein, A. H. (1989). *Managing technology in the decentralized firm.* New York: Wiley.

Sosa, M., Eppinger, S., & Rowles, C. (2004). The misalignment of product architecture and organizational structure in complex product development. *Management Science, 50* (12), 1674–1689.

Szakonyi, R. (1994). Measuring R&D effectiveness - I. *Research Technology Management, 37* (3), 27–32.

Szakonyi, R. (1994). Measuring R&D effectiveness - II. *Research Technology Management 37* (3), 44–55.

Takeuchi, H., & Nonaka, I. (1986). The new new product development game. *Harvard Business Review, 64* (1), 137–146.

Thamhain, H., & Wilemon, D. (1987). Building high performing engineering project teams. *IEEE Transactions on Engineering Management.* Vol. EM-34, No. 3, 130–137.

Thompson, J. D. (1967). *Organizations in action.* New York: Sidney.

Tushman, M. L. (1979). Managing communication network in R&D laboratories. *Sloan Management Review, 4,* 37–49.

Van de Ven, A. (1986). Central problems in the management of innovation. *Management Science, 32* (5), 590–607.

von Boehmer, A., Brockhoff, K., & Pearson, A. W. (1992). The management of international research and development. In Buckley, P. J., & Brooke, M. Z. (eds.), *International business studies.* Oxford: Blackwell, 495–509.

von Hippel, E. (1988). *The sources of innovation.* New York: Oxford.

von Zedtwitz, M., & Gassmann, O. (2002). Market versus technology drive in R&D internationalization: Four different patterns of managing research and development. *Research Policy, 31* (4), 569–588.

Wheelwright, S., & Clark, K. (1992). *Revolutionizing product development—Quantum leaps in speed, efficiency, and quality.* New York: The Free Press.

8

Cash Constraints and Venture Capital Stage Investing in Start-up Companies

TONY DAVILA, GEORGE FOSTER, and MAHENDRA R. GUPTA

T he fundamental need for funding in start-up firms comes from the entrepreneur's wealth constraints and risk preferences that demand external funds to finance the firm from inception until it becomes cash-flow positive. During the initial stages of a firm's life, before the uncertainty of the venture is reduced and alternative sources of funding become available, venture capitalists provide these funds.[1] While wealth constraints explain the initial funding of a start-up firm, they do not explain why the funding happens through sequential investments rather than happening through a single lump sum transfer.[2]

Sequential funding is a salient characteristic of venture capital investing.[3] Start-up firms do not receive all the funding they need to achieve profitability in their first round of venture funding. Rather, venture capitalists invest through sequential rounds, and their investment today does not commit them to future funding. Sequential funding allows venture capitalists to periodically update their information about the firm, monitor its progress, review its prospects, and evaluate whether to provide additional funding or abandon the

The assistance of Trinet and VentureOne for this research is gratefully appreciated. We are grateful for the comments of participants in the Stanford University research workshop. Financial support is from The Center for Entrepreneurial Studies at the Graduate School of Business, Stanford University, and Morgridge Fellowship. Research assistance was provided by Nicole Ang, Jiangyun Liu, Barbara Lubben, and Jakub Wilsz.

project. Sequential financing provides venture capital with a real option.[4] This option can be exercised or abandoned over time as the uncertainty about the start-up firm is resolved. Sequential financing is also advocated as a governance mechanism to reduce the costs associated with the separation of ownership and management implicit in venture-backed start-ups.[5] The threat of liquidation disciplines managers and reduces managers' incentives to divert resources to themselves at the expense of investors.[6] In this chapter, we use a sample of venture-backed start-up firms to provide evidence on two issues associated with venture funding:

(1) An uninformed examination of funding rounds may suggest that all funding rounds serve the same purpose—to provide cash to a cash-constrained firm. However, academic theory predicts differences in the role of cash constraints over funding stages.[7] The initial round of venture capital provides the funding that start-up firms need to grow.[8] They remove cash constraints that hold back the development of the firm. Funding in later rounds comes in before the firm faces cash constraints and its purpose is associated with governance. Thus the cash that flows to the start-up firm in these late rounds provides the leverage that venture capitalists need to exercise control over the firm and curve managers' incentives to divest cash for lower-value-added activities. In particular, the threat of hitting cash constraints disciplines the agency relationship, even if in most cases these constraints are not hit. The difference in the role of these funding rounds is reflected in employee growth.[9] Our analysis shows that in early rounds, headcount growth significantly increases in the months after the funding round compared to the months prior to the event. This is consistent with early rounds of removing cash constraints that impede the firms' ability to hire and pay new employees until the cash from the funding event is available. For late rounds, the growth rate in months prior and subsequent to a funding event is not significantly different, suggesting that cash does not constrain firm growth around these events. We also find that larger amounts of funding in a round are associated with faster growth.

(2) Employees extract different information from these two types of funding rounds about the potential of the company; they convey signals of different value to employees.[10] The fact that a company receives venture capital for the first time gives a very strong signal to employees about the future of the company, and employee turnover decreases significantly around this initial round. Follow-up rounds are also important signals to employees about the quality of the company, but the signal is weaker as the company matures and uncertainty about the attractiveness of the business model decreases. Our analysis shows that employee turnover decreases much more around the first funding round than in later rounds.

To examine these two issues, we gathered information about a sample of start-up firms on the evolution of employees on a monthly basis—hires and terminations every month—and on the date and amount of venture capital received. Our sample includes 170 start-up firms with 268 funding events.

THE SEQUENCED STRUCTURE OF VENTURE CAPITAL FINANCING

Venture Capital

Venture capital firms are financial intermediaries focused on providing capital to small, innovative, fast-growth start-up companies that are typically high risk and not amenable to more traditional financing alternatives. Venture capital firms have certain unique characteristics that separate them from traditional sources of funds. First, their investments (start-up firms) involve higher levels of uncertainty, asymmetric information, and typically higher intangible assets and growth opportunities.[11] Second, venture capitalists take an equity position in the company and play an active role in the governance of the firm.[12] They typically are on the board of directors and regularly monitor performance.[13] This monitoring goes beyond what a traditional financing institution does and includes spending time at the companies, frequent meetings with managers, and being involved in the definition of the companies' strategies, hiring decisions,[14] and top management compensation.[15] In addition, venture capitalists bring their experience in evaluating the prospects of start-ups through their screening of potential investments,[16] their collaboration with other start-ups, their understanding of the solutions to the problems that these firms may face, and when start-ups are best positioned to raise money. They also assist with their reputation in the capital and product markets.[17] Finally, they provide access to a strategic network that includes potential clients or suppliers, management talent,[18] additional funding, strategic partners,[19] and infrastructure providers like accounting firms, law firms, and public relations firms.

Rounds of Financing

A salient characteristic of venture capital investing is its reliance on sequential financing rounds. At each round of financing, venture capital firms supply new financial resources to the start-up in exchange for a percentage of the equity of the company. These rounds of financing are discrete events that happen over the life of the company as a private entity. Rounds of funding are critical in the relationship between venture capitalists and the start-ups they invest in. They are not a mere transfer of financial resources, but involve the redefinition of the governance structure of the firm and provide a signal about its prospects. This new ownership structure affects the control structure of the company as well as the payoffs of a future liquidity event (whether it is a public offering or a trade sale).

Entrepreneurial studies have shown the significant role of cash constraints in the decision to engage in entrepreneurial work as well as in the investment in any entrepreneurial endeavor.[20] In venture-backed start-ups, this cash constraint is the starting point for the initial investment and the creation of an agency relationship between venture capitalists (investors) and the management team. The role of this initial round is to solve the cash limitation that the entrepreneur faces. But follow-up rounds fulfill additional roles; otherwise, venture capitalists would provide all the capital in this initial round.

A proposed explanation is based on the real option embedded in the investment process of sequenced venture funding. Each funding round provides enough capital to reach the next funding round where venture capitalists, in light of new information, decide whether to provide a new round of funds to the firm or to exercise their abandonment option.[21] Such an option does not exist if all funding is provided upfront.

Sequenced funding and the threat of liquidation associated with it can be also be used to decrease costs associated with the separation of ownership (venture capitalists) and control over decision making (management)—what is called in the academic world agency costs. Because managers do not bear all the consequences of their decisions—for instance, they may decide to overspend in the building to gain personal status because shareholders rather than managers themselves bear the cost of the building—they may pursue actions that are in their best personal interest but not in the best interest of the company. The separation between what is best for management and what is best for shareholders gives raise to agency costs. Sequenced funding decreases the agency costs associated with management having private information that they can use to allocate their effort between generating information about the project and private consumption. Sequenced funding allows the venture capitalist to update his beliefs about the success of the project at the end of each period and decide whether to fund the next round.[22] Sequenced funding also decreases the problem associated with management behaving opportunistically and renegotiating with the venture capitalists for a larger share of the value once the investment has been made and their effort is needed to deliver the value.[23] Sequential funding is also better than upfront funding because of contracting limitations. An upfront contract cannot include all possible contingencies that will emerge over the life of a company. Sequential funding alleviates this limitation: because it does not require making all information explicit, new information gets embedded in the next round of funding.[24] Otherwise, the venture capitalist would need to price protect himself, reducing the rents to the management team. Thus, sequential funding helps entrepreneurs capture a larger share of the value that they generate.

These models separate an initial round where an entrepreneur bound by a cash constraint receives funding and where an agency relationship is established from follow-up rounds. These follow-up rounds rely on the threat to the entrepreneur of hitting his cash constraint to curve agency costs. In contrast to the initial round, where the cash constraint is binding, this constraint is not binding in equilibrium for follow-up rounds.

All these arguments suggest different roles for initial versus follow-up rounds. In all cases, the sequential funding is not intended to remove unexpected cash constraints; only the initial round supplies cash to a cash-hungry company; follow-up rounds exist to curve down the loss in value that emerges from the separation between the investor (venture capitalist) and management (the entrepreneur) that leads to agency costs. Follow-up rounds provide cash that the company needs to grow, but in contrast to the initial round, cash in follow-up rounds is supplied before it is needed to avoid halting growth for reasons unrelated to the strategy of the company. The threat of hitting a cash constraint allows sequential funding to fulfill its governance role. These arguments suggest that on average, companies will receive follow-up rounds before they need the cash; but for the threat to be credible in a few cases, venture capitalists will wait until the start-up runs out of cash to provide the needed liquidity.

This pattern is reflected in headcount growth around funding events. Headcount is the main use of cash in many start-up firms; therefore, cash constraints are reflected in the inability of these firms to grow their headcount until funds become available. Even if the likelihood of a funding round is credible enough for new employees to be willing to join the company, the lack of funds precludes growth until funds are received. This scenario is consistent with early rounds. In contrast, start-up firms that do not face cash constraints can fund their growth as soon as the signal that the firm will receive additional funds associated with the funding event becomes credible. This scenario is consistent with arguments for late rounds of funding, when cash constraints are used in the bargaining process to reduce agency costs, but funding comes before these constraints are binding.

When the cash constraints are not binding, headcount should be unrelated to when the funding happens. Conversely, when cash constraints are binding, headcount shows a significant change in its growth pattern as soon as money becomes available. In particular, headcount growth will be significantly larger in the months after a funding round compared to the months previous to the event.

Signaling

Another relevant effect of funding rounds within a company is their value as signals about the quality of the company. The role of signals has long been part of the economics literature as mechanisms to reduce uncertainty.[25] Funding not only makes cash available to the company, but also indicates that informed and sophisticated investors—venture capitalists—trust the future of the company. Before each round of financing, venture capitalists perform a thorough analysis of the company they intend to fund. They access information internal to the company and match this information with their experience and knowledge of the industry to evaluate its prospects. This piece of information signals the quality of the company. Employees are more likely to stay if this signal is positive.

This signal mechanism is valuable not only to external constituencies such as customers, suppliers, and partners, but also to internal employees. Internally, a round of financing brings new information that adds to the beliefs that employees have about the quality of the company and its attractiveness as a workplace. The funding round indicates that outside experts having access to different and probably richer information than employees find the company attractive to invest in. If the uncertainty about the future of the firm is large, the updating of employees' beliefs associated with the early funding rounds may be significant enough to affect their decisions to remain in the firm. The value of this signal decreases over the life of the venture as uncertainty decreases. The uncertainty about the viability of the business model decreases and the value of signals decreases as companies mature. Therefore, the signaling value of funding rounds is higher in early rounds, compared to late rounds when the uncertainty about the prospects of the start-up firm has been reduced. Employees' decisions about remaining in the company are a good indication of the value of the signal, and employee turnover will decrease when a positive signal—such as a funding round—happens. As uncertainty decreases, the relevance of the signal to employees' decisions to remain in the firm decreases and the impact upon turnover becomes less significant.

DESCRIPTION OF THE SAMPLE AND VARIABLES

Sample

We gathered the sample from a Professional Employer Organization (PEO). The company specializes in providing outsourced human resource services to small firms, mainly in the San Francisco Bay Area but also throughout the United States. Over time, it has developed a strong relationship with venture capital firms and is perceived as a cost-effective full-service solution for the human resources needs of small companies. Companies using its services typically outsource all their human resources needs. Outsourcing non-core activities like payroll is perceived as a way to focus scarce management attention on more high-value-added activities.

The database provides the number of employees in each company in the sample per month and the number of new hires and number of employees who left the company. It includes information about companies that were in the system at some point between January 1994 and December 1999, and we collected information through May 2000. The database grows over time as the PEO, itself also a start-up, grew over this time period. To identify those firms in the sample that received venture funding, we matched the names of the firms against two proprietary databases that follow the venture capital industry: VentureOne and Venture Economics. We found 194 firms that were both in the PEO database and at least in one of the venture capital databases. From VentureOne and Venture Economics, we gathered data on the dates of rounds of financing (including IPO), the amount of funding, as well as information regarding the age of the company. Because firms disclosed the information in these databases on a voluntary basis, not all information is available. In particular, the date of founding is available for 170 firms. In total, the sample includes 4,155 firm-months observations with 268 of these firm-months having a financing event. The companies in the sample have a total of 465 financing rounds.

Several caveats regarding the sample are relevant. The sample is not a random sample of venture-backed start-ups. Only companies that choose to outsource their human resources needs are included. Finally, the time period examined may be "abnormal" in that venture capital investments were particularly large in what has become known as the Internet bubble timeframe.

A total of eighty-five venture-backed firms left the database during the observation period. Some firms went out of business. Another set of firms left because the PEO's value proposition was no longer viewed as cost effective— either because they changed their human resource strategy or because they outgrew the services provided by the PEO. An analysis of companies exiting indicates that these companies were relatively smaller or had stayed relatively longer in the database. This exit pattern apparently reflects two types of start-ups. One type is smaller companies. The other is older companies; this is consistent with the probability of bringing human resource management inside increasing with age.[26] The loss of smaller companies may bias the sample toward more successful start-ups, while the loss of older ones may introduce a bias toward companies in the early stages of their lives. However, neither of these two effects is expected to affect the behavior around the rounds of funding.

Table 8.1 presents descriptive statistics for the sample. The sample is heavily biased toward high technology industries (Panel A), consistent with the focus of venture capital funds. Headcount-related expenses are typically the single largest cost category for these firms in their formative years.[27] Panel B summarizes the average number of rounds for companies founded in different time periods. The median number of rounds is two. Companies founded in the 1997–99 period have fewer rounds, in part due to being in existence for a shorter period and in part due to going to IPO in faster time. Panel C presents financing statistics for the sample. The amount of funds raised increases from $4.46 million (median $3.00 million) for early rounds (which include seed and first rounds) to $12.25 million (median $8.55 mllion) for later rounds (second to fourth rounds). The mean post-money valuation increases from $10.03 million (median $7.28 million) for early rounds to $59.98 million (median $37.50 million) for later rounds. The companies in the sample had 465 financing events, 220 early round events, 225 late rounds, and twenty fifth and sixth rounds. Panel D provides timelines on the database.

Out of the 465 venture funding events, we have headcount growth information for 268 of them. Panel A in Table 8.2 describes the distribution of

TABLE 8.1.   Descriptive Statistics for Firms in the Sample

Panel A: Industry Statistics

	Venture-backed Firms
Communications and Networking	28
Electronics and Computer Hardware	8
Semiconductors	8
Software	51
Information Services	35
Healthcare and Biotechnology	19
Business and Consumer Services and Products	<u>21</u>
Total	**170**

Panel B: Number of Financing Rounds for Companies in the Sample

Founded	Mean	Median	Minimum	Maximum	Standard Deviation	♯ of Companies
Before 1994	3.10	3	1	7	1.97	20
1994–96	3.36	3.5	1	6	1.42	70
1997–99	2.13	2	1	5	1.10	80
Total	**2.75**	**2**	**1**	**7**	**1.47**	**170**

Rounds of Financing	Amount raised (in millions of dollars)			Post-money Valuation (in millions of dollars)			Number of Rounds
	Mean	Median	Standard Deviation	Mean	Median	Standard Deviation	
Early Rounds	4.46	3.00	6.64	10.03	7.28	9.84	220
Late Rounds	12.25	8.55	8.30	59.98	37.50	80.94	225
Additional Rounds	23.47	23.47	12.35	181.05	161.00	113.13	20
Overall	**$9.08**	**$5.00**	**$12.35**	**$46.56**	**$20.50**	**$76.52**	**465**

Panel D: Evolution of the Database over Time

Year	1994	1995	1996	1997	1998	1999	2000	**Total**
Venture-backed Firms Year End	19	29	64	47	98	109	101	**194**
Number of Employees	389	832	1,832	3,755	5,426	9,371	6,477	**27,193**
Bi-monthly Data Points	5,400	11,446	23,264	51,798	74,980	116,120	49,270	**585,497**

TABLE 8.2. Descriptive Statistics for Research Variables

Panel A: Events in the Sample

Number of Months	4,155
Number of Months with Financing Event	268
Number of Early Round Events (rounds zero and one)	79
Number of Late Round Events (rounds two, three, and four)	165
Number of Other Rounds (round five and six)	12
Number of IPOs	12

Panel B: Size, Growth, and Turnover for Venture-backed Startups

	Mean	Standard Deviation	10% Quartile	90% Quartile	Median
Employee Growth (per month)	1.63	8.10	−1	6	1
Number of Employees	31.38	34.66	4	70	21
Turnover	0.058	0.166	0	0.111	0
Time in the sample (in months)	26.1	16.5	9	52	23

Panel C: Correlation Table

	Turnover	Ln (size)	Ln (age)
Growth	−0.29	0.27	−0.12
Turnover		0.05	0.16
Ln (size)			0.39

these events; seventy-nine correspond to early rounds (seed and first round), 165 are late rounds (second, third, and fourth), and twelve are fifth and sixth rounds. An additional twelve events correspond to companies in the sample that went public but remained in the sample. We have an additional 3,887 firm-month observations with no funding event. Panel B presents descriptive statistics on the variables used in the study. Venture-backed companies have thirty-one employees on average with an average monthly growth of 1.80 employees. Panel C presents the correlation among the variables in the research.[28] Growth is positively correlated with lower turnover, suggesting that growth may proxy for success and thus employee retention. Growth is also correlated with size but negatively with age. Turnover as well as size increase with the age of the company.

Headcount Growth and Employee Turnover

Employee growth, which we use to capture the existence of a binding cash constraint, is constructed as follows. For each month, we count the number of employees in each company in the sample. We use this count to estimate the change in the number of employees. A limitation of this measure is that it does not include outside consultants and contractors. We do not have hard data to evaluate the potential impact of this limitation. However, the PEO management believes that the start-ups in their database do not use these outside contractors significantly.

A start-up's ability to secure venture funds sends a strong signal about the prospects of the start-up to both the external and internal constituents in the organization. We use employee turnover as a measure of the signaling value of venture funding within the company. Turnover is measured as follows. The database has information at the employee level and allows us to track when a particular person left a company. To estimate turnover in a specific month, the number of people who left the company during that month is divided by the headcount at the end of the previous month. This is computed for each month on a company-by-company basis. Given the importance of salary to employees, we view our estimate of turnover as being a reliable measure.

ROUNDS OF FUNDING INFORMATION

The date of each funding round provides the event to anchor the evolution of headcount and turnover variables. Figure 8.1 illustrates how funding events in calendar time are translated into event time for the particular case of a funding event that happened in February 1999. We classify the various rounds of financing as early or late rounds of financing. Early rounds are seed and first rounds and proxy for the initial round described in theoretical models where cash constraint is binding. Second, third, and fourth rounds are classified as late rounds and proxy for follow-up rounds. This classification is similar to VentureOne's classification. A small number of companies go through a fifth and sixth round (twelve observations). We separate these rounds because they may be used for different purposes compared to early and late rounds. In particular, they may be used as a mezzanine round before the initial public offering. Alternatively, they may be an interim stage due to the IPO environment not being viewed as "friendly."[29]

FIGURE 8.1. Event Study Research Design

In addition to the date of each funding round, we also collected the amount of funding received. Theory has little to say on how amount of funding affects the evolution of firms. But we can conjecture that where firms are cash constrained (early rounds), larger amounts of funding allow firms to pursue more aggressive growth strategies once they receive the resources. In late rounds, where there are no cash, this association will not exist. If firms with cash resources on hand have very good knowledge of the amount of funding forthcoming, then they can adapt their growth strategy to this variable in the months prior to the funding event. If this is the case, then growth after the funding event relative to growth prior to the event is not associated with the size of funding. However, if the firm is uncertain about the amount of funding that it will receive in a round, the actual realization of this variable affects its growth path going forward. In particular, larger amounts of funding allow firms to pursue a more ambitious growth strategy. This inflection in the growth path will be realized close to the date of the funding round, when the funding terms are fixed.

To fully identify the effect of the funding event, we adjust our analysis for the size of the company measured as number of employees, age of the company, and industry.

EVIDENCE

The Differential Role of Cash Constraints over Funding Rounds

To examine whether growth increases significantly after an early funding round, but not after a late round, we examine the path of employee growth in the months prior and subsequent to the funding event.[30]

For each of the 268 venture-capital financing events in our sample, we identify the month in which the event happened (termed Month 0). We restrict the study to Month 0 and the six months surrounding this event month (prior three months and subsequent three months) when we expect the impact of funding to be most significant to the start-up. We choose three months as a window likely to capture the time period when the information about an upcoming round becomes progressively more credible and the time period when the firm implements the changes associated with having new funds. We identify three different time periods around a funding event—three months prior to the event, the event month, and three months subsequent to the event. We examine absolute growth in number of employees per month.[31]

Figure 8.2 plots growth in employees for early (Panel A) and late rounds (Panel B) (see Appendix A reports the statistical analysis). Each figure plots the mean growth in the three months before the funding round, the month of the funding round, and the three months after the funding round. In addition, it plots the growth 1.5 standard deviations above and below the mean (labeled as minimum and maximum). In early rounds, there is a clear growth

Panel A: Early Rounds

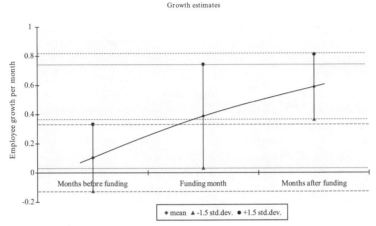

Panel B: Late Rounds

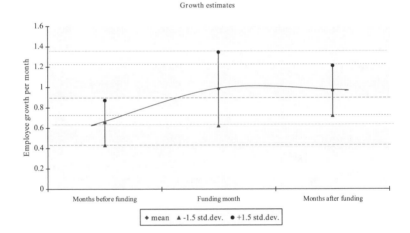

FIGURE 8.2.   Employee Growth around Early and Late Funding Rounds

pattern from the months before the funding to the months after the funding, with the difference between growth in the months before and growths in the month after very significant. In later rounds, growth per month is larger, as is expected in older start-up firms, but there is no clear growth pattern; moreover, the growth in months before, funding month, and months after the round of funding are not significantly different. This pattern suggests that firms ramp up hiring in these later rounds before the cash infusion takes place rather than having to wait for the actual cash coming, which is the pattern for early rounds. This evidence is consistent with early rounds releasing cash constraints that limit the growth of start-up firms, while late rounds serve as monitoring or real-option mechanisms where cash constraints are not binding in equilibrium.[32]

The Effect of Funding Amount

We extend the previous analysis to examine the effect of funding amount on employee growth around funding events. A significant relationship suggests that the amount of funds influences firms' growth strategies.[33]

Figure 8.3 presents the results (also see Appendix B). It plots the additional change in employees from three months before the funding to three months after the funding for each additional million dollars in funding. Again, minimum and maximum describe the 1.5 standard deviation interval. Together with Figure 8.2, this evidence indicates that not only is the funding relevant to the release of the binding cash constraint in early rounds, but it is also associated with the growth path of the firm. For late rounds, where cash constraints are not binding, the results also show a positive association between growth and amount of funding. This evidence suggests that firms adapt their growth strategy to the funding obtained.

The Differential Signaling Value of Funding Events

Figure 8.4 examines turnover centered on the month when a funding event happens (Month 0) (see also Appendix C). Again, the figure plots the

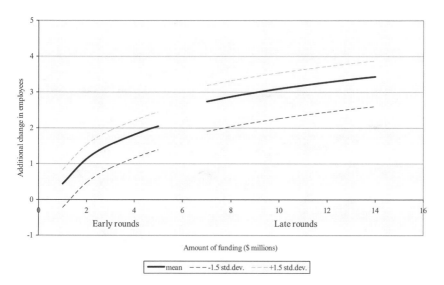

FIGURE 8.3. Amount of Funding and Employee Growth

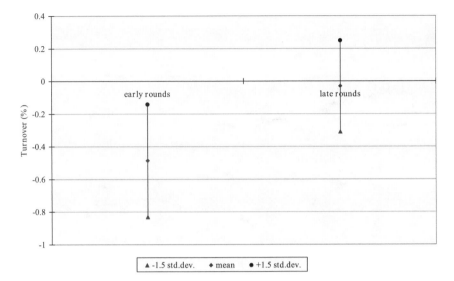

FIGURE 8.4. Employee Turnover around Rounds of Funding

mean turnover, and minimum and maximum indicate 1.5 standard deviations from the mean. Turnover is significantly lower in early rounds but not different from zero in later rounds. This observation indicates that the signaling value of an early round has much more information than in later rounds. If the uncertainty of a start-up firm decreases over its life, the value of an external positive signal is more valuable early on. Initially, employees may assign a significant value to the decisions of external investors; at this stage, uncertainty is large and any piece of information from players with access to a different information set has a significant impact on the employees' updating of the firm's prospects. However, the value of an additional signal is less relevant in updating employees' beliefs in late rounds when the uncertainty has decreased. We also compared turnover in early rounds with turnover during the months prior to these rounds. It might be the case that the employee pool in early rounds is different from the employee pool in later rounds. The turnover in the early rounds window is significantly smaller than in the months prior to these rounds.

We further examined whether the amount of funding had any effect on turnover (see Appendix C). The evidence indicates that the existence of an early round is enough to decrease turnover, and the amount of the round is insignificant. In contrast, turnover around later rounds decreases with the amount of funding. This evidence suggests that larger amounts in late rounds have information value to employees.

CONCLUSION

This chapter addresses the role of cash constraints over the sequenced funding structure of venture capital investments. Cash constraints are an important topic in entrepreneurial finance because of their role in inhibiting new ventures' growth. While this effect is important in early rounds of venture-backed companies, sequential funding theory assigns a different role to these constraints in late rounds of funding. We find very different patterns between early rounds and late rounds of venture funding. The pattern of employee growth in early rounds is consistent with the role of external funding as releasing cash constraints. For late rounds, the pattern is also consistent with theory predictions where cash constraints are part of the bargaining between the various players—entrepreneur, existing investors, and external investors— but in equilibrium are not binding. We also find that the amount of funding is significantly associated with growth for both early and late rounds. We also document that the signaling value of a funding event is significant in early rounds of funding when uncertainty about the prospects of the firm is larger. In late rounds, the event itself is not significant, but the amount of funding has signaling value.

NOTES

1. For a detailed discussion of funding alternatives available to start-up firms, see P. A. Gompers and J. Lerner, *The Venture Capital Cycle* (Cambridge, MA: MIT Press, 1999).

2. Throughout the paper, the term sequential funding is used to refer to the successive rounds of funding that happen in a venture capital funding environment. The term sequential funding is in contrast to staged funding, which is used to refer to the possibility of staging the disbursement of cash within a funding round. This staging may be linked to meeting intermediate milestones.

3. For a classic article on the characteristics of venture capital, see W. A. Sahlman, "The Structure and Governance of Venture-capital Organizations," *Business Economics* 29 (1990): 35–37.

4. The idea of sequential funding as a real option has been elaborated from an academic perspective in D. Bergemann and U. Hege, "Venture Capital, Moral Hazard, and Learning," *Journal of Banking and Finance* 22 (1998): 703–735.

5. The costs associated with the separation of ownership and control are called agency costs. For a seminal article on this topic, see M. C. Jensen and W. H. Meckling, "Theory of the Firm: Managerial Behavior, Agency Costs, and Ownership Structure," *Journal of Financial Economics* 3(4) (1976): 305–360. For the application of agency costs to venture capital backed start-ups see A. R. Admati and P. Pfleiderer, "Robust Financial Contracting and the Role of Venture Capitalists," *The Journal of Finance* 49 (1994): 371–402.

6. For a theoretical elaboration on how the liquidity constraint limits agency costs, see P. Bolton and D. S. Scharfstein, "A Theory of Predation Based on Agency Problems in Financial Contracting," *The American Economic Review* 8 (1) (1990): 93–106.

7. See, for instance, references in prior footnotes and S. Wang and H. Zhou, "Staged Financing in Venture Capital: Moral Hazard and Risks," *Journal of Corporate Finance* (2002):131–156.

8. For a discussion on how cash constraints limit the growth of early start-up firms, see D. S. Evans and B. Jovanovic, "An Estimated Model of Entrepreneurial Choice Under Liquidity Constraints," *Journal of Political Economy* 97 (4) (1989): 808–827.

9. Payroll expenses are typically the largest use of cash in these firms and cash constraints are reflected in the ability to grow headcount.

10. Venture capital funding rounds also have signaling value to external parties. See L. W. Busenitz, J. O. Fiet, and D. D. Moesel, "Signaling in Venture Capitalist— New Venture Funding Decisions: Does it Indicate Long-term Venture Outcomes?" *Entrepreneurship, Theory and Practice* 29 (1) (2005): 1–28.

11. For an academic analysis of the characteristics of venture-backed start-up firms, see P. A. Gompers, "Optimal Investment, Mmonitoring, and the Staging of Venture Capital," *The Journal of Finance 50* (1995): 1461–1489.

12. For a list of the various roles that venture capitalists have, see H. J. Sapienza, A. K. Gupta, "Impact of Agency Risks and Task Uncertainty on Venture Capitalists-CEO Interaction," *Academy of Management Journal* (37) (1994): 1618–1632. Also see Martin Haemmig in this book.

13. For the governance role of venture capitalists, see J. Lerner, "Venture Capitalists and the Oversight of Private Firms," *The Journal of Finance* 50 (1995): 301–319, and K. M. Robie, M. Wright, et al., "The Monitoring of Venture Capital Firms," *Entrepreneurship Theory and Practice* (1997): 9–27.

14. Venture capital-backed firms have been shown to professionalize their management team faster than regular firms. See T. Hellmann and M. Puri, 2001, "Venture Capital and the Professionalization of Start-up Firms: Empirical Evidence," *Journal of Finance* 57 (1): 169–197.

15. Top management incentives in venture-backed firms also present some unique characteristics. See S. N. Kaplan and P. Stromberg, "Financial Contracting Theory Meets the Real World: An Empirical Analysis of Venture Capital Contracts," (2000) *NBER Working Papers 7660*.

16. See, for instance, J. Hall and C. W. Hofer, "Venture Capitalists' Decision Criteria in New Venture Evaluation," *Journal of Business Venturing* 8 (1993): 25–43.

17. See, for example, W. L. Meggison and K. A. Weiss, "Venture Capital Certification in Initial Public Offerings," *Journal of Finance* 46 (1991).

18. See on this issue W. Bygrave and J. Timmons, *Venture Capital at the Crossroads* (Boston: Harvard Business School Press, 1992).

19. On this issue, see J. A. C. Baum, T. Calabrese, and B. S. Siverman, "Don't Go It Alone: Alliance Network Composition and Start-Ups' Performance in Canadian Biotechnology," *Strategic Management Journal* 21 (2000): 267–294.

20. The cash constraints that entrepreneurial firms face are shown in D. Holtz-Eakin, D. Joulfaian, and H. S. Rosen, "Entrepreneurial Decisions and Liquidity Constraints," *RAND Journal of Economics* 25 (2) (1994): 334–347.

21. This real option structure can also be embedded within funding rounds. In particular, the disbursements associated with a funding round can be contractually staged over the achievement of certain intermediate milestones. This chapter only examines the empirical effects of the real option structure associated with interfunding rounds and not intrafunding (effects within) rounds.

22. These arguments are developed in an analytical model in D. Bergemann and U. Hege, "Venture Capital, Moral Hazard, and Learning," *Journal of Banking and Finance* 22 (1998): 703–735.

23. This problem is the "hold-up" problem where a party captures most of the value after the other party has invested because the former is necessary for value to be delivered but the latter is not. See D. V. Neher, "Staged Financing: An Agency Perspective," *Review of Economic Studies* 66 (1999): 255–274.

24. For an analytical development of this argument, see L. Kockesen and S. Ozerturk, "Staged Financing and Endogenous Lock-in: A Model of Start-up Finance," Working paper, Columbia University (2002).

25. Some classical pieces on signaling are G. A. Akerlof, "The Market for 'Lemons': Quality Uncertainty and the Market Mechanisms," *Quarterly Journal of Economics* 84 (1970): 488–500; M. A. Spence, *Market Signaling: Information Transfer in Hiring and Related Screening Processes* (Cambridge, MA: Harvard University Press, 1974); D. M. Kreps, *A Course in Microeconomic Theory* (Princeton, NJ: Princeton University Press, 1990).

26. For evidence on this pattern, see J. N. Baron, D. M. Burton, and M. T. Hannan, "The Road Taken: Origins and Evolution of Employment Systems in Emerging Companies," *Industrial and Corporate Change* 5 (1996): 239–275.

27. Prior evidence indicates that employee growth is positively associated with growth in pre-money valuation across sequential venture capital funding rounds. See A. Davila, G. Foster, and M. Gupta, "Venture Capital Financing and the Growth of Start-Up Firms," *Journal of Business* Venturing 18 (2003): 689–708.

28. All correlations are significant at the 1 percent level.

29. The database includes company-month observations with information on headcount and turnover as well as funding. If a company joined the PEO system after several rounds of funding, we do not have headcount information for the months when these early rounds happened. However, we identify whether a funding event happened right before the company joined PEO, and we can identify the first months of headcount and turnover information as being post-funding event months. Similarly, we do not have information for companies that had funding rounds after they left the headcount database; but if a funding event happened just after the company dropped out of the database, we can flag the last months in the database as pre-funding event months.

30. We use a pooled regression specification: $Employee\_growth_{j,t} = \alpha + \Sigma_{i=prior, event, subsequent} \gamma_i Early\_Round_{j,t} * Month\_Dummy_{i,j,t} + \Sigma_{i= prior, event, subsequent} \eta_i Late\_Round_{j,t} * Month\_Dummy_{i,j,t} + \Sigma \beta_i Control\_Variables_{j,t} + \varepsilon$. In addition to using relative growth as a robustness check (see Appendix A), we also examined for the possibility of "momentum." It has been argued that past growth fuels future growth. We use an instrumental variable approach to proxy for the lagged dependent variable; we also control for

autocorrelation in the residuals using an AR(1) model and use a Prais-Winsten estimator. Results are comparable.

31. Appendix A also includes the statistical analysis for growth relative to company size at the beginning of month −3.

32. While theory predicts particular roles for early and late funding rounds, there may be additional roles unrelated to cash constraints. For example, Microsoft and eBay [reportedly] sought venture capital funding not because of cash constraints or agency problems within the current governance structure, but because having a seasoned investor would increase their chances of a successful IPO.

33. We also examine this question using statistical analysis with the following specification separately for early and late rounds: $Employee\_growth_j = \alpha + \gamma \ Funding\_amount_j + \Sigma \ \beta_i \ Control\_Variables_j + \varepsilon$. We also run the specification with the dependent variable defined relative to size at the beginning of month −3. We also run a similar specification with employee growth defined as the difference between number of employees in month +3 and in month −3. Conclusions do not change.

APPENDIX A
Funding Events and Monthly Headcount Growth

	Employee Growth		Relative Employee Growth	
	Coefficient	t-stat	Coefficient	t-stat
lnsize	0.798***	12.27		
lnage	−0.633***	−10.01	−0.036***	−11.63
efm	0.104	0.68	0.024**	2.00
ef0	0.388	1.64	0.017	1.05
efp	0.588***, ++	3.95	0.049***, +	5.23
lfm	0.651***	4.43	0.025***	4.27
lf0	0.984***	4.09	0.026***	3.05
lfp	0.966***	5.94	0.028***	5.10
Communications and networking	−0.458**	−2.23	−0.007	−0.89
Electronics and computer hardware	0.071	0.26	0.016	1.27
Semiconductors	−0.628***	−2.67	−0.006	−0.53
Software	−0.515***	−2.66	−0.013*	−1.83
Information services	−0.106	−0.47	−0.001	−0.09
Biotechnology	−0.747***	−3.95	−0.020**	−2.56
Constant	1.371***	5.29	0.182***	14.89
Adjusted R^2	0.12		0.11	
♯ of observations	3,843		3,815	

- Employee growth is the difference in size between sequential months.
- Relative employee growth is employee growth relative to size at the end of the previous month.
- *lnsize* is the log of size at the beginning of the month, *lnage* is the age at the beginning of the month,
- *efm* (*lfm*) is a dummy that takes value of one for the three months prior to an early (late) funding event,
- *ef0* (*lf0*) is a dummy variable that takes value of one for the month of an early (late) funding event,
- *efp* (*lfp*) is a dummy variable that takes value of one for the three months subsequent to an early (late) funding event.
- *Hardware IT* includes "communications and networking," "electronics and computer hardware," and "semiconductors;" *software IT* includes "software" and "information services." The reference industry is "business and consumer services and products."

Dummy variables controlling for months prior and subsequent to rounds fifth and sixth and IPO events included but not reported. To avoid the influence of outliers, we eliminate the top and bottom 5% of the dependent variable's observations. The specification controls for autocorrelation in the White-adjusted residuals. ***, **, * indicates significantly different from zero at the 1%, 5%, and 10% respectively. ++ indicates significantly different from *efm* at 5%, + indicates significantly different from *efm* at 10%.

APPENDIX B
Employee Growth Prior and Subsequent to Funding Events

Panel A: Early Rounds

| | Employee growth | | Relative employee growth | |
	Coefficient	t-stat	Coefficient	t-stat
lnsize	1.700	1.16		
lnage	−0.926	−1.27	−0.110	−1.34
lnamt	1.554***	3.10	0.140**	2.45
Hardware IT	−1.848	−0.62	−0.505	−1.67
Software IT	0.736	0.28	−0.174	−0.68
Biotechnology	−0.875	−0.34	−0.020	−0.06
Constant	0.315	0.10	0.638**	2.01
Adjusted R^2	0.07		0.08	
♯ of observations	51		50	

APPENDIX B (CONTINUED)

Panel B: Late Rounds

	Employee growth		Relative employee growth	
	Coefficient	t-stat	Coefficient	t-stat
lnsize	0.803	0.83		
lnage	1.906	1.58	0.046	0.91
lnamt	2.209***	2.66	0.041	1.35
Hardware IT	−3.941	−1.40	−0.134	−1.21
Software IT	−2.026	−0.76	−0.140	−1.43
Biotechnology	−6.353***	−2.60	−0.233	−1.58
Constant	−6.668	−1.39	0.033	0.15
Adjusted R2	0.07		0.00	
♯ of observations	141		140	

- Employee growth is the change in employees in months $[+1, +3]$ minus the change in employees in months $[−3, −1]$.
- Relative employee growth is relative to company size at the beginning of month $−3$.
- *lnsize* is the log of size at the beginning of the month,
- *lnage* is the age at the beginning of the month,
- *lnamt* is the log of the funding amount.
- *Hardware IT* includes "communications and networking," "electronics and computer hardware," and "semiconductors;" *software IT* includes "software" and "information services." The reference industry is "business and consumer services and products.

To avoid the influence of outliers, we eliminate the top and bottom 2% of dependent variables' observations. Standard errors are White-adjusted. ***, ** indicates significantly different from zero at the 1% and 5% respectively.

APPENDIX C
Rounds of Financing and Employee Turnover

Panel A: Signaling Value of Funding Events

	Turnover	
	Coefficient	t-stat
lnsize	0.004***	3.92
lnage	0.007***	6.38
ef	−0.005**	−2.11
lf	−0.000	−0.17

APPENDIX C (CONTINUED)

	Turnover	
	Coefficient	t-stat
Communications and networking	−0.009***	−2.94
Electronics and computer hardware	−0.014***	−3.09
Semiconductors	−0.013***	−3.02
Software	−0.004	−1.45
Information services	0.000	0.04
Biotechnology	−0.008**	−2.27
Constant	−0.000	−0.08
Adjusted R²	0.04	
♯ of observations	3,904	

- Turnover is defined as the number of people leaving the company in a particular month relative to the number of employees at the beginning of the month.
- *lnsize* is the log of size at the beginning of the month,
- *lnage* is the age at the beginning of the month,
- *ef* (*lf*) is a dummy that takes value of one for months [−3, 3] around an early (late) funding event.
- The reference industry is "business and consumer services and products."

Dummy variables controlling for months around late rounds and IPO events included but not reported. To avoid the influence of outliers, we eliminate the top and bottom 2% of the dependent variable's observations. The specification controls for autocorrelation in the White-adjusted residuals. ***, **, * indicates significantly different from zero at the 1%, 5%, and 10% respectively.

Panel B: Signaling value of Funding Events and Funding Amount

	Turnover	
	Coefficient	t-stat
lnsize	0.004	
lnage	0.007***	−11.63
ef	−0.007**	−2.02
lf	0.008*	1.84
Efaf	0.002	0.82
lfaf	−0.004**	−2.38

APPENDIX C (CONTINUED)

	Turnover	
	Coefficient	t-stat
Communications and networking	−0.009***	−2.88
Electronics and computer hardware	−0.013***	−3.03
Semiconductors	−0.012***	−2.89
Software	−0.005	−1.55
Information services	0.000	0.11
Biotechnology	−0.008**	−2.22
Constant	0.000	0.10
Adjusted R^2	0.04	
♯ of observations	3,904	

- *Efaf* (*lfaf*) is *ef*(*lf*) times the amount of funding. Other variables and specifications as in Panel A.

9

Sector-Focused Incubation: A Tool for Promoting Technology Innovation and Commercialization

JAMES ROBBINS

N umerous opportunities arise every year for the commercialization of technology innovations from early-stage, or start-up, technology companies and from innovators within established corporations. While innovation can occur in many forms, the introduction of technology innovation into the marketplace is a primary process for making innovation work. One proven strategy for moving great ideas to commercialization is the "technology incubator."

A technology incubator is a specialized type of business incubation organization whose mission is to provide business resources and professional services geared toward improving the success of early-stage technology businesses. Their goals are to bring innovative technology to the marketplace and to produce successful firms.

This chapter identifies some of the challenges related to bringing innovation to the marketplace, explains how technology incubation can help solve these challenges, and provides examples of such incubation programs being used to assist emerging technology start-ups and corporations in commercializing technology innovations.

CHALLENGES TO INNOVATION

The majority of potentially revolutionary ideas fail to successfully translate into market-changing realities. Despite the existence of multiple business and government entities, nonprofit organizations, and other agencies, which have an interest in implementing successful technology innovation, many innovative ideas and the technology developers who champion them fail to create processes that can bring such innovation into the marketplace.

There are numerous barriers to technology innovation and commercialization that prevent innovations from reaching the marketplace. Some of the biggest problems include:

- failure to protect intellectual property,
- founding teams with poor business skills,
- inadequate understanding of commercial markets,
- failure to develop adequate business and financial plans, and
- inadequate capitalization.

In addition, those innovations developed within established companies often encounter corporate processes that discourage innovation and entrepreneurship, hamper introduction of new technology into the marketplace, and often shelve viable new technology if it is inconsistent with the markets for existing mainstream corporate products.

Designing an innovation strategy is one key step to solving such challenges. The first role of an innovation strategy is to "increase the efficiency of the innovation process" in order "to move great ideas from concept to commercialization with speed and minimum use of resources."[1] A key element of successful innovation strategy must include approaches to support the start-up and growth of small technology businesses.

SMALL BUSINESSES DRIVE INNOVATION

Recently, there has been increasing recognition that small businesses are the engine of innovation and economic change. Small businesses represent a growing share of the country's highly innovative firms (defined as those with fifteen or more patents), increasing from 33 percent of the pool in 2000 to 40 percent in 2002. Small businesses also represented 65 percent of the companies in a U.S. Small Business Administration (SBA) report's list of most highly innovative companies in 2002.[2]

This SBA report finds that small firms' contributions to technological innovations are best measured industry-by-industry. Their impact is particularly significant in emerging research and technology-intensive fields. In biotechnology, for example, small firm research and technologies are said to be used by large firms at a rate of 60 percent higher than expected, and 41 percent of all biotech patent citations go to small firms. In fact, 66 percent of patent citations from large biotech companies and 79 percent of those from small companies are associated with the earlier work of small firms. This finding conforms with the generally held notion that small firms lead the creation and technological growth of emerging industries before larger firms take on dominant roles through consolidations, mergers, and acquisitions. The study also finds that larger firms are more likely to use the patents and technologies generated by small firms than acquire the firms in their entirety.[3] Thus, efforts to stimulate and improve innovation efforts within small technology start-ups are key to making innovation work.

TECHNOLOGY INCUBATORS IMPROVE BUSINESS SUCCESS

Technology incubation programs accelerate the successful development of innovative concepts in entrepreneurial companies through an array of targeted business support resources and services, developed or orchestrated by incubator management and offered both in the incubator and through its network of contacts. They provide the start-up companies with education and assistance in all aspects of their development, including business planning, financing, marketing, sales, management and board development, revenue models, market entry, and strategic partnerships. Technology incubation programs help address many of the technical, market, and business risks that are commonly faced by high-tech entrepreneurs, while providing a supportive environment in which their businesses can grow.

There are nearly 1,000 business incubators in North America and over 3,500 worldwide. A growing number of these are technology incubators focus on new, innovative technology-based companies. According to the National Business Incubation Association, 37 percent of U.S. incubators are technology focused. Of those, almost half focus on information technology and electronics.[4]

Incubation provides multiple benefits not only to the start-ups, but also to other companies and to the community in which it is located. The major benefit for start-ups is dramatic improvement in the success rate of incubated business compared to other small businesses. A recent study by the National Business Incubation Association (NBIA) indicates that businesses that participate in an incubator program *have a success rate of approximately 80 percent over a five-year period*, compared to only 20 percent for non-incubated businesses.

Corporations benefit by creating technology partnerships with emerging young technology companies and by mining incubators for innovations and potential acquisition opportunities. Increasingly, corporations are using relationships with incubators as part of a distributed research portfolio, hoping to identify and take advantage of potentially disruptive technologies.

Perhaps the greatest beneficiaries of technology incubators are the communities in which they are located. As companies graduate from technology incubators, they tend to locate nearby, creating high-level jobs and economic development. Research on this issue showed that more than 84 percent of the businesses locate within five miles of the incubator site after graduating from the incubator program.[5]

When the incubators are focused on specific technologies, they assist in the development of innovation clusters, which can provide a region with a reputation for supporting technology focused on a particular technology area.

SECTOR-FOCUSED ECONOMIC DEVELOPMENT FACILITATES INNOVATION

Innovation clusters, or sectors, may be defined as geographic concentrations of interconnected companies, suppliers, service providers, and others in a particular industry or sector.[6] Many economists have studied the impact of industry clusters on innovation and economic development. These economists often recommend researching evolving technology clusters in a region and linking economic development investments to technology clusters that will help shape innovation in that region. Economists such as Michael Porter at Harvard and groups at SRI in California have developed research methods to identify innovation clusters and measure their growth in metropolitan regions throughout the United States and internationally. Cluster-based economic studies have been used as the basis for regional economic studies in many of these metropolitan regions across the country, and many of these studies have identified incubation, and especially sector-focused incubators, as an important tool in their economic development portfolios.

SECTOR-FOCUSED INCUBATION IS AN EFFECTIVE INNOVATION TOOL

As economic cluster opportunities are identified in city or regional planning studies, sector-focused incubation has become an effective tool for stimulating the growth in the targeted cluster(s).

Sector-focused incubators target business opportunities in a specific industry sector—for example, life science, software, communications technology, agricultural technology, clean energy, etc.—and then concentrate their mission, operations, activities and services on the unique challenges and opportunities that face early-stage companies in that industry.

In a sector-focused incubator, each new company is screened to ensure it is both related to the sector and not directly competitive with other businesses in the incubator. These criteria foster collaboration and synergies among the businesses, and because all are in the same industry, they often leverage one another's technologies and cross-sell products. By directing their efforts in a particular industry, incubator managers can provide a greater depth of assistance and resources that are more specifically tailored to the needs of a company.

Sector-focused incubation concentrated on a particular industry sector attracts investors, business executives, professional service providers, faculty and others with expertise in the area of focus. It also increases the opportunities and interest in technology collaboration and partnership by corporations.

Therefore, a sector-focused incubator can provide the focal point from which groups with the best expertise can meet and help move innovation from early-stage technology development to full commercial scale.

Software Business Cluster

As an example of the effectiveness of sector-focused incubation, the Software Business Cluster (SBC), a software-focused incubator in San Jose, California, has assisted more than 120 companies since its creation in 1994. It operates as a project of San Jose State University, which also operates the Environmental Business Cluster, an incubator focused upon clean energy technology commercialization, and the BioScience Center, an incubator focused on the convergence of life science and IT. Prior to the creation of the SBC, fewer than ten software companies existed in San Jose. At present, more than ninety software companies reside in San Jose and the majority of them were incubated at the SBC. Over $550 million in venture capital has been invested in the companies started in the SBC, with four companies going IPO. Over 1,500 employees now work in San Jose in companies started at the SBC. The SBC is widely credited for stimulating software innovation in San Jose, establishing a process for helping young companies turn their technology into profitable businesses, and creating a culture where entrepreneurial activity and technology innovation can flourish.

Open Technology Business Center

Another example of a sector-focused incubator is the Open Technology Business Center in Beaverton, Oregon. Focused specifically upon open source software, it was developed in partnership with the Open Source Development Laboratory (OSDL), where Linus Torvalds, the creator of Linux, currently works and continues to innovate. A primary purpose of this sector-focused incubator is to assist companies in commercializing technology from OSDL and to stimulate partnerships between the large corporate sponsors of OSDL and the emerging young technology companies that are starting up in the Open Technology Business Center.

Environmental Business Cluster

The Environmental Business Cluster in San Jose, California, has the largest private technology commercialization program for clean energy companies in the U.S. Technology innovation in energy areas as diverse as solar, wind, wave, hydro, electric vehicles, hydrogen fuel cells, and energy efficiency products are all receiving assistance moving through the innovation cycle at the EBC. The EBC has strong partnerships with the National Renewable Energy Lab and the California Energy Commission. Again, in this case, the incubator has partnered with research programs, where innovative technologies are being developed through research grants, and it is helping to move these innovative new technologies through the commercialization process, working with up to twenty-five such start-ups at any given time.

National Alliance of Clean Energy Incubators

Sector-focused incubation is also being used on a national level to foster innovation and technology commercialization. For example, the National Renewable Energy Lab (NREL) has worked with the ten incubators around the U.S. to form the National Alliance of Clean Energy Incubators. This national network of incubators stretching across the U.S. provides locations in all regions of the country for the referral of technologists with clean and renewable energy solutions that need help commercializing their technology. Thus, they can receive technical assistance with their innovations from NREL and the Department of Energy and business assistance for the start-up company from an incubator in their region.

The National Alliance of Clean Energy Incubators has the following goals:

- Access to capital investment
- Business mentoring from energy experts and business leaders
- Facilitation of strategic alliances
- Marketing and public relations assistance
- Technology support services

The Alliance of Clean Energy Incubators also works with NREL to run an annual Venture Investment Forum for clean energy start-ups that are selected through a national competition. It gives the companies selected the opportunity to present their business models to over 250 investors and corporations. The presenting companies receive mentoring from the incubators and other business mentors. These incubation programs are helping to accelerate the rate at which clean energy technology is reaching the marketplace.

TechBridge

In a similar manner, the Chesapeake Innovation Center (CIC), the nation's first homeland security technology incubator, in partnership with the National Security Agency and more than ten other major corporations, has formed TechBridge. TechBridge is an incubation program that enables the CIC to introduce emerging homeland security technology companies from incubators around the U.S. to major homeland technology users, such as the National Security Agency, the Department of Homeland Security, state and federal government agencies, and major corporations such as Northrop Grumman, Bearing Point, Arinc, Boeing, and others.

The CIC performs targeted technology scouting and market intelligence into emerging technology companies for the government agencies. It provides access to major partners, market acceleration, and strategic business assistance to innovative technology companies in the homeland security sector.

Incubators bridge the gaps that exist between technology innovation, business development, and market entry. The incubator itself aims to be an innovative organization that promotes learning within a framework designed to meet certain characteristics that have been recognized to accelerate and support innovation, including:

- Specific processes or programs for client companies (entrepreneurs)
- A systems approach to commercialization that recognizes the complex organization dynamics of start-ups
- A shared vision of the technology sector's importance and the need for entrepreneurial activity to support innovation in the sector
- Flexibility and agility in response to problems that enhance innovation and create an environment conducive to market success
- A timely on-site process to anticipate and minimize the risks associated with business start-up and commercialization
- A collaborative and interactive environment that maximizes creativity while minimizing destructive tensions.[7]

CORPORATIONS AND INCUBATION

Corporations also use technology incubators to accelerate innovation. Fundamentally, the assistance provided by technology incubators can assist private entrepreneurs and companies to address the "innovation gap" identified by Henry Chesbrough in his book *Open Innovation*. As Chesbrough notes, corporations should make use of external innovation, allow others to share their corporate innovation concepts, use start-ups as sources of learning for technology alternatives, and interact with start-ups to stimulate innovation.[8]

Panasonic

The Panasonic Incubator was created in 1999 by Panasonic Ventures, an arm of Matsushita Corporation in Japan and parent to Panasonic Technologies, the U.S. consumer products company. Cited as a best practices incubator by the National Business Incubation Association, the U.S. professional incubation association, and subject to a case study published by the Harvard University Business School, the Panasonic Incubator was formed to help this $67 billion international firm create technology partnerships between innovative emerging Silicon Valley technology start-ups with disruptive technology and the corporation's innovative research groups in Japan. Now called the Panasonic Collaboration Center, its mission is clearly focused upon attracting and working with disruptive technologies:

CASE STUDY: THE PANASONIC TECHNOLOGY COLLABORATION CENTER

The Panasonic Digital Concepts Center (PDCC) has established the PDCC Technology Collaboration facility in Silicon Valley to promote technology partnerships focused on embedded Linux-based applications and middleware solutions for exciting new consumer electronics products.

The Center will provide early-stage start-ups with the opportunity to:

- Collaborate with a global Fortune 100 company, a leader in consumer electronics.
- Benefit from access to Panasonic engineering and technology expertise.
- Generate revenue through customer and partner relationships with Panasonic in the U.S. and Japan.
- Access potential investment though Panasonic's investment fund and network of venture firms.
- Expand their access to the Linux community in Silicon Valley and on the West Coast, focused on consumer electronic software for Linux.
- Obtain critical business building assistance and mentoring support from Panasonic to support the growth and success of their companies.
- Participate in industry programs supported by Panasonic and gain visibility into other Open Source trends on the West Coast.

Linux is an important platform for Panasonic to deliver device interoperability and standardized product development. Targeted applications include ubiquitous networking and user interface solutions in addition to other applications that are essential for the new digital era. Panasonic seeks software that drives interoperability and ease of use for home audio/video products, as well as mobile (3G handsets) and automotive entertainment products.

The Panasonic Digital Concepts Center has a proven track record of assisting start-up companies. Our new Technology Collaboration Center in San Jose is co-located with several Panasonic technology units and designed to facilitate interaction with product development engineers from the U.S. and Japan. A limited number of companies will be chosen to join this new and highly selective program.

Monsanto

The Nidus Center for Scientific Enterprises is a corporate incubator that is sponsored by Monsanto with the goal of creating an agricultural biotech and life sciences innovation center in St. Louis. Its mission is to speed innovative ideas in the life sciences market by:

- Nurturing entrepreneurs
- Protecting and growing innovative ideas
- Commercializing new technologies, and
- Attracting investment capital to their partners[9]

Nokia

A different approach to innovation was taken by Nokia. Its U.S. division, Nokia Innovent, was established to foster innovation through collaboration between Nokia and disruptive technology start-ups, those technologies that would change the technology base for Nokia products. Innovent offered a collaborative environment that promised to leverage Nokia's market and technology leadership with very early-stage disruptive technology innovators in the U.S. The stated goal was to "accelerate innovation" in communications technology. A significant part of the strategy was to use business incubators on the East and West Coasts to help them identify entrepreneurs, present them to Nokia Innovent, and offer those entrepreneurs a set of incubation services once Innovent chose them as collaboration partners. Nokia believed that incubators could provide both the sourcing assistance to identify emerging technology companies and the business start-up services to accelerate their growth while Innovent introduced them to innovation and partnership opportunities within the parent company.

Nokia also had a corporate venture group, Nokia Ventures, that could be used to assist with the incubation process in appropriate cases. Behind this effort was the belief that Nokia itself needed to constantly innovate and reinvent itself and that such technology collaborations would help "transform and renew our core businesses" by helping the company combine its internal research and development innovation efforts with external entrepreneurship in areas of disruptive technology that were outside their current research efforts. Nokia believed that helping disruptive technology start-ups commercialize their technology was an investment in their own culture of innovation.[10]

BEST PRACTICES IN TECHNOLOGY INCUBATION

The programs employed by best practice technology incubators are entrepreneurship strategies designed to facilitate innovation and technology commercialization. Peter Drucker, in *Innovation and Entrepreneurship*, says that "Such entrepreneurship strategies are central to successful innovation, and entrepreneurship as a force for innovation always needs to be market driven."[11]

The best incubation programs focus on the challenges facing start-ups and provide networks to entrepreneurs to help them engage in their work. Incubators recognize that networks are the basic unit of innovation and must include members both inside and outside of the technology start-up that is engaged in technology innovation.[12]

Services and programs are designed to foster the startup and growth of companies in the targeted sectors. From services that simplify business start-up, such as shared conference rooms, to one-on-one coaching, seminars, and a network of expertise, services and programs are the core value of technology incubators.

At the same time, the companies in the incubator are an entrepreneurial community. Programs that facilitate networking among the fifteen to twenty-five companies in the typical incubator help to build peer relationships during this critical growth stage. Programs will be designed to encourage the interaction among the client companies.

The network of contacts and relationships established by a sector-focused technology incubator will attract participants from the sector. Entrepreneurs will find technology business expertise and experience, and specialized sector knowledge of the technology markets and how to access them. In addition to having flexible office and lab space to accommodate growth, entrepreneurs will find services that simplify business start-up, such as one-on-one coaching, seminars, and a network of expertise, services, and programs on site. They will typically have access to this expertise from area-based professional service providers and local research institutions.

In addition to entrepreneurs and early stage companies, other participants in the incubator generally will include established corporations and university researchers and faculty. The incubator will serve as a clearinghouse to exchange ideas on technology needs and to connect with companies and universities that can create just-in-time solutions to start-up problems. University faculty and researchers can engage with the entrepreneurs to share their technological innovations. They can also find entrepreneurs who will partner with them to commercialize their technology innovations. A set of incubation center programs will facilitate networking among all of these various participants. The combination of the services and the network of expertise and relationships will foster the creation of successful technology companies.

Programs developed by best practice technology incubators generally include:

- *One-on-One Coaching and Mentoring*—twelve to twenty experienced business people offering pro bono assistance to Center businesses.
- *Entrepreneurship Seminars and Programs*—aimed at risk management for start-ups.
- *Networks of Expertise: Business and Technical Professionals*—utilizing experienced professionals from technology business.
- *Technology Forums*—building relationships with established technology companies, universities, and research labs.
- *Prototype and Testing Lab Programs*—a place to gain an understanding of commercial technology needs.
- *Student Intern Program*—assistance for start-ups from student teams.
- *Venture and Debt Investment Programs*—a process to ready companies for venture and debt investors.
- *CEO/Founder Roundtable Discussions*—regularly scheduled meetings to allow the CEOs of the start-ups to share issues with their peers.
- *Industry Brown Bag Lunch Discussions*—monthly lunch seminars by local business service professionals.
- *Peer-to-Peer Network Facilitation*—Facilitated discussions among incubator companies.

In addition to the specific networking process established by technology incubators, all technology incubators offer a suite of programs and services for their client start-up companies. The National Business Incubation Association has found that the following programs are commonly found among successful technology incubators:

- Business mentoring
- Marketing and public relations assistance
- Business plan assistance
- Networking assistance
- Access to Internet services
- Linkage to strategic partners and customers
- Assistance obtaining financing
- Management team development
- Referrals to IP and legal professionals
- Technology commercialization assistance
- Linkage to federal labs and local colleges and universities[13]

TECHNOLOGY COMMERCIALIZATION

Sector-focused technology incubators typically also have industry-focused commercialization programs for their technology start-ups. The Environmental Business Cluster (EBC) in San Jose, California, operates the largest private technology commercialization program for clean energy technology start-ups in the United States, excluding national labs and major universities. With over twenty-five technology start-ups at any given time and contracts with the U.S. Department of Energy and the California Energy Commission, the EBC has developed a commercialization roadmap to help clean energy innovation companies take their technology to the marketplace. The EBC's technology program outline is typical of such incubation efforts:

CASE STUDY: ENVIRONMENTAL BUSINESS CLUSTER TECHNOLOGY COMMERCIALIZATION PROGRAM

The services that are provided include:

1. *Market analysis assistance*
   Size, demographics, maturity, number of players, etc.
2. *Market surveys assistance*
   Revenue expectation, adoption rates, customer reactions, etc.
3. *Assessment of Intellectual Property status*
   Suitable protection, patent possibilities, legal documents, etc.
4. *Review of operations structure*
   Employee agreements, consulting agreements, incorporation status, board of directors, investor agreements, etc.
5. *Business planning*
   Cash flow, P&L, business plan development, sales and marketing strategies, employment plans, etc.

6. *Web design & Web hosting*

  Site design, site content planning assistance, content management recommendations, assistance in understanding hosting arrangements, etc.

7. *Investor presentations (PowerPoint)*

  Thirty-minute pitch, presentation rehearsals, due diligence preparation, executive summary preparation, term sheet review, etc.

8. *Customer presentations (PowerPoint)*

  Presentation development, demonstration development, value proposition, development agreements, etc.

9. *Design of marketing/sales collateral material*

  Message preparation guidance, graphic design recommendations, trade name assistance, copyright protection assistance, etc.

This commercialization program includes assistance from EBC staff and university interns for market research, market study, business plan preparation, graphics design, Web development, and other related activities as well as individual consulting assistance from specialists assigned to start-up companies by the EBC, based upon specific needs.

CONCLUSION

Many investigators have demonstrated that technology incubation can accelerate the transfer and commercialization of technology by linking talented entrepreneurs with ideas for innovation to individuals with the market wisdom and economic resources to commercialize their innovations.[14]

Sector-focused incubation has impacted numerous communities, as it helps them develop innovation clusters that bring them recognition for their emerging technology companies. The potential for such incubation programs as a tool to further innovation, entrepreneurship, and technology commercialization is still growing. Technology incubators have proved that they can stimulate the development of technology clusters, and such clusters will promote regional innovation. They should be considered a tool for technology commercialization and implemented to stimulate new business formation.

According to Victor Sidel, researcher at Stanford University's Center for Work, Technology and Organization, "[i]ncubators have the potential to house some of the most dynamic and exciting companies of the future."[15]

NOTES

1. Davila, T., M. Epstein, and R. Shelton. 2005. *Making Innovation Work.* Upper Saddle River, NJ: Wharton School Publishing, p. 121.

2. *Small Firms and Technology: Acquisitions, Inventor Movement, and Technology Transfer.* U.S. Small Business Administration. 2005. U.S. Government Printing Office.

3. Ibid.

4. Wolfe, Chuck, Dinah Adkins, and Hugh Sherman. 2001. *Best Practices in Action*, National Business Incubation Association, Athens, OH.

5. Molinar, Lawrence. 1997. *Business Incubation Work*. Athens, OH: NBIA Publications.

6. Devol, Ross. 2000. *Blueprint for a High-Tech Cluster*, Los Angeles: Milken Institute.

7. Davila et al., p. 212.

8. Chesbrough, Martin. 2003. *The Innovation Gap: Open Innovation and Strategic Investing*. Presentation to the International Business Forum.

9. Richards, Sally. 2002. *Inside Business Incubators & Corporate Ventures*. New York: John Wiley & Sons, p. 157.

10. The author worked with Nokia Innovent on their collaboration strategy. 2004. *Innovation is our DNA*. Nokia Corporation Brochure. Keilalahdentie, FIN.

11. Drucker, Peter F. 1985. *Innovation and Entrepreneurship*. New York: Harper & Row, p. 251.

12. Davila et al., p. 11.

13. Tornatzky, Louis, Huh Sherman, and Dinah Adkins. 2003. *Incubating Technology Businesses—A National Benchmarking Study*. Athens, OH: National Business Incubation Association.

14. Lewis, David. 2005. *The Incuation Edge*. Athens, OH: NBIA Publications.

15. Richards, p. 25.

10

Measuring Innovation: A Framework for Action

HERNÁN ETIENNOT and JOSÉ MARÍA CORRALES PEÑALVA

T he importance of innovation for both society and organizations' survival is widely accepted. In addition, scientific management developed by Taylor in 1911 highlighted the relevance of measurement systems. Knowledge of both concepts evolved and improved during the 1900s, but benefits of joining them and creating a performance measurement system for innovation were first neglected, later questioned, and accepted only in the last decade.

This chapter aims at providing the criteria and steps needed to set up a measurement system that helps to enhance innovation.

The chapter is structured as follows: first, it discusses the evolution of performance measures for innovation. Second, it introduces strategy as leading the innovation measurement system, and the business model as the framework required to identify key metrics. Third, the chapter emphasizes the importance of cascading down this business model to the different organizational levels. Finally, it uses the Balanced Scorecard concept to design the measurement system because it covers both previous dimensions: the business model and its drill down.

EVOLUTION

Innovation is a critical business activity because it helps organizations survive, renew, and grow. With product life cycles becoming shorter and the pressure to develop competitive advantages increasing, organizations have discovered the significant roles of flexibility and adaptation. In this sense, innovation is a mechanism for adapting products, services, and processes to new environmental requirements and, going a step further, innovation to create new environmental conditions (Damanpour & Evan, 1984). The focus on innovation research has shifted from wondering "whether" this adaptation happens to "when" and "how" it takes place (Eisenhardt & Tabrizi, 1995). This evolution reflects not only the importance of innovation for business firms, but also the significance of performing it properly.

Innovation has evolved from being considered an inspirational task, neither manageable nor measurable, to a process that can be mapped, measured, and guided (Drongelen & Bilderbeek, 1999). Initially, the measurement system in R&D was considered an act of mistrust toward scientists (Werner & Souder, 1997b). In the 1980s, innovation measures became frequent in most U.S. firms (Werner & Souder, 1997b). They were not used as a mechanism of evaluation, but as a diagnostic mechanism to find opportunities for improving the innovation process (McGrath & Romeri, 1994). The beliefs that in order to innovate, creativity should not be constrained by measurement concerns, and that each project was unique and thus not comparable, was questioned (Brown & Svenson, 1998; Shields & Young, 1994). The dominant approach today understands innovation as a manageable process where metrics are required to know whether the organizational innovation activities are effective and in order to promote communication and learning.

The measurement system consists of "the acquisition and analysis of information about the actual attainment of company objectives and plans, and about factors that may influence this attainment" (Drongelen & Bilderbeek, 1999). It should be understood as an instrument for continuous improvement and not for determining whether performance is satisfactory or negative. It is closer to a diagnostic tool than a tool to judge subordinates. This key idea underlies this chapter: a measurement system should enable innovation instead of restricting it and should work as informational stimuli that enhance intrinsic motivation by confirming capabilities or providing a guideline for improvements (Amabile, 1997). In this sense, the measurement system contributes to: a) communicating strategy; b) controlling the innovation progress; and c) facilitating discussion.

Sometimes, performance assessment is interpreted as a computational problem that requires measuring everything possible. Each approach to measuring performance provides feedback to the organization and influences its behaviors (Eccles, Nohria, & Berkley, 1992). A bad measurement system may be harmful, and often companies use counterproductive metrics (Barnett & Cahill, 2006). Actually, measuring things that are not related to the intended strategy may promote non-desired behaviors that gain legitimacy and at the end implicitly redefine the strategy (Hauser & Katz, 1998; Hauser & Zettelmeyer, 1997). This is the case of R&D efficiency measured according to patents obtained per R&D expenses. While this measure is suitable for many projects and especially for technological ones, promoting the overall number of patents can destroy the financial corporate performance by focusing too much on applying for patents, instead of increasing the patent quality and thus the intangible value of the company (Lin & Chen, 2005).

The importance of measuring innovation performance, for both practitioners and academics, is evident from efforts that the Product Development & Management Association made to research this topic (Griffin 1997b; Griffin & Page, 1996), and also in the survey conducted by the Industrial Research Institute in 1993. In the latter, 248 executives considered that "measuring and improving R&D productivity and effectiveness remain the biggest problem for respondents" (Meyer, Tertzakian, & Utterback, 1997).

In academia, the discussion about this topic started in the 1980s, increased in the 1990s, and is part of regular discussions in this decade. Yet, concepts are still confusing and ambiguous (Gatignon, Tushman, Smith, & Anderson, 2002). That no conclusions or specific recommendations can be found beyond that innovation is a complex problem because efforts are not observable, and outputs are uncertain. And even when they can be seen, there is a significant lag between the people's effort and their outputs. Another conclusion is that innovation requires integrated measurement systems with financial and nonfinancial metrics, tailored to each innovation activity, each organizational level, and each innovation strategy (Werner & Souder, 1997a). The literature covers the topic from different frameworks—value chain, life cycle, portfolio, real options, etc.—distinct perspectives—product development, basic research, joint R&D or innovation in general—and several types of innovation—radical, incremental, semi-radical or commercial versus administrative.

Among practitioners, there is a growing acceptance that innovation needs to be measured, but moving from needs to solutions is still weak. For new product development (one of the most measurable activities of innovation), best practice firms only measure performance against objective in 63 percent of the projects, and the remaining companies only do it in less than half of their cases (Griffin, 1997b). Moreover, recent studies report that the most innovative managers are unsatisfied with measurement systems because they do not track their activities and contributions (Hertenstein & Platt, 2000). Besides, many managers consider that there are possibilities to improve the use of measurement systems by extending them to still-uncovered activities like design (Driva, Pawar, & Menon, 2000).

While most of the literature on innovation measurement systems has been focused on product development; innovation is a broader concept that can be applied to logistics processes, administrative systems, advertising campaigns, financial instruments, basic research, etc. (Damanpour, 1991). Among innovation activities, we can distinguish basic research, applied research, new product development, engineering, service design, etc. (Hauser & Zettelmeyer, 1997; Shields & Young, 1994). In this chapter, we will bring up conclusions from these different fields to a common and broad concept of innovation measurement.

STRATEGY LEADING THE MEASUREMENT SYSTEM

The purpose of a measurement system is to support management actions for implementing strategy. The company strategy is the starting point to define the measurement system, much like a person needs the final picture to complete a puzzle. It is almost impossible to design and understand a measurement system without a clear idea of organizational goals and strategy (Schmitt, 1991). Moreover, many authors consider that the most important metric of a measurement system is the one that let managers know the fit between innovation and business strategy (Griffin & Page, 1996; Schmitt, 1991).

The strategy defines how organizations compete with a unique value proposition (Porter, 1996). It should specify what technologies the company needs to master and what products and customer segments are the target for innovation activities (Loch & Tapper, 2002). It is top management's responsibility to decide the innovation strategy, and to create a shared vision about how it fits within the business (Schmitt, 1991). According to the innovation strategy selected, top management determines whether innovation will focus on new business models or new technologies, the mix of radical and incremental innovation, as well as the economic effort allocated to innovation.

The idea that more innovation is always better is wrong. A company can follow a strategy of being an aggressive innovator to create new markets or focusing on incremental innovation to keep growing and to dominate existing markets. The right strategy depends on environmental uncertainties, market opportunities, and corporate competences. Moreover, an innovation strategy is not one dimensional, an aggressive innovator will pursue certain incremental innovations, and a more conservative firm may still bet on radical innovations. It is just a matter of focus and emphasis; thus, the innovation portfolio will be diversified among different types of innovation projects. Moreover, the innovation strategy selected by the company will change over time, moving from aggressive to incremental, and waiting for the time to switch to aggressive innovation again.

The intended strategy becomes tangible through the business model. The most important part of the strategy relies not only on how the organization positions itself with regard to competitors and customers, but on the activities it will perform (Porter 1996). Once the strategy is defined, it is important to make explicit management's idea on how to achieve innovation and how it fits into the business. The business model explains how pieces of the business match together (Magretta, 2002). Strategy can be ambiguous, and operational decisions make it specific. Thus, the business model makes explicit— in operational terms—management-dominant logic (beliefs, theories and

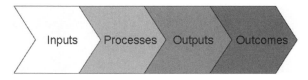

FIGURE 10.1.   Input-Process-Outputs-Outcome Model

propositions) (Prahalad & Bettis, 1986) about how the strategy should be implemented.

A business model for innovation is a coherent frame to translate ideas into value creation. It is defined through the value chain of inputs, process, outputs, and outcomes. Innovation requires specific processes and resources to both develop new ideas and obtain the intended outputs and outcomes. A business model for innovation contributes to reducing the time of analysis and to filter ideas and behaviors, enhancing management focus, coordination, and coherence (Chesbrough & Rosenbloom, 2002; Prahalad & Bettis, 1986). An example of how this value chain works are the conclusions from Langerak, Hultink, and Robben (2004): having a market-oriented culture (input) does not affect organizational performance directly but affects it through developing a more competitive product and improving launching activities (process); these two activities subsequently enhance the product performance (output), which is the factor that finally has a positive impact on the organizational performance (outcomes). A similar approach to the innovation measurement system was taken in previous works (Brown & Svenson, 1998; Schumann, Ransley, & Prestwood, 1995)

Inputs "... are the raw materials or stimuli a system receives and processes" (Brown & Svenson, 1998). They are the antecedent conditions required for intended innovation. Inputs involve culture, motivation, knowledge variety, skills, experience, and attitudes, but also the financial resources and infrastructure available (Cardinal, 2001). Inputs are very important for basic research and radical innovation, when the process or output required is highly uncertain. In these situations, input measures—leading metrics of performance—are critical. For example, given an amount of total R&D expenditure, the higher the percentage allocated to basic research, the more likely is radically innovative output (Mansfield, 1980).

Processes are activities and behaviors that determine how innovation performs. Mechanisms of process control—centralization and formalization—is one of the most discussed topics on innovation, because of the idea that control may reduce the generation of ideas and risk-taking attitudes, even though it enhances the implementation (exploitation) (Cardinal, 2001). Thus, process control is more related to incremental innovation because there is less uncertainty about what is expected and how to get it. Process measures are real-time metrics that identify when it is required to change the course of actions (Davila, Epstein, & Shelton 2005).

Outputs are results that the organization gets after combining and transforming some inputs through its processes. Outputs are measures that focus on delivery, transfer, and application of technology (Schumann, Ransley, & Prestwood, 1995) in nonfinancial terms, like patents, customer satisfaction, new products, etc. A strong emphasis on output will focus researchers in short-term and low-risk projects. In contrast to inputs, outputs measures are lagging metrics, because deviations are known once the match is played. Therefore, they are good for projects with low uncertainty. One important problem of the output measures is the ability to distinguish failures because of innovation activities from those due to marketing or manufacturing activities (Davila, 2003; Loch, Stein, & Terwiesch, 1996).

Outcomes reflect the economic value created that the firm is able to appropriate for itself. Many companies achieve very high performance in the technical aspect or in customer satisfaction, but they cannot get money out of it; they are not able to retain part of the value created. The problem with outcome measures is that they are seen at the end of the game—a long time after decisions were made and effort expended. Therefore, these measures are useful only for applied engineering, where this lapse is the shortest one and there is a minimal uncertainty.

Summarizing, the strategy pursued by each company will in turn determine the measure system required (Griffin & Page, 1996). A measurement system for radical innovation emphasizes inputs as well as nonfinancial and subjective metrics, and deemphasizes process, outcomes, and output metrics. In contrast, a measurement system for incremental innovation increases its focus from process to output and outcomes, and uses more objective measures. Thus, a radical innovation project relies to a larger extent on the subjective assessment of experts, while an incremental innovation project is assessed based on measures of value creation, return on investment, profits, or cost reduction.

The business model will, in turn, determine which measures should be used. The better the management logic describing how the business works, the better the measurement system and management information will be. The business model is a story about how a company does business (Magretta, 2002), and the "words for labeling and defining measures and units tell a story about the manager's organizational world" (Eccles, Nohria, & Berkley, 1992).

The influence of strategy on performance measures is well illustrated by the case of Volvo Aero Corporation (Karlsson, Trygg, & Elfström, 2004). Volvo Aero develops and manufactures high-technology engine components for aircraft, rockets, and gas turbine, in cooperation with the world's leading engine manufacturers. The company changed from a functionally oriented firm—depending on military projects—to a business-oriented partner in the aerospace market. The company started in 1932 with the development and production of aircraft engines for the Swedish military force. The search for market opportunities in the civil engine began in the 1970s. A vigorous marketing initiative was launched under the slogan of "Going Commercial." The company increased its commercial sector and was mostly oriented to engine development and manufacturing, basically for military forces and increasingly for commercial clients. The goal was to develop technologies in order to increase the performance of military engines and get spillovers from there. During the 1980s, the research was aimed to develop equally product-related technologies for both commercial and military engines. The measure for evaluating progress was product performance improvement. During the 1990s, the strategy turned to a stronger commercial approach, the company changed its name from "Volvo Flygmotor" to "Volvo Aero" (because the Swedish name was difficult to communicate at the international level), and it was also reorganized in business units. The research activities were more focused on specific products of different business units. Measures related to markets needs, time-to-market, and risk management gained importance. Special care was devoted to the process of increasing internal efficiency, cutting down cost and lead time, etc. To ensure inputs supported the strategy implementation, the company also promoted the creation of different interest groups, made up by universities and other firms within the research area.

DIFFERENT SUBJECTS, DIFFERENT MEASURES

The organizational structure shapes the measurement system. Whether we are evaluating a profit or a cost center determines the type of financial performance to be measured. While the first type of center would be measured based on earnings, the latter would be better measured by deviations with respect to standard costs or budgeted expenses. Similarly, the organizational unit evaluated depends on whether the company is organized by business or customer segments. This is the case of the full-service communications agency Hill, Holliday, Connors, Cosmopulos, Inc. The firm was traditionally organized by profit centers representing the different products and services in the industry (advertising, public relations, market research, etc). When the market became more competitive and customers more cost conscious, the firm had to change from profit centers around products to profit centers around customers. Although the measured variable remained the same, the definition of how to measure changed from profits per business unit to profits per customer group, going from competitive behaviors among business activities to cooperative behaviors to get the highest customer share of pocket (Eccles, Nohria, & Berkley, 1992).

Different organizational levels require different measures. Whether measuring at the level of the project, product family, program, business unit, or corporate organizational innovation (Davila & Wouters, 2005; Griffin & Page,

1996; Meyer, Tertzakian, & Utterback, 1997; Schumann, Ransley, & Prestwood, 1995), measurement systems ought to provide information required by the particular level as well as information aligned with objectives and responsibilities of higher levels. The final purpose of each organizational unit is to contribute to fulfill the corporate goals.

Finally, strategy has to cascade down to each organizational level (Loch & Tapper, 2002). The process of cascading down strategy is intended to provide strategic alignment (Schumann, Ransley, & Prestwood, 1995). The value chain from inputs to outcomes has to be translated into value with measures and goals at each organizational level. Each of these levels has a measurement target with the objective of contributing to the goals of the levels it reports to. Consequently, the measurement system has to disaggregate the goals from these upper levels into various metrics, giving them a different scope and specific metrics. Similar to a puzzle—where each piece has it own characteristics, colors, and content, but where every piece also links to the neighbor pieces—in the measurement system, some measures are aggregated at each higher level, while others are level specific.

One of the reasons for practitioners' dissatisfaction with measurement systems is the tradition of selecting a measure and applying it to every organizational level. Unfortunately, empirical evidence suggests that companies measure just one organizational level, which frequently is the team level, and do not recognize different needs from measurement systems at different levels (Drongelen & Bilderbeek, 1999). The increasing risk aversion and discount factor associated with lower organizational levels is widely accepted in innovation research, and also its consequences on decision making. The closer to business and corporate levels, the more a unit's manager can diversify the risk.

The corporate level is the most aggregate level, and the one where goals cascade from (Bremser & Barsky, 2004). At the corporate level, the measurement system focuses on outputs and outcomes. Once the corporate level defines goals and the strategy to achieve them, each business unit in accordance with the corporate level is responsible for establishing its contribution to value creation, profit, and innovation; whether it is radical or incremental; or whether it is focused on technical aspects or on the business model.

The business unit has also specific characteristics that should be taken into account. At the business unit level, the problem is about how individual units position themselves to compete within its industry (Langfield-Smith, 1997). The business units take care not only of a specific project but also of the project portfolio that allows a sustainable innovation activity. Because of this, the business units support less risk than the project manager, but more risk than the corporation or its shareholders, who can diversify among different business units or in the capital markets. Another well-documented problem of business units is that benefits from their research activities may be collected by another business unit, while costs are not. This implies that central

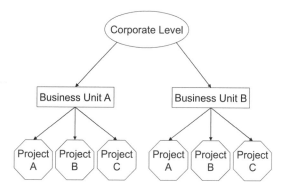

FIGURE 10.2. Cascading Down the Measurement System

subsidies are expected from the corporation in order to counteract the rational undervaluing of risky projects and recognize collateral benefits (Hauser & Zettelmeyer, 1997).

The project level is where the field of measurement systems is most developed. Project characteristics such as goals, complexity, and newness should be taken into account when benchmarking with competitors (Griffin, 1997a). The objectives at this level are operational. Many conditions are determined by the organization, and the project manager only deals with the quantity of resources or their mix in the project team. But it is very difficult to create a completely different culture for his or her team, or to go through a very distinct stage-gate process.

BALANCED SCORECARD TO MEASURE THE BUSINESS MODEL AT DIFFERENT ORGANIZATIONAL LEVELS

Strategic measurement systems, such as Balanced Scorecard, are useful measurement tools. They bring together the two dimensions discussed previously, that is, the value chain and the organizational level. Strategic maps translate strategic goals into a coherent set of operational terms—to communicate the strategy to every member within the organization, linking it to personal objectives; to integrate the business with financial plans, and finally to learn from the feedback if the strategy is in fact working (Bremser & Barsky, 2004; Kaplan & Norton, 1996).

Prior work has used Balanced Scorecard as an appropriate tool for designing a measurement system for innovation (Bremser & Barsky, 2004; Drongelen & Bilderbeek, 1999; Loch & Tapper, 2002; Neufel, Semeoni, & Taylor, 2001; Schumann, Ransley, & Prestwood, 1995). While Balanced Scorecard is mainly used for business units, the logic of the Balanced Scorecard offers a model applicable for any business process (Davila, Epstein, & Shelton, 2005). This

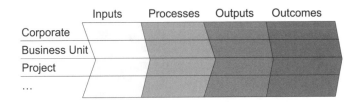

FIGURE 10.3. Full Model of a Measurement System

kind of integrated techniques has been considered more accurate, comprehensive, effective, and versatile (Werner & Souder, 1997a).

The Balanced Scorecard measures performance on multiple value drivers. Measuring a single driver would result in optimizing one business dimension at the expense of others (Eccles, Nohria, & Berkley, 1992). The Balanced Scorecard includes financial and operational measures linked by causal relationships that operationally describe the business model of a company (Kaplan & Norton, 1992). It measures performance in the short and long term, usually through many perspectives: financial performance, customer relations, and internal business process as well as learning and innovation (Kaplan & Norton, 1992, 1993, 1996).

The use of multiple measures systems is illustrated by the case of Sealed Air Corp., the leading global manufacturer of a wide range of protective and specialty packaging products. It completely redefined its measurement system from one focused on earning per share to another with five dimensions, among which customer satisfaction was the first, cash flow the second, then world-class manufacturing, innovation, and finally earning per share (Eccles, Nohria, & Berkley, 1992). With this change, the company evolved from a short-term to a long-term focus, reflecting management beliefs that customer satisfaction was the leading indicator of financial performance.

The essential idea of the Balanced Scorecard is to track the business model. The logic behind the previous four dimensions is to get information about how well the value chain is managed. Do we have the required resources? How well do we transform resources in output? Are our products and services well accepted by customers? How much do we get from the value of these outputs? These questions are parallel to the input-process-output-outcome described previously.

The Balanced Scorecard is designed as a cascade of goals. Each hierarchical level sets goals that contribute to those of the upper level, linking each other in a causal relationship that facilitates the implementation and communication of the strategy (Kaplan & Norton, 1992, 1993, 1996). The design of each level of the Balanced Scorecard should be assigned to the specific organizational level, aiming not only to get commitment but also to promote the use of the measurement system as an enabling tool for improving their own work and reinforcing the manager's intrinsic motivation (Amabile, 1997).

Special care should be taken not to distort the measurement system's roles with too much emphasis on using it for evaluation or reward purposes. While the benefits of using specific metrics are not questioned, they can be underweighted when a superior has to evaluate a subordinate's performance (Lipe & Salterio, 2000). The specific metrics for divisional level are commonly nonfinancial metrics, which usually predict financial performance. When they are underweighted, financial metrics generally gain importance and employees put their focus on short-term and low-risk activities.

The issue of operational versus financial metrics is also related to their objectivity. Financial metrics are quite common because they are easy to measure and are considered more objective (Eccles, Nohria, & Berkley, 1992). But even these metrics are open to subjectivity through the period, unit, and definition applied. Additionally, when measurement systems are used to diagnose and not to reward, a subjective measure of an important variable is better than a more objective evaluation of something irrelevant or that might generate undesired behaviors. The idea is "... to measure what is really important, not just what is easy to measure. Vaguely right is better than precisely wrong" (Hauser & Katz, 1998). Many aspects of innovation like the strategic fit, the relevance of an idea, or customer satisfaction can not be evaluated objectively, and in many cases the evaluation is not quantitative but qualitative.

DESIGNING THE MEASUREMENT SYSTEM AT DIFFERENT LEVELS

The goal of this section is to go one step beyond the previous discussion and talk about the implementation of measurement systems for innovation activities. Because the measurement system is contingent to each firm and its conditions, this section analyzes its implementation in different parts of the business model for specific organizational levels. Because of the extension that a task like this could take, we focus on those issues that we consider of higher relevance. The cascading process covers the two most discussed organizational levels in the literature: the business unit and the project level.

Inputs

Business Units

At the business unit level, the goal is to maintain a good portfolio of projects that reinforces and improves the company's strategic position. Because the ratio between successful projects and the overall number of projects analyzed is low, a large number of proposals are needed to avoid problems over the long term. Therefore, a common metric is the number of ideas received and the ratio of conversion into projects.

Environmental screening is a critical activity to improve the number of ideas submitted and the quality of the information process. The heterogeneity of information sources is a key issue for environmental screening. External networks as well as the quantity and type of contacts with institutions like universities, government, professional associations, etc. might be leading indicators of innovation. It is important to monitor whether the company has an adequate number of professional members and partner institutions. It is also important to promote diversity and a balanced distribution of these contacts among managers within organization.

The number of internal proposals is also a good metric. It reflects not only the possibility of new projects but also the organizational culture regarding internal commitment with innovation and risk taking. But maximizing this metric with no balancing metric is dangerous. To reward people based on the number and quality of their ideas might give rise to a syndrome of "not invented here," thus losing important opportunities from the outside (Hauser, 1998).

The balance between the degree of focus on internal versus external innovation, or the diversity required for the environmental screening, is determined by the importance of radical versus incremental innovation in the company's portfolio. The more weight radical innovation has, the more need to update the external environment and follow new trends.

Structural variables are also important indicators of the company's abilities to innovate. Besides the common financial and tangible resources, there are many other inputs through which organizations might develop its advantages for innovation:

The organizational structure—its degree of autonomy or centralization of R&D activities—promotes different types of innovation. For example, radical innovation is more frequent in centralized organizations with high concentrations of scientists, while incremental innovation is more common in large, complex, and decentralized organizations with formal processes (Ettlie, Bridges, & O'Keefe, 1984).

Organizational culture is another important structural resource. A culture with emphasis on market orientation is an important factor for organizational innovation (Langerak, Hultink, & Robben, 2004). At the same time, this type of culture increases the innovation stimulus by promoting more contacts with customers and cross-departmental teams, and enriching projects with other perspectives.

Employees' attitudes are good proxies for organizational culture. As we have already explained, ideas submitted by employees are a traditional output measure of the innovation culture. Also, a subjective evaluation of attitude can be obtained from human resources climate surveys, external audits, rankings of industrial magazines, etc. Even employees turnover influences innovation. A very high turnover implies low possibilities of creation and exploitation of knowledge. But a very low turnover provides high possibilities of reducing the external stimulus, the not-invented-here syndrome, and the emphasis on incremental innovation.

The traditional example of culture promoting innovation is 3M, which allows employees to use 20 percent of their work time on their own projects, using corporate resources. Additionally, if the project grows and becomes a new business, they may become partners of that business. Another feature of 3M culture is the tolerance for failure. Because people are risk averse, employees will not take the risk of innovative projects if they are not able to rely on the organizational support and/or if their effort is not compensated and they can be penalized for unpredictable failures.

Projects

Projects have certain metrics that cascade down from the business unit, while others are specific to each project. For radical projects, in addition to external stimulus, metrics should focus on knowledge diversity (Bonner, Ruekert, & Walker, 2002). Therefore, a metric could be the number of scientists employed and the different specialties of team members.

Customer orientation can be measured using customer involvement or the proportion of funds received from business units instead of from central management. Many companies use a "tin cupping" model to collect funds for projects, which forces them to be focused on customer needs. However, it should be carefully managed because too much customer orientation may lead the organization to exploit actual knowledge, avoiding exploration or basic research. This could be dangerous for a company with an intended aggressive innovation strategy.

The R&D expenditure is considered an important input for innovation. Once again, we have to call attention to the importance of strategy and environmental characteristics. Capital market responses to the announcement of increasing R&D expenditure is positive for high technology and market uncertainty, and negative for low technology and market uncertainty (Lin & Chen, 2005).

Process

Business Units

One of the most studied topics about innovation portfolio management in business units is how to select the right set of projects (Cooper, Edgett, & Kleinschmidt, 2001; Hauser 1998). This selection might reinforce or deviate from the intended strategy, creating management commitment in the medium term (Cooper, Edgett, & Kleinschmidt, 2001; Loch & Kavadias, 2002). This is a difficult problem because of its multifaceted and multiperiod features.

Portfolio management is the process that the business unit's manager must constantly check. It is "... a dynamic decision process, whereby a business's list of active new product and R&D projects is constantly up-dated and revised. In this process, new products are evaluated, selected and prioritized;

existing projects may be accelerated, killed or de-prioritized; and resources are allocated and re-allocated to the active projects" (Cooper, Edgett, & Kleinschmidt, 2001).

There are many mechanisms to select projects such as financial methods, strategic methods, portfolio maps, road maps, scoring models, check list, etc. (Cooper, Edgett, & Kleinschmidt, 2001).

An important criticism of most of these models is that they work with only one or two dimensions; meanwhile, portfolio management is a multifaceted concept. Practitioners have tried to overcome this problem using multiple methods, but they still prioritize one dimension over the others—for example, financial mechanisms that are the most often used by practitioners, score projects based on their returns or their net present value, real option or any other mechanism—but they do not consider strategic fit based on innovation type or implementation stage. Data envelopment analysis overcomes this problem by analyzing projects with respect to the multidimensional surface of efficiency. It evaluates how distant the different projects are from this surface built on the relation between outputs (like cash-flow or net-present value) and inputs (like required investment, life cycle stage, or innovation type) (Linton, Walsh, & Morabito, 2002).

Instead of searching for the most efficient individual project, the portfolio management relies on having a well-balanced portfolio of projects. The right balance of projects and an adequate ratio of projects per resources available are the variables that better discriminate best from worst performers (Cooper, Edgett, & Kleinschmidt, 2001). For example, graphical methods may determine how well balanced the project is with regard to innovation type, dominant technology, value creation, risk, etc. Different strategies may concentrate on certain dimensions or be more dispersed in others. Technology concentration might reinforce the competitive position of a firm by preempting the potential competitors and taking advantages of economies of scale; while diversity might increase the possibility of exploiting more business opportunities in different markets due to economies of scope (Lin & Chen, 2005).

An additional issue to keep in mind is the interrelation among projects (Chien, 2002). When selecting projects through project ranking tools, potential benefits, like synergy and risk reduction are not considered; problems such as total available resources or interdependences are also often ignored. The unit of analysis for portfolio management must be the portfolio itself, instead of projects. The evaluation should be made by comparing the attributes of one portfolio versus others; and not the additional attributes of the selected project for one portfolio versus the rest.

Projects

At the project level, the process control focuses on how projects evolve through different stages. The metrics vary depending on the project goal.

How to execute incremental innovation projects is more predictable, and what is expected for each stage has lower uncertainty. Metrics on expected profits and performance, customer target, and other project attributes can be examined at the end of each stage to decide whether to let the project move forward or kill it. Project performance can be monitored through stage-gate process metrics, such as milestones accomplished, time for completion, overlapping stages, budget fulfillment, productivity, and subjective evaluations of task performance.

Basic research projects are different. Uncertainty does not allow detailed forecasts of financial and technical performance. Moreover, the more the project is oriented toward basic science, the less is known about possible applications. Evaluations generally rely on the results of experiments and prototypes. But more important is the subjective evaluation of experts about the task originally performed and the project potential.

Output

Business Units

The goal of innovation activities is to achieve a satisfactory level of outputs that in turn generates outcomes. The organization has to succeed in both commercial and technical dimensions. Additionally, depending on the aggressiveness of the innovation strategy, it will be important to measure innovation activity, like number of patents filed, quantity of new products released, sales originated by new products, products approved, products designed, awards won, projects completed, and proportion of first-to-market products.

Outputs at the business unit level are measured based on platforms or product families that aggregate many projects. The commercial outputs might be evaluated at the platform level in terms of the commercial productivity of related projects and, at the business unit overall level, by metrics like revenues and market share of new products, number of publications, number of citations, etc. Technical outputs are measured at the organizational level, in terms of platform efficiency—that is, the relation between the cost of developing a new upgrade, with respect to the cost of developing the technological platform from which the project derives (Meyer, Tertzakian, & Utterback, 1997).

Projects

The two dimensions—technical performance and value to customer—are also important to evaluate projects (Cohen & Eliashberg, 1996). Depending on the type of innovation pursued by the project, the balance between these two dimensions and the variables used in each of them will change (Griffin & Page, 1996). For example, products that are launched to a market with high margin and large demand benefit from putting higher priority on technical performance rather than time-to-market.

Customer-based measures help improve the decision making when trading off short and long-term impact. Depending on the research stage and the project innovativeness, it might be evaluated through surveys of customer acceptance and satisfaction, market share obtained, repetitive customers, gross margin of new products, possibility of commercialization, etc. For example, radical innovation would be measured by customer acceptance and satisfaction, while incremental innovation depends on the market share, revenues, and revenue increases.

At the project level, technical output is related more to product or process innovation than to the innovation activity itself. It is traditionally measured by benchmarking technical performance, rate of defective products, easy use, design, process stoppages, user's claims, proportion of redesigned parts, patents filled, number of citations, etc.

Outcomes

Business Units

Although the organization may expect technical and commercial outputs, it is important for any business firm to create value for its shareholders. Several issues make measuring shareholder value difficult, and various techniques have been proposed to get a more accurate evaluation of how any innovation activity contributes to value creation.

The common issues associated with measuring value creation in innovation are timing, separability, and uncertainty.

The issue of timing comes from two factors: a) the long lapse between the investment and the returns required to come up with a reliable measure of value, and b) the decision about the window of time to measure value creation. This is the case of the Kodak instant picture, which might be considered a success if we measure the 35 percent of market share and the total market increase in two years. But once we include the long-term financial cost of infringing the patent owned by Polaroid, this product was a failure for Kodak (Griffin & Page, 1996).

The problem of separability is related to the difficulty of evaluating the spillovers of an innovation into other products. Even with failures, the organization as a whole learns and gets value. Separability in cases of radical innovation is even harder, because generally it opens a large number of new opportunities for which it is difficult to assess the impact of the original innovation. Experts will usually give a better estimate of value creation than financial or operative measures.

The problem of uncertainty is quite different. It is easier to evaluate value creation for an incremental project because the investment-return lapse is shorter, the price-change or manufacturing cost reduction is more easily identifiable, and resources and process required are more accurately estimated. For radical innovation, all these factors are more difficult to estimate, mainly due to the uncertainty about inputs required, optimal process, and expected outcomes.

Return on investment (ROI) is one of the most widespread metrics, but it usually biases managers toward low risk projects or underinvestment in R&D. Many similar accounting-based measures such as profit from new products over R&D expenses and residual earnings are commonly used with similar effects (McGrath & Romeri, 1994).

Recently, real option valuation has been proposed as an alternative metric. The logic behind option valuation is that some uncertainty about possible outcomes generates value (Hauser & Zettelmeyer, 1997). The flexibility of the investment decision sequence raises the opportunity of benefiting from favorable outcomes and limiting the negative ones.

Projects

The contribution to value creation is not the immediate purpose of every single project (Griffin & Page, 1996). Depending on whether the project is more oriented to basic research or incremental innovation, its contribution to value can be more diffused. In more applied or incremental projects, the contribution to value creation is easier to identify.

At the project level, we can measure outcomes. But, too much emphasis on these metrics may lead behavior towards less uncertain projects, with safer but lower positive returns. Traditional metrics for project contribution are reduction in manufacturing costs or in capital requirements, increases in selling price or net profit, and time-to-profit.

CONCLUSION

A measurement system for innovation is an enabling instrument that contributes to continuous improvement of innovation activities. It is not easy to develop because of specific characteristics of innovation activities, like multiperiods, multidimensions, separability, and observability. There is no universal measurement system for innovation activities, as well as there is not a unique measure or measurement system for all organizations. The development of these systems should consider their specific features, the intended innovation strategy, the business model in which managers' decisions are taken, and combining common and specific attributes at different organizational levels.

REFERENCES

Amabile, T. M. (1997). Motivating creativity in organizations: On doing what you love and loving what you do. *California Management Review, 40* (1), 39.

Barnett, M. L., & Cahill, G. (2006). Measure less, succeed more: A Zen approach to organizational effectiveness. *Philosophy of Management, 6.*

Bonner, J. M., Ruekert, R. W., & Walker Jr., O. C. (2002). Upper management control of new product development projects and project performance. *Journal of Product Innovation Management, 19* (3), 233–245.

Bremser, W. G., & Barsky, N. P. (2004). Utilizing the balanced scorecard for R&D performance measurement. *R & D Management, 34,* 229–238.

Brown, M. G. & Svenson, R. A. (1998). Measuring R&D productivity. *Research Technology Management, 41* (6), 30.

Cardinal, L. B. (2001). Technological innovation in the pharmaceutical industry: The use of organizational control in managing research and development. *Organization Science, 12* (1), 19–36.

Chesbrough, H., & Rosenbloom, R. S. (2002). The role of the business model in capturing value from innovation: Evidence from Xerox Corporation's technology spin-off companies. *Industrial & Corporate Change, 11* (3), 529–555.

Chien, C. (2002). A portfolio-evaluation framework for selecting R&D projects. *R & D Management, 32* (4), 359–368.

Cohen, M. A., & Eliashberg, J. (1996). New product development: The performance and time-to-market tradeoff. *Management Science, 42* (2), 173–186.

Cooper, R. G., Edgett, S., & Kleinschmidt, E. (2001). Portfolio management for new product development: Results of an industry practices study. *R & D Management, 31* (4), 361.

Damanpour, F. (1991). Organizational innovations: A meta-analysis of effects of determinants and moderators. *Academy of Management Journal, 34* (3), 555.

Damanpour, F., & Evan, W. M. (1984). Organizational innovation and performance: The problem of "organizational lag." *Administrative Science Quarterly, 29* (3), 392.

Davila, A. (2003). Short-term economic incentives in new product development. *Research Policy, 32* (8), 1397.

Davila, T., Epstein, M. J., & Shelton, R. D. (2005). *Making innovation work: How to manage it, measure it, and profit from it.* Upper Saddle River, NJ: Wharton School Publishing.

Davila, T. & Wouters, M. (2005). Management accounting in the manufacturing sector: Managing cost at the design and production stages. Working paper, University of Twente, Enschede, the Netherlands.

Driva, H., Pawar, K. S., & Menon, U. (2000). Measuring product development performance in manufacturing organisations. *International Journal of Production Economics, 63* (2), 147–159.

Drongelen, I. C. K., & Bilderbeek, J. (1999). R&D performance measurement: More than choosing a set of metrics. *R & D Management, 29* (1), 35.

Eccles, R. G., Nohria, N., & Berkley, J. D. (1992). Toward robust performance measurement. In Eccles, R. G., Nohria, N., and Berkley, J. D. (eds.), *Beyond the hype: Rediscovering the essence of management.* Boston: Harvard Business School Press, 145–169.

Eisenhardt, K. M., & Tabrizi, B. N. (1995). Accelerating adaptive processes: Product innovation in the global computer industry. *Administrative Science Quarterly, 40,* 84–110.

Ettlie, J. E., Bridges, W. P., & O'Keefe, R. D. (1984). Organization strategy and structural differences for radical versus incremental innovation. *Management Science, 30* (6), 682–695.

Gatignon, H., Tushman, M. L., Smith, W., & Anderson, P. (2002). A structural approach to assessing innovation: Construct development of innovation locus, type, and characteristics. *Management Science, 48* (9), 1103–1122.

Griffin, A. (1997a). The effect of project and process characteristics on product development cycle time. *Journal of Marketing Research (JMR), 34,* 24.

Griffin, A. (1997b). PDMA research on new product development practices: Updating trends and benchmarking best practices. *Journal of Product Innovation Management, 14,* 429–458.

Griffin, A., & Page, A. L. (1996). PDMA success measurement project: Recommended measures for product development success and failure. *Journal of Product Innovation Management, 13* (6), 478–496.

Hauser, J. R. (1998). Research, development, and engineering metrics. *Management Science, 44,* 1670.

Hauser, J., & Katz, G. (1998). Metrics: You are what you measure! *European Management Journal, 16* (5), 516.

Hauser, J. R., & Zettelmeyer, F. (1997). Metrics to evaluate R, D&E. *Research Technology Management, 40* (4), 32.

Hertenstein, J. H., & Platt, M. B. (2000). Performance measures and management control in new product development. *Accounting Horizons, 14* (3), 303.

Kaplan, R. S., & Norton, D. P. (1992). The balanced scorecard—Measures that drive performance. *Harvard Business Review, 70* (1), 71.

Kaplan, R. S., & Norton, D. P. (1993). Putting the balanced scorecard to work. *Harvard Business Review, 71* (5), 134.

Kaplan, R. S., & Norton, D. P. (1996). Using the balanced scorecard as a strategic management system. *Harvard Business Review, 74* (1), 75.

Karlsson, M., Trygg, L., & Elfström, B.-O. (2004). Measuring R&D productivity: Complementing the picture by focusing on research activities. *Technovation, 24* (3), 179.

Langerak, F., Hultink, E. J., & Robben, H. S. J. (2004). The impact of market orientation, product advantage, and launch proficiency on new product performance and organizational performance. *Journal of Product Innovation Management, 21* (2), 79–94.

Langfield-Smith, K. (1997). Management control systems and strategy: A critical review. *Accounting, Organizations & Society, 22* (2), 207–232.

Lin, B.-W., & Chen, J.-S. (2005). Corporate technology portfolios and R&D performance measures: A study of technology intensive firms *R & D Management, 35,* 157–170.

Linton, J. D., Walsh, S. T., & Morabito, J. (2002). Analysis, ranking and selection of R&D projects in a portfolio. *R & D Management, 32,* 139.

Lipe, M. G., & Salterio, S. E. (2000). The balanced scorecard: Judgmental effects of common and unique performance measures. *The Accounting Review, 75* (3), 283.

Loch, C. H., & Kavadias, S. (2002). Dynamic portfolio selection of NPD programs using marginal returns. *Management Science, 48* (10), 1227–1241.

Loch, C. H., Stein, L., & Terwiesch, C. (1996). Measuring development performance in the electronics industry. *Journal of Product Innovation Management, 13* (1), 3–20.

Loch, C. H., & Tapper, U. A. S. (2002). Implementing a strategy-driven performance measurement system for an applied research group. *Journal of Product Innovation Management, 19*, 185–198.

Magretta, J. (2002). Why business models matter. *Harvard Business Review, 80* (5): 86–93.

Mansfield, E. (1980). Basic research and productivity increase in manufacturing. *American Economic Review, 70* (5), 863–873.

McGrath, M. E., & Romeri, M. N. (1994). The R&D effectiveness index: A metric for product development performance. *Journal of Product Innovation Management, 11*, 213.

Meyer, M. H., Tertzakian, P., & Utterback, J. M. (1997). Metrics for managing research and development in the context of the product family. *Management Science, 43* (1), 88.

Neufel, G. A., Semeoni, P. A., & Taylor, M. A. (2001). High-performance research organizations. *Research Technology Management, 44* (6), 42.

Porter, M. E. (1996). What is strategy? *Harvard Business Review, 74* (6), 61–78.

Prahalad, C. K., & Bettis, R. A. (1986). The dominant logic: A new linkage between diversity and performance. *Strategic Management Journal, 7* (6), 485–501.

Schmitt, R. W. (1991). The strategic measure of R&D. *Research Technology Management, 34* (6), 13.

Schumann, P. A. J., Ransley, D. L., & Prestwood, D. C. L. (1995). Measuring R&D performance. *Research Technology Management, 38* (3), 45.

Shields, M. D., & Young, S. M. (1994). Managing innovation costs: A study of cost conscious behavior by R&D professionals. *Journal of Management Accounting Research, 6*, 175.

Werner, B. M., & Souder, W. E. (1997a). Measuring R&D performance—state of the art. *Research Technology Management, 40* (2), 34.

Werner, B. M., & Souder, W. E. (1997b). Measuring R&D performance—U.S. and German practices. *Research Technology Management, 40* (3), 28.

11

Management of Innovation and Product Development Processes

RALF SAUTER

OVERVIEW OF INNOVATION AND PRODUCT DEVELOPMENT PROCESSES

The importance of innovation and product development process in securing long-term business success is undisputed. "It is not products but the processes that create products that bring companies long-term success. Good products do not make winners; winners make good products" (Hammer & Champy, 2001, p. 27). In order to repeat and control the market success of product innovation processes, the cooperation between different functional departments must be organized in a process-oriented manner. Today, having process-oriented structures with clearly defined tasks and milestones is a prerequisite for efficiently undertaking standalone projects as well as multiple, parallel-running projects.

The process model in Figure 11.1 depicts the typical operational process of customer-independent product development with important milestones. Later on, examples of customer-dependent product development processes will be cited from the automotive supplier industry.

Innovation and product development processes can be separated into project-specific and cross-project processes. The goal of cross-project processes in innovation and multiproject management is to align product portfolio and project resources with corporate strategy. Their purpose is to instigate strategically important innovation and product development projects and make sure that they receive adequate attention in the organization. By contrast, product

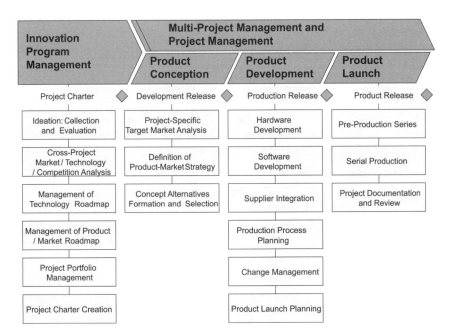

FIGURE 11.1.   Process Model of Product Development

conception, product development, and product launch processes are about the creation of new products within individual projects.

Innovation Program Management

Innovation program management encompasses active ideation—the collection and systematic evaluation of ideas. Product ideas with a high degree of market relevancy are systematically gathered, assessed, prioritized, and rendered usable for the company. Ideation processes include elements both within and outside of the company. Typical external company elements are current clients, target clients, competitors, sales partners, and technology. Internal elements focus on leveraging the innovation potential of the company by employing well-suited processes. For example, some companies periodically conduct "Market and Technology" workshops. Through the use of creative ideation techniques, interdisciplinary teams from sales, product management, development, and production generate and preselect innovative ideas.

Cross-project analyses of markets, technology, and competitors have a dual purpose. First, these analyses serve to prudently observe market trends, promote the methodical search for innovation, and optimally position individual company products. The second purpose is to utilize the market intelligence gathered as a foundation for evaluating new ideas for products. When companies are able to effectively read market trends in the early phases of defining and assessing new product concepts—in essence, being able to gauge the potential success of prospects—they can prevent resources from being wasted and avoid projects being abandoned during conception and even in the development phase. Sound knowledge of the market also remains a prerequisite for formulating a specific project charter. This in turn is the premise for an efficient project execution. Today, shorter and shorter time-to-market intervals often do not allow project teams to conduct comprehensive market research and segmentation. In cases in which pertinent market segmentation data already exists, the project team can limit its analysis of the target market to certain key aspects.

The processes implemented in the management of technology, the product/market roadmap, and the project portfolio are especially vital in the strategic alignment of the company. The positioning of future products must be defined based on the current product program and the newly selected ideas. Which products, in which markets, and at what time become central issues. Critical for the success of projects that result from roadmaps (and of subsequent product development projects) is the proper allocation of resources. We need to ask three crucial questions:

- Are the necessary development resources available?
- Are the timetables realistic?
- Does the current project portfolio support the corporate strategy?

In the true sense of a continual management process, decisions about whether to expedite, abandon, or delay development projects must be made. Another important aspect is the realization of platform and modularization strategies. The complexity and myriad of variants can best be actively influenced during the processes when modules or platforms are reflected in the roadmap.

The process by which individual project charters are created is of utmost importance for the efficient and systematic execution of development projects. In a project charter, tasks, work packages, goals, teams, and product specifications are defined, based on the product/market and technology roadmaps. Past experience shows that the more succinct and clear-cut a project charter is and the earlier the project team—especially the project leader—gets involved in shaping the charter, the smoother the product conception phase will run.

Single and Multiproject Management

Multiproject management works as the interface between individual development projects and is responsible for the systematic incorporation of project ideas stemming from portfolio management. While portfolio management primarily governs the general allocation of development resources according to the overall company strategy—including product and technology road-maps—multiproject management oversees the detailed provision of resources as needed by individual projects.

A typical situation in which project managers often find themselves is requiring more resources than planned to reach a certain critical milestone. Multiproject managers must then decide if resources committed to other projects can be temporarily siphoned or bought off altogether.

Product Conception

The product conception process relates to the individual product development projects and commences as soon as the project charter gets final approval from management. The process is carried out by interdisciplinary project teams that forge a concrete product concept.

In the first step, the project-specific analysis of the target market, validating, realizing, and objectifying market demands take center stage. The analysis of target customers (demands, pricing issues, etc.) together with the analysis of the target market (competing products, market trends, market potential, etc.) mold the basis for the conception and development of successful products.

Part of the product/market strategy definition is to answer the question of how to place the future product in the target market, ensuring success over the competition.

This process is closely linked with the design and assessment of alternative concepts. The systematic pursuit, evaluation, and selection of practical solutions prevent having to prematurely rely on existing or well-established approaches that might not optimally meet the demands of the current market situation. Typical evaluation criteria for the selection of a concept are, for example: practical feasibility, fulfillment of customer demands, and target costs, as well as the acceptance/attractiveness of employed technologies.

Because in the product concept phase according to the 80/20 rule, 80 percent of the product life cycle costs are determined, and the emphasis in this phase should be placed on target costing activities.

Product Development

Since hardware and software development in many companies is for the most part certified according to recognized international standards (DIN ISO or CMMI), the following exposition will concentrate on the remaining processes. Integrating suppliers into processes is extremely critical for success, especially in projects with a low level of production intensity and with large target cost gaps that need to be closed through the procurement of parts, modules, and/or components from low-wage countries or in projects with a high dependency on systems suppliers. Often, a technically promising and profitable concept can only be realized by systematically integrating key suppliers from the outset of the development process. Moreover, this collaboration helps to alleviate quality problems. When purchasing complex systems, key suppliers should be fully involved already in the product conception phase. The same holds true for the timely design and optimization of production planning.

The change management process is responsible for identifying, evaluating, collecting at regular intervals during the development process, communicating, and implementing the necessary changes to the product concept. Development projects frequently suffer delays because too late into the process—during the integration of components—the team realizes that the components do not fit together appropriately. The reason for this mistake is either inadequate or total lack of effective communication. Depending on the scope of change, for example those affecting the fulfillment of customer demands, both sales and portfolio management must be part of the communication process.

The product launch planning process ensures that the positioning of the product in the target markets as defined in the product/market strategy is supported from the outset through a suitable marketing strategy. In addition, it ensures that the launch process does not get set back because of a missing marketing concept. Shorter development phases prove useless if the right marketing is not in place or if sales and distribution gives inadequate support, ultimately slowing down product entry into the marketplace. Moreover, product-related actions in the sense of an appropriate marketing mix (product, price, place, promotion) are to be coordinated with the general marketing activities of the entire company.

Product Launch

The product launch process encompasses, in addition to the activities already mentioned in the previous phases (marketing process, provision and allocation of resources, production adjustments), the management of the product ramp-up, preproduction, and serial production. These processes depend to a large extent on the number of adjustments needed in production—from minor equipment changes to building a completely new production facility.

From a management point of view, project review and documentation are of utmost importance. A critical (yet positive) postproject review by the interdisciplinary team should be conducted, for example, six months after product launch. This review serves as feedback to learn from mistakes and to work out improved measures for the future. All too often, however, this step is neglected in the grind of day-to-day operations.

The innovation and product development processes require the harmonized interplay of many different operational areas of the company. Moreover, these processes are primarily creative in nature. Hence, standardizing the way people work in the sense of specific directives is neither possible nor worth striving for. In the final analysis, each product development process is unique in itself, and can be summarized by the following sentence: "Product innovation is 50 percent process, structure, and method and 50 percent incalculable human imagination." The following sections will show in detail how a company, based on its corporate product strategy and with the help of the previously mentioned reference model, can spearhead, optimize, and control its innovation and product development processes.

STRATEGIC ORIENTATION OF INNOVATION AND PRODUCT DEVELOPMENT PROCESSES

How well the innovation and product development processes are carried out is a primary driver of company success, provided that they are optimally aligned with the overall corporate strategy and direction. The corporate strategy, together with the current business model, imposes specific directions on how innovation process can be designed. For instance, management of innovation is pivotal to the success of companies that follow the strategy of being the product and technology leader. In addition, it is essential for these companies to "institutionalize" innovation routines through certain key processes. The remaining innovation and product development processes must also be designed so that innovation culminates into finished products and services. On the other hand, companies that follow a cost leadership strategy design their processes differently. In this case, technological innovations are second order in nature, and these companies focus on employing existing technologies or acquiring those developed by third parties. Consequently, certain processes in the product development are often outsourced.

In industries with short product life cycles, like telecommunications and consumer electronics, innovation management aligning innovation and product development processes is extremely important. The following case study of a telecommunications company underscores this point.

Case Study: Telecommunications Equipment Manufacturer Innovation Program Management

A telecommunications equipment manufacturer, leading in several segments in the industry, faced the problem that despite having allocated substantial resources to development process over several years, the success of new innovations still had not hit the bottom line. A detailed analysis revealed that the company had difficulty in effectively implementing a concerted innovation program.

So-called "submarine projects" surfaced every once and a while (some successful, some less successful)—ad hoc products developed by the misappropriation of funds and without the approval of management were proof of these projects happening. In addition, constant delays in meeting deadlines indicated that the innovation program management was not able to set the appropriate priorities. Comments such as "we don't have the resources or enough time to do a market analysis" suggested that the allocation of resources was not focused enough. Decisions either to abandon existing projects, to halt running projects, or to speed projects through increased allocation of funds were often made too late and without strong convictions. Concise product and technology roadmaps that could have served as guides to effective decision making were missing. Moreover, project priorities already in place were misaligned with the demands of the product/market strategy. As a result, the majority of projects did not have a charter. Without a clearly defined charter, most projects were predestined from the outset to fail. All of the aforementioned shortcomings created a domino effect. For example, a project experiencing a delay due to insufficient resources led to other projects being delayed and forfeiting resources.

The situation was remedied by implementing an effective project portfolio management (Figure 11.2). A process was developed for systematically finding and evaluating project ideas. To ensure the transparency in decision processes with the least amount of bureaucracy, a project portfolio management committee, made up of middle and senior management, was given the authority to react flexibly and quickly to new events and make the necessary decisions.

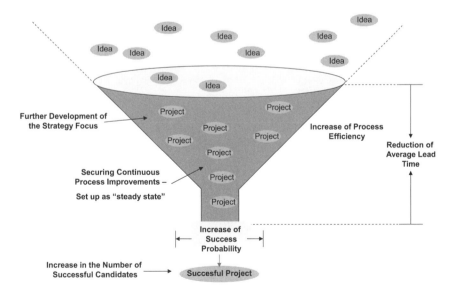

FIGURE 11.2. The Need for Project Portfolio Management

In many industries, being the leader in product and technologies goes hand in hand with being the leader in cost control. Often, innovative products alone do not guarantee success in the marketplace. The following case study exemplifies the dichotomy that many companies experience: the delicate balance between developing innovative, cutting-edge products and at the same time keeping costs at an absolute minimum through lean product development processes.

A power train engineering firm, a leader throughout the world, faced the challenge of keeping its product and technology leadership in a slowly growing market segment within an industry with reasonable margins but with increasing pressure to cut costs from new products coming from Asia. It became clear during a strategic realignment of the company that maintaining ample profitability by catering to a premium segment of the market would not be sustainable over the long term. Reasonable profitability could only be reached by producing for the mass market. However, past attempts to develop products for the masses had failed, because the company was not able to produce them cost effectively. In addition, products for the mass market had more functions than their cheaper competitor.

The strategy that was successfully implemented can be ascertained from the strategy map in Figure 11.3, which clearly illustrates the cause-and-effect relationships between elements key to sustainable profitability.

The strategy centered around two approaches to improving the cost situation that are apparent in the strategy map:

- market-oriented product development
- setting up production in low-wage countries

Market-oriented product development was intended to reduce costs by avoiding overengineering of products. Based on prior experience and in order to achieve cost savings, a low-cost culture was created and optimally leveraged. Past experience had shown that developers always wanted to create new, cutting-edge products employing the latest (more expensive) technologies. Moreover, they shied away from working on low-cost products. Hence, the company implemented a completely new corporate culture. The company culture moved from a technology-driven mentality to a customer- and market-oriented one.

The transformation of the corporate culture in conjunction with the implementation of a strict market-oriented product development process would have still been insufficient to sustain profitability. The Company was fully convinced that market-oriented products would only be successfully developed after the developers and researchers in charge had gained a clear understanding of what the target consumer wanted. This awareness was achieved by integrating developers in project-related target market analyses and by having them in regular contact with customers. In addition, lower costs, associated with products produced in large quantities, were achieved by setting up

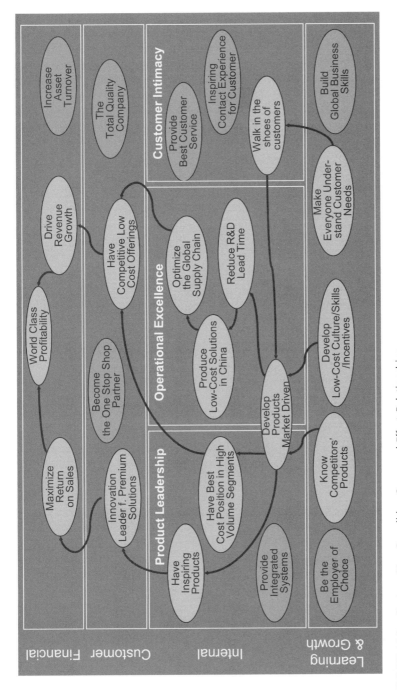

FIGURE 11.3. Strategy Map Describing Cause-and-Effect Relationships

a production facility in China. This step was only possible through the creation of sturdy product concepts and associated supply chain processes.

Another aspect vital to the alignment of innovation and product development processes with corporate strategy is organizational structure. The guiding principle here is "structure follows strategy." This principle is especially true for the interfaces between functional units (production, development, sales, etc.) and project organization.

Questions surrounding the structure of project organization in conjunction with heavyweight project management are beyond the scope of this chapter. Which organizational form best suits project needs depends on project priorities, the degree of innovation, and the style of corporate leadership. Figure 11.4 highlights the major advantages and disadvantage of four widespread project organizational types.

The following prerequisites are necessary before a heavyweight project management—and, consequently, the project organization—can be of value:

- Project team has a very relevant presence in the company and the project leader has direct access to senior management
- Team interaction takes place on a regular basis through frequent meetings—once if not twice a week
- The company practices participatory leadership: team involvement in strategic aspects such as resource allocation, patents, etc.
- Team members possess the right balance between hard and soft skills and are adept at project management
- Team leverages not only its own pool of knowledge, but also employs best practices from other teams
- Important projects have priority over day-to-day operations
- Supervisors measure and control project team performance

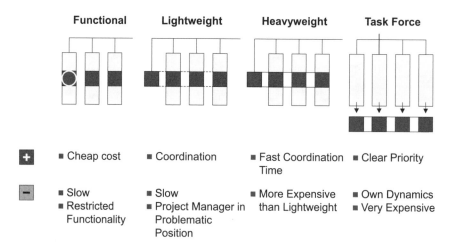

FIGURE 11.4. Different Types of Project Management Organization

One of the biggest challenges is creating the balance between project organization on the one hand and a functional, regional organization on the other. The project team often finds itself caught in the middle: project objectives conflict with the interests of line functions and regional organizations. For example, discussions surrounding resource allocation or product demands either cripple the project's progress or lead to different functional areas, calling the project results into question. The following case study underscores how important the interplay is between the line (chain of command) and project responsibility and how it affects the success of a product launch.

Consumer Electronics 4U Corp. (CE4U): Product Launch of a New Camera

At corporate headquarters, a product development team had developed a new camera to replace its successful camera already on the market. The new model was planned to be launched in the U.S. Corporate executives, however, had neglected to inform their U.S. branch about the new model until it was much too late.

To increase the chances of the new model successfully entering the U.S. marketplace, a market analysis should have been conducted. Because the U.S. branch never got funds allocated to perform this market research, the project was unnecessarily delayed by several months. The project team in charge of the new camera model had decided to conduct a market study on its own without relying on local support from the U.S. It was no surprise that the U.S. sales department rejected the "positive" results from the analysis. The U.S. branch doubted that the product truly met the demands of the U.S. consumer.

After several rounds of discussions about the likelihood of the product succeeding, it was finally decided to continue its development. The suggestions that the regional U.S. branch made to do another market study fell on deaf ears. The project team had pushed through their agenda over that of local interests.

Eventually, development came to a close and the product was launched. Needless to say, the product was not successful in the very important U.S. market.

A well-functioning multiproject management could have solved the conflict. Success is about efficient communication and understanding among the projects and the organizational units about how project implementation should proceed. When these interfaces do not work, either the project manager or the individual functional areas are circumvented—in essence being left out of the process. In order for a multiproject management to function properly, additional aspects play a major role. For example, clearly defined escalation processes need to be in place, ensuring prudent and fast decision making during conflict situations. Moreover, management must constantly be abreast of the latest changes to each individual project. This process should be carried out in the most pragmatic way possible. Certain bureaucratic regulations and overly detailed project plans were also responsible for the ineffective multiproject management at this consumer electronics manufacturer.

DESIGNING INNOVATION AND PRODUCT DEVELOPMENT PROCESSES

Situation

The central issue is how to design innovation and product development processes. On the one hand, creativity for innovation requires a nonbureaucratic and flexible course. Complicated and superfluous procedural issues can stifle creativity. On the other hand, coordinating large international product development often makes a structured product development process absolutely necessary. Many companies have process/procedural handbooks that stipulate in detail how the product development process should be carried out and documented. In most of the cases, these prescribed processes are simply ignored—they become useless.

Goals

Experience shows that the right approach lies somewhere in the middle. It's not about trying to define "standard product development processes," but rather about anchoring certain process standards in the organization.

It makes little sense to develop standard product development processes that encompass predefined, uniform process steps and identical procedures that do not take into account project-specific differences and nuances. The goal is to define company-specific process standards that make uniform interfaces transparent, support a uniform philosophy (e.g., orientation on results or the market), and simultaneously include as few "must dos" as possible.

Benefits

What are the benefits of anchoring the same process standards across the organization? In international companies, creating a uniform language is especially important for operations to run efficiently. By the same token, uniform process standards in an organization define responsibilities, procedures, milestones, and benchmarks, helping to ensure that misunderstandings are avoided and facilitating the efficient and smooth running of operations. Setting up these uniform standards is particularly crucial for the development of complex systems, because they guarantee not only a functional system concept, but the frictionless interplay between hardware, software, and service aspects. Moreover, uniform structures are the prerequisite for identifying best practices, for effectively cooperating with partners, and for providing appropriate IT support. According to the process standards, teams also receive

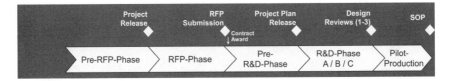

FIGURE 11.5. Project Phases in Product Development

milestone documents, reports, and examples from past projects. The ultimate goal must be to anchor a transparent and, thus, a controllable as well as measurable product innovation process. Figure 11.5 shows the project phases of an American automotive parts supplier.

Many companies answer the question of whether they have a uniform product development process with a "yes." But looking at the manuals they have on their shelves or to the information on their intranet, the answer to the question of whether these standards are followed on a daily basis is all too often "no." Overly detailed process definitions are frequently an insurmountable barrier to anchoring the standards in the company. It is also quite common for teams to have tasks delegated to them regardless of the type of project. For example, process descriptions ignore that it does not necessarily make sense in every case to conduct a Failure Mode and Effects Analysis (FEMA), a Quality Function Deployment, or a comprehensive simulation. A bureaucratic product development process that takes too much of the team's time and that is not actively supported by management is a process that is not alive. When the schedule for product launch gets tight and resources become scarce, certain work units that are absolutely essential to the project, such as a detailed market analysis for a new product, go by the wayside.

The situation can be remedied by having process standards focus on essential work units, milestones, and management instruments and by deciding at the outset of a project which additional activities need to be carried out specifically for that project. Agreeing on these activities through a project portfolio management committee has proven to be very efficient for companies. This ensures that resources are properly allocated. Moreover, conducting regular milestone and gate meetings with great discipline is also very decisive. This means that requested reports, presentations, and analyses are completed and distributed on time and that the entire management team is present. The golden rule is: the next project phase will not receive approval to start until all open questions have been sufficiently answered. Another interesting mechanism is the implementation of automatic policy with so-called "if-then" rules. The following rule, for example, supports the culture of attaining results: if there is a cost gap that is larger than X percent at a certain point in the project, then interdisciplinary cost optimization workshops need to be conducted and evaluated ideas must be documented.

CONTINUOUS MANAGEMENT OF INNOVATION AND PRODUCT DEVELOPMENT PROCESSES

Two key aspects are at the forefront of continuous innovation and product development management processes. The first aspect ensures the proper allocation of resources to individual projects and makes sure that projects run smoothly. Experience has shown that problems in this area are often outside the actual product development execution and are found in the planning phases before projects get underway. The most critical issues and ways to solve them have already been discussed at length. Suffice it to say here that a transparent, pragmatic, and nonbureaucratic management of the project must be guaranteed. Figure 11.6 depicts a target costing status report that was completed by a project team every two weeks.

The initial retrospective cost calculations are compared to current cost estimates. In addition, target costs are evaluated according to cost type, milestones, and miscellaneous items, and estimates by the team are also used and not just those from the team leader. There is even more transparency when individual items/activities that deviate from the allowable costs are examined in a separate report. The goal is to close the cost gap, making the difference between the initial and actual cost estimates as small as possible. Besides documenting performance and progress in black and white, these reports also serve to motivate team members.

These reports, which are geared toward ensuring market success, also shed light on the progress of critical work units and on the status of resources in a project. Instruments like target costing, specific market research, customer

Target Costing / Target Cost Achievement		Product: Project Manager:		Customer: Project Nr.:			Date:	
		Initial Calculation		**Actual Calculation**		**Target Cost Splitting**		
		%	US $ p. Unit	%	US $ p. Unit	Delta (US $)	Target (US $)	Responsible
1 Price per Unit (without savings)			22,30		22,31			
1a + Other Revenues					0,01	2,00	2,01	
2 - Target Profit	% v. 3	5,0%	1,06	5,0%	1,06			
3 = Allowable Costs	1-2		21,24		21,24			
4 - Target Overhead	5+6+7		2,59		2,01			
5 - Business Unit Overhead	% v. 13	6,9%	1,78	6,9%	1,19			
6 - R&D Costs (Project related)			0,69		0,69			
7 - Terms of Payment	% v. 1 ca. 0,59%		0,13	ca. 0,59%	0,13			
10 = Controllable Costs for the Team	3-4		18,64		19,23			
12 Target Cost Gap	10-13		-7,10		1,93			
13 = Transfer price	14+15		25,74		17,30			
14 + Production Overhead	% v. 17	13,5%	3,06	7,5%	1,21			
15 = Production Cost 1	17+16		22,68		16,09			
16 + Defective Units				1,0%	0,16			
17 = Production Cost 2			22,68		15,93			
18 + Operating Costs for Machines			3,91		3,11			
19 + Preparation Costs for Machines			2,93		0,01			
20 + Direct Labor			2,72		1,47	-0,22	1,61	
21 + Material Handling				2,0%	0,22			
22 + Material Costs for parts			5,09		11,11	-0,99 10%	12,45 11,83	
23 Material Costs for raw material			8,04					

FIGURE 11.6. Example of Target Costing Status Report

sentiment models, target cost splitting, alternative assessment methods, etc. are intergraded in the project plans as work units. The substance and use of these instruments are presented during the relevant gate meetings. Target costing instruments and their use in market- and profit-oriented control is well documented and, hence, will not be discussed in any greater detail here.

OUTLOOK

Experience shows that the mere introduction of target costing, quality function deployment, or product development processes alone does not guarantee success. The strategic alignment and design of process in the creative realm of innovation and product development process demand an approach that coincides with the corporate strategy and culture and have a guiding validity beyond the scope of just one single project. Moreover, sustainable development of processes over time—whether they are market- or profit-oriented—requires a long-term change process to be in place. This process begins with management. It is only when the upper echelons of the corporate structure continuously synchronize projects clearly with the demands of the markets and customers that product innovations can bring about long-term competitive advantages.

REFERENCE

Hammer, M. & Champy, J. 2001. *Reengineering the corporation: A manifesto for business revolution.* New York: HarperCollins.

Index

About the Editors and Contributors

Tony Davila is a faculty member at IESE Business School, University of Navarra, and the Graduate School of Business at Stanford University, where he specializes in performance measurement and control systems for innovation management. He consults for large companies and Silicon Valley start-ups and has published in leading journals, including *Research Policy* and the *Harvard Business Review*. With Marc J. Epstein and Robert Shelton, he is co-author of *Making Innovation Work*.

Marc J. Epstein is Distinguished Research Professor of Management, Jones Graduate School of Management, Rice University, and was recently visiting professor and Hansjoerg Wyss Visiting Scholar in Social Enterprise at the Harvard Business School. A specialist in corporate strategy, governance, performance management, and corporate social responsibility, he is the author or co-author of over 100 academic and professional papers and more than a dozen books, including *Counting What Counts*, *Measuring Corporate Environmental Performance*, *Making Innovation Work* (with Tony Davila and Robert Shelton), and *Implementing E-Commerce Strategies* (Praeger, 2004), and co-editor and contributor to the multi-volume set *The Accountable Corporation* (Praeger, 2005). A senior consultant to leading corporations and governments for over twenty-five years, he currently serves as editor-in-chief of the journal *Advances in Management Accounting*.

Robert Shelton is principal at PRTM Management Consultants. He advises executives in a wide variety of industries and speaks on issues of innovation and business strategy to corporate, government, and university audiences around the world. He previously served as managing director at Navigant Consulting, vice president and managing director with Arthur D. Little, and managing director of the Technology Management Practice at SRI International, and his work has been cited in such publications as the *Wall Street Journal* and CNN Financial News and has been broadcast on NPR. With Marc J. Epstein and Tony Davila, he is co-author of *Making Innovation Work*.

José María Corrales Peñalva is professor of accounting and control at IAE Business and Management School, Universidad Austral, Buenos Aires, Argentina, where he serves as head of the accounting and control area and executive education director. He is also a consultant to multinational companies.

Hernán Etiennot is professor of management and control at IAE Business and Management School, Universidad Austral, Buenos Aires, Argentina. He is also public accountant for the Universidad Católica Argentina. His research interests focus on incentives, innovation, and enabling mechanisms of control. He has had experience with local and multinational organizations in Argentina. Before joining IAE he held both financial and marketing positions in different financial institutions.

George Foster is Paul L. and Phyllis Wattis Professor of Management; director of the Executive Program for Growing Companies; and Dhirubhai Ambani Faculty Fellow in Entrepreneurship (2005–2006) at the Graduate School of Business, Stanford University, where his research and teaching interests include globalization strategies, sports management and marketing, entrepreneurship/early-stage companies, and financial analysis and valuation. His publications include over thirty research articles, three monographs, and multiple editions of several textbooks: *Financial Statement Analysis, Cost Accounting: A Managerial Analysis*, and *The Business of Sports*. His awards include the AICPA Award for Outstanding Contribution to the Accounting Literature, the Competitive Manuscript Award of the American Accounting Association, Distinguished Teaching Award at Stanford Business School. Foster is actively involved in the business community, especially with venture capital-backed startup companies, and has served on the board of directors of several companies. He is also involved with sporting organizations around the globe, including directing executive programs for the National Basketball Players Association and for the National Football League.

Oliver Gassmann is professor for technology management at the University of St. Gallen, Switzerland, and director at the Institute of Technology Management. After earning his doctorate in 1996 he worked for Schindler Corporation, headquartered in Switzerland, initially as a project manager for technological core competencies in Europe and the United States, and, between 1998 and 2002, as vice president, technology management, responsible for corporate research worldwide. In addition, he serves as a member in several economic and academic boards, including Economiesuisse, CTI Swiss Innovation Agency, the audit committee of Schindler, and the editorial board of *R&D Management*. He has published ten books and over 130 publications on innovation; his work has been published in English, German, Chinese, and Japanese.

Mahendra R. Gupta is dean and Geraldine J. and Robert L. Virgil Professor of Accounting and Management at the Olin School of Business, Washington

University, St. Louis. His current research explores issues in strategic cost management, benchmarking, customer profitability, entrepreneurship, and performance measurement. He has been a consultant to various manufacturing firms and government agencies, and serves on the editorial boards of *The Accounting Review, Journal of Management Accounting Research, Accounting Horizons,* and *International Journal of Applied Quality Management.* His articles and working papers have been published in a variety of journals, including *Journal of Accounting and Economics, Journal of Marketing, Contemporary Accounting Research,* and *Journal of Cost Management.*

Martin Haemmig, adjunct professor, has conducted extensive research over the last five years on over one hundred international venture capital firms in Asia, Europe, Israel and the United States. He has since expanded his research scope to international investors, and startup companies through joint projects between CeTIM (Centre of Technology & Innovation Management at their university sites in Munich and Rotterdam), Stanford University Business School, and the University of California. In addition to the above schools, he also lectures at the ETH Zurich, as well as at China's Tsinghua, Peking and Renmin University. Martin Haemmig is an advisor to the World Economic Forum in its venture capital working group for "Nurturing the early stage investment climate in China." His book, *The Globalization of Venture Capital* (Haupt) has been translated into Chinese by Fudan University (Fudan Press).

Julie H. Hertenstein is associate professor of accounting at Northeastern University. Her previous experience included information technology management positions at Pacific Telephone and Burlington Industries. Her research focuses on the influence of financial and non-financial information, particularly accounting information and expertise, on new product development and new product success. As a senior research fellow with the Design Management Institute, she also focuses on the measurement of design performance. Dr. Hertenstein's articles appear in leading journals, including *Advances in Management Accounting, Journal of Product Innovation Management, Accounting Horizons, Management Accounting, International Journal of Strategic Cost Management, Business Horizons, Case Research Journal,* and *Design Management Journal Academic Review.* She is a co-author of *Accounting: Text and Cases, 9th Edition* (Irwin, 1994), and has written numerous cases published in leading accounting and information technology textbooks.

Pradip N. Khandwalla taught at McGill University, Canada, for several years before returning to India in 1975; thereafter, he was professor at the Indian Institute of Management, Ahmedabad, until his retirement in 2002, where he held the L&T Chair in Organizational Behavior from 1985 to 1991, and served as director from 1991 to 1996. He is also a member of the Institute of Chartered Accountants of India. His area of specialization is organizational theory, with research, teaching, training and consulting interests in the areas of organizational design and management of excellence, innovative turnaround management, management restructuring, effective management of public enterprises and strategic organizations, and individual and management creativity and innovation. He has been a consultant/trainer to a large number of organizations in India and around the world. He has authored over a dozen professional books and eighty papers and articles in Indian and foreign journals. His books, several of which have won awards, include: *The Design of Organizations, Fourth Eye: Excellence through Creativity, Excellent Management in the Public Sector, Turnaround Excellence: Insights from 120 Cases, Corporate Creativity: The Winning Edge*, and *Lifelong Creativity: An Unending Quest*. He has also authored three books of poems, a book on one-act plays, and translations of poetry and short stories. He has served on the editorial/advisory boards of several of the world's leading journals of management and organizational research, including *Administrative Science Quarterly, Journal of Management, Organizational Science*, and *Organization Studies*. He has served as a member of the board of directors of over a dozen corporations, and currently he is on the boards of Bank of Baroda, Grow Talent, Gujarat Gas, and Micro Inks, and on the governing councils of the Academy of HRD, Centre of Organization Development, Eklavya Teachers' Training College, MICA, Shri Ram School-Aravalli, and other institutions. He has served as a member of the National Renewal Fund, Government of India, and as a trustee, India Brand Equity Fund, and on a variety of other public-sector boards and commissions.

Ralph Maurer is a doctoral student in the department of management science and engineering at Stanford University, with a focus on organizational theory. His work experience includes time with Apple Computer, Deluxe (film industry), and as an IT consultant. Ralph is currently conducting research on the relationship between organizational identity and property in creative industries.

Kandarp H. Mehta is a doctoral student in the general management department at IESE Business School, Barcelona, Spain. Before joining the doctoral program at IESE Business School, he served at ICFAI Business School, Ahmedabad, India, where he taught courses in the area of finance and strategy in the MBA program. He has also conducted corporate creativity workshops with Pradip Khandwalla.

Ikujiro Nonaka is professor in the Graduate School of International Corporate Strategy at Hitotsubashi University and a Xerox Distinguished Faculty in Knowledge at the University of California-Berkeley. He has published numerous books and articles on knowledge management in Japanese and English, including *The Knowledge-Creating Company* (co-author, Oxford, 1995), *Managing Industrial Knowledge* (co-editor, Sage, 2001), *Handbook of Organizational Learning and Knowledge* (co-editor, Oxford, 2001), and *Hitotsubashi on Management* (co-editor, Wiley, 2004).

Vesa Peltokorpi is the Center of Excellence (COE) project director in the Graduate School of International Corporate Strategy at Hitotsubashi University. He has published several articles in international reviewed journals. His research interests include shared cognition, cross-cultural psychology, and knowledge management.

Marjorie B. Platt is professor and group coordinator of accounting at Northeastern University. She is also a certified management accountant (CMA). A senior research fellow with the Design Management Institute, her current research focuses on how managers use financial and non-financial information in the process of making business decisions, particularly those that deal with new product design and development and the evaluation of design performance. In addition, she publishes and consults on the prediction of corporate bankruptcy and financial distress. Her most recent articles have appeared in *Journal of Product Innovation Management, Advances in Management Accounting, Accounting Horizons, Case Research Journal, Journal of Business Research, Journal of Business Finance & Accounting, Journal of Economics and Finance,* and *Design Management Journal Academic Review.*

James Robbins founded Business Cluster Development (BCD) in 1993. BCD has helped over thirty organizations with the formation of sector-focused incubators or innovation centers. He is executive director of the Environmental Business Cluster in San Jose, which specializes in technology commercialization of clean and renewable energy technology, and has the largest private technology commercialization program for clean energy start-ups in the United States. He is also chairman of the board of directors of the National Business Incubation Association. Robbins has thirty years of experience in the fields of new business formation, innovation hubs, organizational design, technology development, and law. In addition to starting his own business to assist communities in the development of sector-focused incubators and innovation centers, he has worked for San Jose State University, Digital Equipment Corporation, the U.S. Supreme Court, and was a trial attorney.

Ralf Sauter is a member of the board of Horváth & Partners USA, and heads the global consumer and industrial goods practice. Horváth & Partners is the European market leader in state-of-the-art solutions in the fields of budgeting and management accounting, strategic management and innovation, and process management and organization. Dr. Sauter has over ten years of consulting experience, and has led several engagements that focused on strategy implementation, planning, budgeting, reporting and reporting systems. He has worked with such internationally renowned companies as Sara Lee, Continental, Audi, Siemens, Mercedes Benz, BASF, Atlas Copco, and R+V Insurance. He is the author and co-author of three books and several articles in major international journals, and speaks frequently at conferences.

Maximilian von Zedtwitz is professor at the School of Economics and Management at Tsinghua University in Beijing, China. He is director of the Research Center for Global R&D Management at Tsinghua, and President of AsiaCompete, a training and research firm based in Hong Kong. He also serves as an adjunct and visiting professor at Rutgers University, and the University of St. Gallen, Switzerland. Prior to relocating to China in 2003, he was a faculty member at IMD in Lausanne, Switzerland, and a visiting scholar at Harvard University. His research and teaching interests include global innovation, technology-based entrepreneurship, and international strategy.